STRAIGHT TALK ABOUT
PROFESSIONAL ETHICS

Also Available from Lyceum Books, Inc.

STRAIGHT TALK ABOUT PROFESSIONAL ETHICS

Kim Strom-Gottfried
University of North Carolina, Chapel Hill

LYCEUM
BOOKS, INC.

Chicago, Illinois

© Lyceum Books, Inc., 2007

Published by

Lyceum Books, Inc.
5758 S. Blackstone Ave.
Chicago, Illinois 60637
773+643-1903 (Fax)
773+643-1902 (Phone)
lyceum@lyceumbooks.com
http://www.lyceumbooks.com

10 9 8 7 6 5 4 3 2 1

ISBN 978-1-933478-03-6

Library of Congress Cataloging-in-Publication Data

Strom-Gottfried, Kim.
    Straight talk about professional ethics / Kim Strom-Gottfried.
        p. cm.
    Includes bibliographical references and index.
    ISBN 978-1-933478-03-6
  1. Professional ethics. I. Title.
    BJ1725.S83 2007
    174'.93613—dc22
                                            2006100858

To Smith P. Theimann, Jr.,
who lived the values of service, humility, respect,
compassion, excellence, and integrity

Contents

ABOUT THE AUTHOR

Kim Strom-Gottfried, Ph.D., LISW, is the Smith P. Theimann Distinguished Professor of Ethics and Professional Practice at the School of Social Work at the University of North Carolina at Chapel Hill. Professor Strom-Gottfried teaches in the areas of direct practice, communities and organizations, and human resource management. Her practice experience in the nonprofit and public sectors focuses on suicide prevention, intervention, and bereavement. Professor Strom-Gottfried's scholarly interests involve ethics, moral courage, and social work education, and she is active in training, consultation, and research on ethics and social work practice. She has written numerous articles, monographs, and chapters on the ethics of practice. Professor Strom-Gottfried is also the coauthor of *Direct Social Work Practice* and *Teaching Social Work Values and Ethics: A Curriculum Resource.*

PREFACE

Is it ethical to pray with a client?

My agency has a policy against accepting gifts. Does this mean I shouldn't accept a jar of pickles when I visit my home-bound client?

My client is fascinated by disturbing video games involving workplace violence. Do I have a duty to warn someone?

My teenage daughter is dating a former resident of the psych ward where I used to work. What can I do?

My client is asking me not to keep records of his treatment because he is in the military. Isn't it in his best interest if I agree?

I used to treat a fellow professional in my bereavement practice. Is it unethical for us now to refer clients to each other?

If these examples are any indication, ethics is a complex and high-stakes area of professional practice. Too often, though, when practitioners think of ethics, they think of high-minded philosophical discussion far removed from the challenges of their daily lives. Or they become overwhelmed considering so many options that they simply throw up their hands and say, "I'll trust my gut." Or they become so preoccupied with avoiding risk that they make their decisions guided by the question, "Whom would I rather be sued by?" None of these is a recipe for sound ethical decision making. None accounts for the fact that ethical and clinical excellence are intertwined. None of these gives credence to the standards of professional practice exemplified in our codes of ethics. I hope that after reading this text, your take on ethics will be different.

This book discusses risk but is not driven by it. It examines the ethical standards governing social work practice as they might be applied in a variety of situations. It offers a nimble, useful framework for considering ethical dilemmas to help you develop your capacity for critical thinking in arriving at ethically sound decisions. It equips you, the reader, with well-grounded tools to use in preventing ethical difficulties or in weighing options if ethical challenges do arise. It acknowledges and addresses the fact that often the challenge of ethics lies in having the courage to do the right thing, not the ability to discern the right thing. It is written in a lively and conversational manner intended to make ethics accessible to students and experienced practitioners alike. It employs practical guidance, sound resources, and authentic cases featuring an array of roles, settings, and issues. It doesn't just present dilemmas but guides you through the critical thinking needed to resolve them. It doesn't just stick to the easy right-wrong dilemmas, either. Together, we'll address the spectrum of ethical challenges, including the challenges in choosing between competing "goods" and competing "bads." While many of the dilemmas are drawn from direct practice examples, the book covers a variety of ethical dilemmas that arise for supervisors, managers, and planners and in other roles and settings.

How is it organized? The book begins with a discussion of what ethics means and what it means to be ethical. This section lays an important foundation for all that follows, and it contains useful case material as well. The second chapter offers a framework for examining ethical dilemmas and weighing your options for addressing them, and it gives you examples that apply that framework.

Each of the remaining chapters focuses on a particular area of ethics—confidentiality, self-determination, informed consent, and so forth. Each of these chapters uses a consistent format that provides an overview of the ethical concept and the related standards, a case example in which the standard is violated, and another where the standard is upheld. The rest of the chapter is devoted to ethical decision making in a more complex dilemma utilizing the critical-thinking framework introduced in the third chapter. Sometimes there will be one "right" answer; sometimes several will be revealed by the analysis. Sometimes (maybe often) you'll dispute my view of the case or disagree with the outcome. Wonderful! To take a differing perspective, you must be engaged with the question, striving to find a way out that fits with your understanding of ethical practice. Such engagement with ethics can only make us stronger as we consider the views of others and articulate and advance our own. I hope to hear from you as you use this book. Let me know the insights it raised, the dilemmas it brought to mind, and the ideas you have for improving ethical practice in our profession. I am certain we'll all be better for it.

As you read the cases, you may feel you recognize the characters involved. Each case is a composite of a commonly occurring dilemma, a case that has been created from an actual dilemma, or a case that has been made up. No case in the book is, in and of itself, a "real" case, though I hope you find them all realistic and useful. In addition to sending your feedback, please send me your dilemmas so that others can benefit in the future from novel, life-like examples.

Many people deserve credit for the inspiration and creation of this work. Heartfelt thanks go to Beth DuMez for her abiding concern for ethics in our profession; to Kerry Sugrue and Joette Woody for their research and bibliographic wizardry; to Edie Klecka and Tom Meenaghan for invigorating the writing and thinking process; to Joanne Caye, Tina Souder, and Elaine Stevens for sharing their ethical and clinical expertise; to Martin Hall for his research and insights on moral development; to the UNC social work IT staff for responding to all forms of computing crises; to all the people who have revealed their ethical wisdom and struggles at workshops, classes, and consultations so that we all can learn and grow stronger from their examples; to Cyd Wiford for the use of the North Topsail Beach writing sanctuary; to the members of my writers' groups for their support; and to my husband, George Gottfried, for all the sacrificed evenings and weekends and for his abiding enthusiasm for this work.

Part I

The Groundwork for Ethical Practice

Chapter 1

ON ETHICS AND ETHICAL BEHAVIOR

"It's an interesting time to be in the ethics business," a fellow trainer said to me at the outset of a recent workshop. The study of ethics goes back thousands of years—even Socrates pondered the meaning of morality some 2,400 years ago (Rachels, 2003). But the first few years of the twenty-first century have brought a resurgence of interest in the ethics that govern the lives we lead as individual citizens and as professionals in various disciplines. Some of this interest comes from the increasing complexity of our daily lives, from the ascendance of technology that speeds up communication but erodes protections of privacy to scientific advances that were heretofore unimagined. Some of the interest in ethics comes from concerns about liability, focusing on the risk management strategies needed to avoid malpractice claims. The interest in ethics also comes from recent notorious lapses in ethical behavior, such as those associated with corporate accounting fraud, plagiarism by renowned journalists and historians, and unsportsmanlike conduct such as using performance-enhancing drugs or betting on games. Even revered institutions are not immune to disgrace, as the pedophilia scandal in the Catholic Church has revealed. The attention these events have received leads individuals to look for guidance in the ethical dilemmas they confront in their own lives (Cohen, 2002). My particular interest is in the ethical dilemmas that helping professionals experience and the guidance and support they need to do the right thing, often in difficult circumstances. This book is intended to be such a guide, delivering information on ethics and ethical decision making, as well as abundant examples through which you, the reader, can hone your skills.

3

ELEMENTS OF ETHICS

The journey must begin with an understanding of ethics. What are ethics? What does it mean to be ethical? Is being ethical in one's personal life the same as being ethical in one's chosen profession? What is an ethical dilemma? How can one choose the right course of action when faced with such a dilemma?

At its core, ethics involves doing the right thing in a given circumstance—behaving ethically. The challenge comes, of course, in defining the "right" thing. The determination of what is ethical is shaped by many forces, some of which conflict with each other. Ethical dilemmas come in all shapes and sizes. They involve life-and-death questions that involve laws, faith, personal beliefs, and multiple stakeholders. An example might be a patient who declines to undergo a life-saving medical procedure because of religious beliefs. Should her beliefs and personal autonomy be honored even if they may ultimately result in her death? Should the beliefs of her medical team and the opinions of the courts that hear her case carry more weight than her own convictions? These are tough questions that occasionally rise to the level of national attention and debate.

More often, though, we are presented with ethical dilemmas that are smaller in scope but no less difficult to resolve. You see a parent in line at the grocery store viciously strike her child for reaching out to the candy display. Should you intervene and try to minimize harm to the child? Perhaps doing so would make the mother think twice and break a cycle of escalating harsh discipline. Or do you mind your own business, reasoning that your intrusion might shame the mother or infuriate her more, leading to more punishment for the child? Besides, you're just a fellow citizen and have no obligation to put yourself on the line. If only someone in authority would speak up! Why doesn't the clerk or someone else in the line say something?

What about ethics in the workplace? You're a teacher whose student has broken the school honor code by submitting a paper plagiarized from an Internet site. The honor standards are clear, as are the consequences. Enforcing them would result in the student's expulsion and probably some uproar from his parents, friends, and other supporters. Maybe you should give him a second chance. Maybe you should search for a reasonable explanation. But failing to follow the honor code's stipulations is unfair to other students who follow the code and to those who have been properly punished for not following it. And why have a code if there is always an exception, always a rationale, always a reason not to uphold it?

These examples illustrate several important things about ethics: dilemmas crop up throughout our daily lives, often without warning. They demand that we weigh a number of factors in choosing a course of action, and they don't usually give us much time to do so. When I was personally faced with the grocery store incident, I ruminated about what to do until the opportunity to act had passed. Then I rationalized, "Oh well, too late." Had I been better prepared to act, quicker to know what was right, and more courageous in doing so, I would have taken a better course of action—for the child and for my conscience. When I ask myself today, "Did I do the right thing?" the answer, unfortunately, is no.

Some contend that ethical decision making involves not a choice between right and wrong but one between competing "goods" or competing "rights"—that the choice between a good and a bad action does not constitute an ethical dilemma (Kidder, 1995). For example, the decision whether or not to steal a neighbor's furniture is not an ethical dilemma: right and wrong are clearly defined, and doing wrong would be considered both unethical and illegal. But what if the neighbor left a bureau by the curb, ostensibly for trash pickup? Would it be ethical to take it under those circumstances? The decision and the rationale used to discern the right thing in this case involves ethical decision making. Some who subscribe to rule ethics (Rachels, 2003) would maintain that the circumstances do not matter. If it is unethical to take your neighbor's goods, it doesn't matter where they are or why they are there when you decide to lift them.

Others would evaluate the appropriateness of the action based on the consequences—using the circumstances of the case to determine the correctness of an action (Reamer, 2006). They would appraise the situation, weigh the intent of the neighbor, consider the impact on others, and determine what harm or good might come of their actions. This, of course, requires one to be an accurate evaluator of the surrounding circumstances—to be certain that the bureau on the curb *is* trash and not awaiting pickup by a moving company or refinishing service, for example.

Some would evaluate the dilemma by deferring to the law—theft is illegal, but picking up someone else's discarded junk is not. The problem with deferring to the law is that there are many actions in personal and professional life that are not covered by the law. Is it ethical to accept a gift from a client? The law could care less. And even where law exists, it may not always provide an appropriate guide to just action. It is legal for politicians to accept large campaign contributions from the very industries over which they will be drafting regulations, but is it right to do so?

Even when laws are clear, following them may not always be the right course of action. For example, the law says you must stop at a red light. But if you are a volunteer disaster responder rushing to a call in the middle of the night, should you sit there through the entirety of the light? Do the ends (responding to an emergency) warrant the means (breaking traffic laws)? When people of good conscience perceive that the laws themselves are flawed, what is the right course of action? The easy answer is changing flawed laws, but sometimes that change is a long time in coming or blocked by powerful, entrenched interests. The rich tradition of civil disobedience is built on the notion that there must be some recourse for action when laws themselves are unjust. Rosa Parks was breaking the law when she refused to move to the "colored" section of an Alabama bus, but few would have suggested even then that her choice was unethical. The laws in some states prohibit the placement of foster children with homosexual couples. Social workers in those cases must decide whether obedience to the law takes precedence over the needs of children for loving, stable foster homes, particularly when such homes are scarce.

So, the law is of limited help in ethical decision making. Doing something because the law says to do it (or because it says not to do it) is a fairly narrow basis for behavior. It corresponds to the most basic stage in Kohlberg's schema of moral development (Hutchison, 1999). And laws, at their essence, provide only a minimal guide for acceptable behavior—following them is not the same as being an ethical person (Cohen & Cohen, 1999). In fact, in acknowledging the shortcoming of law as guidance for action, Moulton (1924) defined ethics as "obedience to the unenforceable" (p. 4)—that is, *our ethics are those things*

6

that mediate our free will. Ethics are guidance for the situations in which we enforce the laws upon ourselves (Moulton, 1924).

Usually, the complexity of an ethical dilemma emerges in the details. Decisions that on their face may be simple become more difficult when other factual elements are introduced. It is unethical to allow a client to harm himself. What if the client is gravely ill with a terminal illness? What if the client is in excruciating pain that is not diminished by medication? What if the client lives in Oregon, where assisted suicide is legal? What if he has pursued his rights under that statute and has passed the tests for competence and the absence of coercion or clinical depression? What if his family supports his decision even though they grieve the prospect of his death? Is it still ethical for the clinician to intercede to keep the client from carrying out his wish to die with more dignity than he foresees if he lets nature take its course? The devil is in the details.

Some consider all this equivocating on ethics and throw up their hands, demanding a clear answer—"Is it right or not? Just tell me what to do, and I'll do it!" Or they conclude that ethics are situational—that if everything is relative, then any action can be justified. In fact, neither is true. Core ethical standards provide us the guideposts for action. Knowing what they are and what they mean is an essential first step in ethical practice. The challenges occur in those situations when standards collide, or when the standard fails to offer clear guidance for action. In these situations, doing the right thing involves examining the array of options available in upholding the ethical standard and considering, within that particular context, the most ethical course of action. This doesn't mean that anything goes as long as you can rationalize it. It means that, though there are many things to consider in sorting out the proper choice, some choices will be more ethically sound than others. This notion of *contextual* ethical decision making will be discussed further in chapter 2 as you learn the elements to consider in sound ethical practice.

ETHICAL DEVELOPMENT

On what basis do we as individuals develop our sense of right and wrong, or our preference for certain decision-making schemata over others? When we are faced with a difficult decision, what leads us to select one option over another? The consideration of such questions extends as far back as Plato. Throughout history, a range of theories from fields such as philosophy, psychology, and economics have endeavored to explain ethical choices. Examining these perspectives helps us to understand the particular ethical outlook reflected in our own moral development.

Philosophy

A fundamental concept in ethical thinking is whether an action is right objectively, meaning that it is the best action in an absolute sense, or whether it is right subjectively, in which case any decision could be considered right (Graham, 2004). This discussion is a major feature of Plato's dialogues, where Socrates argues that ethics are absolute, while the Sophists generally argue ethics are subjective. Graham (2004) describes Socrates's position as "hard objectivism," and that of the Sophists as "hard subjectivism" (p. 14). Graham (2004) goes on to specify these categories further, adding "soft subjectivism" and "soft objectivism" (p. 14). Soft subjectivism says that in *most* cases an absolute best decision cannot be made, while soft objectivism allows that reason and argument can provide an optimal ethical decision *most* of the time. Graham contends that soft objectivism is the most tenable of the four categories. The appeal of rule-based ethical frameworks to some and outcome-based frameworks to others is apparent in these early musings.

A somewhat different take on ethical behavior is contractualism. Contractualism posits that ethical decisions are essentially those that a society agrees upon in order to function effectively (Graham, 2004). This agreement, or "social contract," as it is sometimes known, "forms the basis of law and morality and can be appealed to as the ground of our social obligation to recognize and accommodate the needs of others" (Graham, 2004, p. 164). Thus, the reasoning behind an ethical act is that it holds society together and prevents what Thomas Hobbes called "a war of all against all" (as cited in Graham, 2004, p. 170).

Psychology

Kurtines and Gewirtz (1995) outline four major psychological perspectives of moral development. The first, and predominant, is the cognitive developmental perspective. Jean Piaget and Lawrence Kohlberg are the primary figures associated with the cognitive developmental perspective. Piaget (1932) argued that individuals' moral development follows a linear progression beginning with egocentrism in young children and gradually advancing to higher forms of decision making where the needs of others are increasingly considered. Kohlberg (1984) built on this work but went one step further. Where Piaget had described developmental "phases," Kohlberg selected the more rigid term "stage." Still, the basic premise remained that of progressively ethical decision making.

Kohlberg's ideas continue to be influential, though theorists within the social constructivist perspective have described his methods and theories as male-centric (Gilligan, 1982). Gilligan (1982) argues that the female "voice" has been ignored in the traditional understanding of morality. The traditional "morality of fairness," which "ties moral development to the understanding of rights and rules," is contrasted with a more woman-centric "morality of care," which is more concerned with "responsibility and relationships" (Gilligan, 1982, p. 19).

The personality/psychodynamic perspective is typified by the ideas of Freud and later Erikson. This perspective is not concerned specifically with behavior or cognition but attempts to understand the whole of a person. Hogan and Emler (1995) state that moral conduct in adulthood "can be largely understood in terms of the concepts of identity and reputation management" (p. 210). Individuals seek to establish an identity as an ethical person while simultaneously cultivating a similar reputation. Thus, someone intent on cultivating the identity of a rebel may choose corresponding ethical behaviors (testing rules, speaking out, etc.) to bolster her reputation. This process may be deliberate, though it may also be instinctual.

The fourth and final psychological perspective, behaviorism, was to some degree a response to the Freudian ideas of instinctual choices. Burton and Kunce (1995) state, "Reasoning about moral issues results from early behavioral training and these judgments may eventually become guides to subsequent action as part of a feedback system" (p. 143). Ethical behavior would thus be perceived primarily as the result of "training" that occurs in homes, schools, churches, and other institutions.

Economics

The concept of rational choice grew out of the field of economics and posits that individuals make choices based on the perceived amount of personal benefit (Zsolnai, 1998). Others' goals, desires, and needs are always considered secondary to one's own. The rational choice theorist might argue that choices that may appear to be altruistic are ultimately guided by personal benefit. For example, even when a person performs a selfless act, the act might have been motivated by the desire to feel good or to improve one's social standing. Under this model, ethical decisions become a risk-benefit calculation that takes into account the decision maker's well-being.

Religion

In Spohn's (2000) comparison of psychological and religious explanations of moral development, the notion of "practice" is highlighted. Ethical development emerges from a set of determined practices such as friendship, service, and worship. Religious practice does not supplant the psychological theories that explain internal mechanisms of ethical behavior, but ethical decision making is reified by religious habits and actions.

It seems likely that religion influences ethical decision making, though to what degree and in what way are probably dependent on one's particular religious orientation. National opinion polls have found that one out of seven U.S. citizens (14%) uses the Bible to make ethical choices (Barna Update, 2002). Whether these individuals would come to the same conclusions in similar circumstances is, however, unclear, as relevant passages are selected and weighed differently depending on the reader's faith and individual makeup.

How, then, do you make ethical decisions? How do you determine right from wrong? Which of these theories (individually or bundled with others) resonates with you as you think of yourself as an ethical being? While this text examines dilemmas and applies standards from the helping professions, the insights, impressions, and growth that result will be laid over your existing moral framework. The moral core on which the scaffolding of professional decision making is built may be explicitly drawn from a faith tradition or personal philosophy, or it may be the result of an unexamined set of preferences and ideals. The key is to appreciate that each of us brings to our practice a personal tradition of ethical thinking that will shape and be shaped by the dilemmas we encounter in practice. This tradition may take an active role in shaping our responses, and it may manifest itself in the personal values we weigh. It may be congruent with the ethical mandates and dramas of social work, or it may be at odds with them. Regardless of the harmony between our personal and professional selves, we can be certain that in a lifetime of decision making, the two will be in constant transformation as each influences the other.

PROFESSIONAL ETHICS

Whether or not it is acceptable to remove a bureau from your neighbor's curb or confront an angry parent exemplifies a question of personal ethics—that category of ethics that governs how we conduct ourselves in our daily lives, in our interactions in the workplace, with our friends and family, and in larger society. The guidelines for personal ethics and their application are a compelling topic and are addressed nicely in other sources, from etiquette columns to texts such as Cohen's *The Good, the Bad and the Difference* (2002) and Dobrin's *Ethics for Everyone: How to Raise Your Moral Intelligence* (2002). The focus of this book, however, is on our professional ethics, and particularly the ethics of social work. Our profession presents us with a unique set of principles to guide our choices, and a broad and complex array of situations in which we must make ethical choices. As such, it is quite different from deciding the fate of our neighbor's trash.

Professional ethics involves those dilemmas that occur in the course of our professional practice. Because of this, different considerations come to bear in those dilemmas from those in the dilemmas we face in our personal lives. Developing a commitment to the ethics of our profession and an understanding of how they apply to commonly occurring workplace situations is a core element of professional preparation. Integrating our professional ethics with our personal ethics is another important part of the process. For example, if a person generally embraces the philosophy "live and let live" or "to each his own," how will this be reconciled with a professional role that may

11

require confronting a client about parenting practices or maintaining household hygiene? When we accept membership in a profession, we also accept the values and standards of that profession as they are put forth through codes of ethics and our professional organizations' credos. The process of professional acculturation helps people decide if they can embrace the values and standards of their chosen fields. Those who find themselves in constant conflict with the core beliefs of the profession must reflect seriously on their suitability for the field they have chosen.

Even individuals who have great compatibility with their professions' standards still experience situations where their personal beliefs and professional ethics collide. Ethical practice, then, requires constant attention to the intersection of the two. If you personally believe that it is wrong for a fourteen-year-old to have a baby, can you work with the young client who refuses to take birth control or who chooses to carry a pregnancy to term? Social workers support client self-determination in all but the most exceptional of circumstances. Clearly it would be unethical to trick the client into taking birth control. But it is also unethical to say, "I can't work with you because you are making life decisions I don't agree with—decisions that violate my moral standards." We may say, "I'm concerned about your choice, and here's why," but that shouldn't rise to the level of threats or coercion, and our concerns should be based on the clinical indications or legitimate dangers involved, not simply an argument of what behavior is right or wrong based on our personal values. We impose such judgments at the risk of foreclosing our own growth and of damaging our relationship with the client, within which conversations of morality may rightly take place (Doherty, 1995).

The principles of acceptance and nonjudgmental practice require us to separate what we would choose or how we would want to live from the choices our clients make. And our service to them is not contingent on our approval of their choices. Aha, you say. What about programs that refuse to serve clients who arrive intoxicated or who pester other clients? On closer examination, we see that those exclusionary criteria are grounded in program policies and sound clinical practice. Terminating a client from a rehab program because he uses, or refusing housing at a homeless shelter to a registered sex offender, should be based on sound ethical and clinical standards rather than personal preferences. Setting such organizational standards isn't the same as imposing our personal values on clients or selectively applying only those professional ethical principles we agree with. Ethical practice requires a high degree of self-knowledge and a high level of comfort engaging in dialogue with other professionals to ensure that we're acting on the norms of the field, not our individual preferences.

Doing the right thing as a professional sometimes feels not like making a choice between good and bad, or between competing goods, but like making a choice between competing bads. A client discloses to her counselor that she committed a crime. To report it to the authorities would break trust and the covenant of confidentiality—both bad outcomes. Being complicit in the client's crime by remaining silent is also a bad outcome. Which bad is better? Which choice is the right one? Professional ethics guide us to ask the questions and weigh the factors that help us to arrive at the best possible decision. They also help us to carry out that decision in a way that is clinically *and* ethically effective. Ethical standards of confidentiality indicate that we reveal a client's confidence only for compelling professional reasons. Standards on informed consent require us to talk with the client at the outset of service about the circumstances under which we might have to break confidentiality, so that if reportable information is revealed after that point, the client understands what the consequences will be.

What is a compelling professional reason for revealing a client's past crime? Some would argue that absent some threat of a continued crime spree, there is none. Most would suggest that it is important for the worker to encourage the client to turn herself in—that doing so is important for her conscience and successful achievement of her other treatment goals. They would argue that reporting the crime *for* the client undermines the fundamental premise of trust on which the helping relationship is based. We owe our clients a greater debt of trust than we owe people in our personal lives. If I know my brother committed a crime, I might be violating a family norm or sibling bond in reporting him, but I am not breaking the covenant of trust on which the helping professions are built.

Still it's not easy. Most of us have sympathy for how difficult it was for David Kaczynski (2005) to come forward and identify his brother

Ted as the Unabomber. It's not easy for professionals, either, to sit with information that makes us uncomfortable and that we wish we never knew. But that is part of the responsibility we accept in undertaking our professions. It's why we need to have supportive, regular consultation with peers and supervisors to maintain our competence and ethical compass. And it's why we need to have health and balance in the rest of our lives, so that we are fit to manage the ethical, clinical, and managerial challenges we face in the workplace. If all this seems difficult now, hang in there. The purpose of this book is to help you become familiar with these threads so you can use them in coming to ethical conclusions in your own practice.

ACTING ON ETHICS

Identifying an ethical dilemma and deciding what to do are only two parts of the ethics puzzle. The third part involves action. As described above, the process by which we enact an ethical decision is critical to the success of that decision. Chapter 2 and each of the application chapters will provide you with guidance on that aspect of ethical action.

Sometimes, however, the issue for the clinician isn't knowing what to do or how to do it, but rather having the courage to do it under adverse circumstances. You are a student, and your internship supervisor suggests you meet at a coffeehouse for your supervision session. You know this is inappropriate, as it puts clients' confidentiality at risk, even if names are never mentioned. It also reflects poorly on your professionalism and your organization if people at neighboring tables come to believe this is how you conduct sensitive business. Yet why don't you feel comfortable saying so to your supervisor? Is it because of the power differential? Is it because you feel it's not your place to contradict your supervisor, who after all is supposed to be socializing *you* to the norms of the profession? Maybe you don't want to make waves, so you agree to the location but vow not to say anything substantive about your clients. The disadvantage in that is that you've protected their confidentiality at the price of receiving meaningful supervisory feedback. And you've failed to improve the ethical climate at your agency by calling attention to what is probably an unintentional but common ethical failing.

The quality that helps us in actually doing the right thing is known as moral courage (Kidder, 2005). It is "the capacity to overcome the fear of shame and humiliation in order to admit one's mistakes, to confess a wrong, to reject evil conformity, to renounce injustice, and also to defy immoral or imprudent orders" (Miller, 2000, p. 254). J. K. Rowling (1997) captures it perfectly in the Harry Potter series when Dumbledore says to Harry, "It takes a great deal of bravery to stand up to our enemies, but just as much to stand up to our friends" (p. 306).

Moral courage means accepting challenges that put one's "reputation, emotional well-being, self-esteem or other characteristics" in jeopardy (Kidder & Bracy, 2001, p. 4). It means having the courage to act on your convictions—having "the quality of mind and spirit that enables one to face up to ethical dilemmas and moral wrongdoings firmly and confidently, without flinching or retreating" (Kidder & Bracy, 2001, p. 5). It is unlike physical courage in that it involves standing up "against the unfair, the disrespectful, the irresponsible, the dishonest, and the uncompassionate" (Kidder & Bracy, 2001, p. 11) instead of standing up to the threat of bodily harm.

The willingness to act on ethical principles is essential to ethical practice. If you are unwilling to stand up for honesty, what good is embracing honesty as an important virtue? For some, the notion of moral courage conjures up images of whistleblowers from the movies such as Serpico, Karen Silkwood, Erin Brockovich, and Jeffery Wigand. We picture the very steep personal price they often must pay in defending their principles. Yet acting with moral courage need not put one's life or livelihood at risk. People display everyday courage in speaking up when a colleague is demeaning a client, when patient information is being discussed in the elevator, or when an agency practice such as the location of the fax machine puts the confidentiality of personal data at risk.

Moral courage is not an excuse to be a whiner or a crank. It is not a reason to tilt at windmills. Not every adverse decision in an organization rises to the level of ethical failing, and complaining about each of them does not make one morally courageous. Similarly, speaking out about misconduct without an appreciation of the forces and risks at play is reckless and unwise. The courage part comes into play when the would-be whistleblower understands what he or she is up against. Moral courage also has to be used with care, as many atrocities have been committed in the name of one person's individual convictions. If you are taking on the status quo, it's important to understand how it became the status quo and explore the basis for your judgment that it is wrongheaded before you take on a campaign for change.

This last point is important because it speaks to the process by which one acts on that courage to become an effective agent of change. Those skills must be used when the ethical dilemma isn't what to do but how to do it. What steps you should take to bring about change depends, to some extent, on the *nature* of the difficulty you are confronting and *who you are in relation to the problem*. For example, if you are the new head of human resources for an organization and you discover widespread discriminatory practices implemented by your predecessor and an organizational culture that rejects diversity, you are in a different position relative to the problems than if you are an employee who quit because of the prejudiced work environment. In the language of organizational change, this problem has both depth and distance—it is pervasive throughout levels of the organization and affects an array of functions (Frey, 1990). As such, it will be more complex to address, even for someone in a position of power. Practicing moral courage requires a skillful application of organizational change strategies.

If you are a guidance counselor attending a meeting concerning a student enrolled in special education and discover that the "professionals" are seated at adult-sized chairs while the two child-sized chairs are left for the student's parents, voicing your discomfort and suggesting another arrangement should be relatively simple. Even if you fail to notice this offensive arrangement or don't speak up about it at the time, raising it at a later date and ensuring it doesn't happen to another family is still better than taking no action at all. That doesn't mean it will be easy, or that others may not chafe at your suggestion, only that it requires less tactical skill than a large-scale change might.

Social work authors Brager and Holloway (1983) discuss strategies for internal organizational change. These can be effectively applied to reversing unethical practices in systems of any size. The first step is extensive initial assessment, which involves understanding where the proposed change fits with existing organizational values, whether it addresses a generally recognized problem, whether it can be implemented incrementally or reversed if it does not work, what it requires in terms of resources, and how widespread its impact will be.

The second step, preinitiation, involves the change agent positioning himself or herself as a force for change, building social capital, developing legitimacy on the issue, increasing the tensions so that others recognize the problem, and sharing leadership on the change effort. Initiation involves developing a coalition publicly committed to the change, moving from allies who already care about the issue to key decision makers, and developing presentations on the change that reduce others' resistance to its adoption. During the implementation stage, a honeymoon period will be followed by resistance to the change as others experience the pain of transformation and long for the familiarity of old patterns. The goals at this stage include acting when support is at its peak, anticipating and addressing obstacles, achieving interim goals, being open and informative, and reducing tensions surrounding the change and the problem it was designed to address. Institutionalization involves standardizing procedures and linking them to already established organizational elements, so that the chances of change being undone are lessened.

Some of the suggestions for enacting ethical decision making (discussed in chapter 2) will also apply to acting with moral courage. The key at this point is to have the will and the intent to uphold the ethical principles you'll be learning. The effort is important regardless of the outcome. In its annual "Person of the Year" issue at the end of 2002, *Time* magazine selected three women it called "The Whistleblowers" (Lacayo & Ripley, 2002). That year, Cynthia Cooper had exposed accounting fraud at WorldCom, Colleen Rowley had been identified as the FBI bureau chief whose warnings about terrorists in aircraft pilot training had gone unheeded, and Sherron Watkins had written a confidential memo to Enron chairman Ken Lay to warn him about the fiscal house of cards the company had created with its subsidiaries. In his explanation of the selection of these women, *Time's* editor spoke of them as "ordinary people who in extraordinary ways tried to restore

17

confidence to business and government" (Kelly, 2002, p. 8). While some may argue that there was more that they might have done, the prevailing message was that they were honored not for what they accomplished, but for their actions. In the end, terrorists flew planes into the Pentagon and World Trade Center, Enron collapsed, and WorldCom filed for bankruptcy. *Time* decided to laud the whistleblowers for having *done the right thing*, irrespective of the ultimate success or failure of their efforts.

After all this talk about risk and reward, you may wonder why anyone should be the giraffe and stick his or her neck out while others are being turtles, especially if the giraffe's success is not guaranteed. There are several reasons—from the personal to the global. On the personal level, you have to live with yourself. You have to decide whether you can feel good about yourself if you let an injustice stand. Second, there's the rust problem. Sometimes a small spot of rust on the car, if it's not rubbed out, will over time take out the whole undercarriage. People sometimes refer to this as the boiled frog phenomenon—a frog in a tub of cold water will make incremental adjustments as the temperature of the water is increased in order to adapt to its environment. Unfortunately, this accommodation will be his undoing because the adjustments will obscure the warning system that tells him it's too hot and time to jump out. It's easy to be a frog and look the other way or rationalize inaction so many times that we fail to see the toxic climate in which we reside. So often, when ethical scandals are reported, outsiders shake their heads and say, "What on earth were they thinking!?" The transgressions are so clear. But that's viewing the tub of hot water from the outside, not from inside where incremental accommodations disrupt the moral thermometer.

Acts of courage help to ensure that an individual's own moral compass does not become clouded by repeated adjustments in an unethical environment. The individual's decision to do the right thing is also important for the organization. In Cohen's (2002) view, we judge the appropriateness of our behavior by those around us. Their behavior is a yardstick by which we evaluate our own. In what he calls "the ecology of ethics" (Cohen, 2002, p. 9), then, individual acts of courage diminish a corrosive organizational environment and reinforce an exemplary ethical culture. Multiply this across the web of interactions and systems that make up our daily lives, and hopefully the result of multiple acts of ethical behavior is a better, more just world.

THE ISSUE OF RISK

Social workers must consider other risks beyond those that come from speaking out about injustice. Often they are concerned with the risk of doing the wrong thing or failing to do the right thing. They worry about a disaffected client or family filing a grievance with their employer, a complaint with their licensure board, an inquiry with their professional association, or a lawsuit for malpractice. They fear damage to their reputation and their livelihood, even if such complaints are unfounded. They fear the cost of defending themselves against such actions, even with the benefit of malpractice insurance. And they worry about the toll such a defense will take on their energy, their reputation, their personal relationships, and their work performance.

These are not unreasonable concerns. Litigation and other charges of professional misconduct exact an incredible toll. To some extent, though, they are the price of doing this business. Professions in which people intervene to address physical and psychic pain, to mend relationships, and to improve others' quality of life are not risk free. Even good practitioners may make mistakes, such as failing to act when they should have to protect a client from harm, or acting when they should not have, for example, speaking to the media about a deceased patient's illness, thus violating her confidentiality. And because we live in a litigious society, it is true that anybody can complain about anything, and a good clinician may be blamed for something for which he bears no fault. Yet practicing so conservatively and carefully that one takes no risks is almost impossible in social work. Making ethical and professional decisions based on risk avoidance is akin to using the law as a standard for ethical practice. It is defensive practice, not practice that reaches for the highest standards of the field (Koocher & Keith-Spiegel, 1998). What does that leave for the rest of us who want to be skilled, ethical practitioners but don't want to be the target of client complaints? Good practice is the best policy.

What does "good practice" mean? In part it means knowing where your competencies lie and where they do not, and avoiding situations where you are practicing outside your scope of expertise. It means being conversant with the practice standards for your field so that you know what the norms are, what tests and assessment protocols are appropriate, and what interventions are empirically supported (Houston-Vega, Nuehring, & Daguio, 1997). It also means being familiar with social work's ethical standards, because they will not only guide practice but support you when you can say, "My actions in this case were in keeping with the standards of my profession."

Beyond these steps, you want to be careful not to practice in a vacuum. Even those licensed to practice independently need ongoing consultation and continuing education to think through clinical and ethical dilemmas and to keep abreast of changes in the field. Consultation helps you discover new perspectives and unconsidered options and is a way to check your perceptions against those of other professionals. Colleagues also provide a sounding board in cases where you may be losing your objectivity or straying onto the slippery slope toward ethical transgressions (Gabbard, 1996).

Beyond ethical awareness and consultation, risk management demands that you keep good records. The saying "If it isn't written down, it didn't happen," captures the thinking behind this principle. Documenting your consultation in a record of supervision, recording your decision-making process in your business files, or noting in the client's chart the options and choices discussed will help substantiate the process you went through when faced with an ethical dilemma and the way that you enacted your decision.

Where is the balance between a person who is reckless in his or her professional practice and one who is so timid that he or she can scarcely act autonomously with the baseline confidence needed to encourage clients? In all probability, we all practice on a continuum between those extremes where bold practitioners practice successfully alongside those who are more risk averse. But to succeed amid the perils in the helping professions, a dose of professional humility is required. It takes a confident, thoughtful, self-aware social worker to say, "I don't know" or "I need help sorting out my choices here."

I'm reminded of a family practice physician I saw many years ago who called me on a Monday morning, when she was supposed to remove a mole from my face later that day. She said, "I've been thinking about you over the weekend, and I'd be more comfortable if we put this in the hands of a specialist." She went on to refer me to a dermatologist, and I continued to see her for the rest of my health care. I also recommended her to everyone I knew. She thought about my case! She was comfortable enough with herself to call and cancel a previously arranged procedure! I could imagine an insecure doctor desperate for business who might not think twice about her suitability for the procedure, or who might feel that calling would undermine my confidence. To the contrary, my trust in her competence and in her integrity increased, and after all, aren't those two qualities all clients want in their caregivers? Knowing our limits, practicing within them, and seeking help from others are all part of competent, ethical, risk-managing practice.

HOW THIS TEXT WILL (AND WON'T) HELP YOU WITH ETHICS

Now that we have a baseline notion of what it means to be ethical, we'll examine in chapter 2 a process for addressing ethical dilemmas and the considerations that will help us unravel complex cases. Chapter 3 and those that follow describe seven core concepts that guide ethical practice in social work. These are self-determination, informed consent, competence, confidentiality and privacy, attention to conflicts of interest, maintenance of professional boundaries, and professionalism. In each chapter you will find examples of standards from the NASW *Code of Ethics* that demonstrate how the concept is operationalized for practice. Each chapter contains examples of cases where the principle is upheld and cases where it is violated, as well as dilemmas to which we can apply the ethical problem-solving process. The cases are drawn from a variety of practice settings and locales such as schools, health-care facilities, and rural areas, and professional roles such as that of researcher, clinician, instructor, and supervisor. The unique characteristics and demands of the role or setting will be examined because those features are important parts of the context in resolving dilemmas.

You will surely find that dilemmas you've encountered are not addressed in the book. No book, especially one short enough to be desirable reading, can address the variety of permutations that evolve in ethics cases. In fact, one of my joys in doing workshops on ethics is hearing all the different issues that participants bring up and working through them to an ethically sound conclusion. So, if you hope to find a final answer, this book will be a disappointment. I hope that, instead of expecting it to be a cookbook or a Bible, you'll see it as a mental barbell—a tool to strengthen your critical thinking, with the goal of improving what Kidder (1995) calls your "ethical fitness" (p. 57). As his notion suggests, ethical fitness involves exercising our minds so that we can adroitly respond when ethical dilemmas arise. The more exercise we get in addressing ethical dilemmas, the more likely it is that future dilemmas will be variations on a theme, rather than novel experiences.

This book may be a disappointment to those of you who are looking for a book that will address conflicting values or broad moral questions, fully acquaint you with the philosophical underpinnings of ethical thought, or take on vexing bioethical questions of the day, such as when life begins or the wisdom of human cloning. These are all substantial, compelling areas of study. They are just not the focus of this book. This text is situated in the area of applied ethics. It is grounded in the ways that ethics guide our practice as helping professionals. I use the term "practice" to mean not only direct practice or clinical practice but also the execution of other tasks such as supervision, administration, case management, and the like. I hope to share with you the tools for arriving at ethically sound decisions and the strategies for enacting them effectively. You'll get a chance to try those tools out on the scenarios and cases I provide and, I hope, will gain a greater comfort, and fitness, in employing those tools wherever your professional journey leads.

Chapter 2

ETHICAL DECISION MAKING

In the early 1980s I took one of the multiple-choice exams new social workers were required to pass for licensure. One of the questions was something along the lines of "A client takes off her necklace and throws it at you. What do you do?" One of the answers was "Keep the necklace," and another was "Throw it back." I don't recall the other two options, though I assume one of them was the right answer. What I do recall is sitting there with my Number 2 pencil and my bubble sheet and thinking, "It depends!" (This was not one of the choices offered by the exam.) And in fact, social work is an "it depends" profession. What we decide to do in any situation depends on a variety of factors, including the setting in which we work, our professional role, our knowledge of the client, the goals on which we are working, and our own competency. Ethical decision making requires that we take the same considerations into account.

There are very few clear proscriptions in professional codes beyond the sanction against having sexual relations with a current client. In fact, even straightforward guidelines such as "Do no harm" turn out not to be all that clear in application. For example, a supervisor in a vocational program finds that the social worker who works for him has hepatitis C and is struggling in fulfilling his job responsibilities. What should fellow employees be told about his condition, not only to explain his failure to carry his share of the team's workload, but also for their own safety? Doing no harm would involve protecting the workforce, but what about the harm to the employee if his condition is exposed? What of the harm to the culture of (and laws on) workplace privacy if individuals' health conditions and performance evaluations are not held in confidence?

As we discussed in the previous chapter, the lack of clear imperatives in professional ethics does not mean that anything goes, that every decision is relative. It doesn't mean that any action is acceptable as long as you can find a rationale for it. It means that *disciplined, critical thinking* is required to uphold ethical standards amidst the complexities of professional practice. It means that you must engage in a deeper examination, because the context or factors at play will shape the wisdom, the alternatives, and the impact of a particular course of action. It doesn't mean that you have the option of deciding whether or not to adhere to a standard such as confidentiality or competence; rather it helps you decide what it means to uphold that standard in any given situation.

Take for example the question "Is it ethical to accept a gift from a client?" The answer is clearly "It depends." On one hand, accepting a gift can lead to a conflict of interest if it impedes the worker from carrying out professional responsibilities such as holding the client accountable for a particular action. It can also lead to *perceived* conflicts of interest if other clients believe that it has led to favoritism for the gift giver. Sometimes gifts can lead to boundary confusion, if the client believes the gift signifies a friendship with the worker, or expects reciprocation as friends would do. Because of the ambiguity involved in answering these questions, some agencies invoke blanket prohibitions on the acceptance of gifts, but this solution seems neither ethically nor clinically sensible.

In defense of accepting gifts, we should note that in some cultures, the giving of gifts symbolizes the client's willingness to proceed in a therapeutic partnership with the worker (Spandler, Burman, Goldberg, Margison, & Amos, 2000). At other times, it is simply an act of regard, or gratitude, as when a client shares vegetables from his garden or bakes the worker a cake, or a child shares some artwork she has created. The timing of the gift can matter too. Is the gift given around a holiday or life event when gifts may be given to others with whom we have a relationship throughout the year? Perhaps your client's gift to you is the same one he or she gave his or her hairdresser, mechanic, babysitter, and housekeeper to mark the end of the calendar year. Sometimes clients present gifts to mark an important occasion in the worker's life, such as a baby gift when the worker returns from maternity leave. Is it unethical to accept gifts in such occasions? Is it facilitative of the clinical process? Is it culturally sensitive?

The social work code of ethics is silent on the issue of gifts, but it cautions against conflicts of interest. Thus, some clinicians resolve the ethical dilemma of gift acceptance by determining that homemade or inexpensive gifts don't cause them difficulties in carrying out their responsibilities. When possible, some clinicians share their gifts with the office, for example by putting a cake in the break room, a baby gift in the play area, or a painting on the wall. Because the gift is then shared with the office, the possibility of a conflict arising because the individual worker profited from the gift is diminished.

Even with inexpensive gifts, the wise worker is attuned to the frequency and circumstances of gift giving, and the effects on the clinical relationship. If these raise concerns, he or she may decline even a homemade or token gift. For example, a client whose issues involve "overdoing" may get caught up in baking for the worker in a way that is countertherapeutic. Or a client who provides vegetables from his garden may need to hear that, while the worker appreciates such thoughtfulness, such gestures aren't necessary remuneration for the worker's service.

And some gifts are never okay. An expensive gift, even if it is given to signify cross-cultural acceptance, raises the potential for problems. Likewise, monetary gifts, heirlooms, and items on which the client's family members might have a claim are also problematic. It is incumbent on the skilled worker to become comfortable at exploring and tactfully declining such offers. The ability to gracefully decline gifts and other overtures is essential, because as we discuss later, *ethical practice cannot be separated from good clinical practice* (Gottlieb, 1994), and the *process* by which we enact our ethical decisions is often as important as the decisions themselves.

So, is it ethical to accept a gift from a client? Sometimes it is and sometimes it isn't, and addressing the "it depends" will help you understand the conditions under which it and other actions are okay and when they aren't. The emphasis on context isn't intended to suggest that every ethical dilemma requires an examination of all the factors impinging on the choice. As you develop as a professional, patterns of practice will evolve that suit you, your field, and the populations and issues with which you work. We assume the patterns you develop will be ethical ones. Within those, though, unique variations will emerge from time to time—challenges you hadn't considered or new client needs that don't fit in your existing model. Having the capacity for ethical decision making will not only help you *establish* habits for ethical practice but will help you *adapt* those habits to novel situations as they arise.

In some ways, it may be helpful to think of ethics as a continuum, where the potential choices and actions are arranged on a spectrum ranging from highly unethical to highly ethical or from ethically unwise to ethically sound. Where your choice falls on that continuum may depend on the factors surrounding the case, or the context, and may depend on your own level of comfort with your options. As such there may be several right answers, but finding them requires a systematic method for addressing the "it depends," and this is where ethical decision-making models come into play. As Reamer (1999) notes, "Reasonable people may disagree. . . . What clients and other affected parties have a right to expect is that social workers involved in the decision will be thorough, thoughtful, sensitive and fair" (p. 91).

ETHICAL DECISION-MAKING MODELS

Ethical decision-making models teach us how to weigh the relevant factors in a dilemma and develop an ethically sound course of action. These models come in various forms (D'Aprix, 2005). One type is the decision tree. The user is led through different courses of action based upon their judgments or answers at various points along the tree (Haas & Malouf, 1995; Steinman, Richardson, & McEnroe, 1998). Other authors present a list of steps in hierarchical but not contingent order (Lowenberg, Dolgoff, & Harrington, 2000), and still others offer ordered decision-making processes, some of which offer schemata where memory devices are embedded in the steps to assist with recall. For example, Congress's (1996) ETHIC model stands for examine values, think about ethical standards, hypothesize about different courses of action, identify who would be harmed and who would be helped, and consult with supervisor or colleagues (p. 31–33).

A challenging aspect of ethical decision-making models is that they are often so cumbersome that people fail to use them or fail to remember what the steps stand for. Another challenge occurs when the user, having proceeded diligently through the steps, still ends up with no clear path to a decision. The key, then, is to adopt a model that helps to reveal the important considerations and yet is simple enough that it can become a ready resource to be used reflexively whenever a dilemma arises.

The model I developed for this book incorporates the steps and features commonly found in decision-making models for the helping professions (D'Aprix, 2005). It requires you to ask yourself six questions to ensure that you think through the considerations necessary to determine an ethical course of action. These questions are modeled on the imperatives for telling a story that we all learned in elementary English class—Who, What, When, Where, Why, and How. It is intended to uncover the various dimensions of the "it depends" but does not give you all the steps for ethical decision making. It is assumed, for example, that as a good practitioner, you will implement the decision and document it, so those elements aren't explicit in the model. It is also assumed that you have the intent to behave ethically and the courage to do so, so you won't be reminded to include that in your considerations. For our purposes, the questions in the model manifest themselves in the following way:

- Who will be helpful?
- What are my choices?
- When have I faced a similar dilemma?
- Where do ethical and clinical guidelines lead me?
- Why am I selecting a particular course of action?
- How should I enact my decision?

These questions are not ranked in an order of priority, or in an order for action. They are offered in this order because they are easier to remember that way. All should be considered, but different circumstances will dictate that you address them at different times in the decision-making process, and that you give different weight to the various choices. Let's examine what each means and then put them into practice with an example.

Who Will Be Helpful?

Even the seasoned practitioner should not make ethical decisions in a vacuum. Discussing the issue with appropriate individuals or entities may bring forth information, obligations, or alternatives we haven't previously considered. Conrad (1990) calls this the "dialogic process." By discussing the dilemma with others, we are able to unravel the knot of issues that may be tied up in the case, we get assistance in examining the case from various perspectives, we open the door to the generation of more creative solutions, and we have the opportunity to anticipate and rehearse how we will carry out our decision.

Who is an "appropriate" person or entity for consultation? Not just anyone. You should consult only those people who are well versed in ethical and clinical practice in the setting where you practice. Hopefully, you have an ongoing collegial or supervisory relationship with them, so that the dialogue takes place in an atmosphere of professionalism, familiarity, and trust. That person should be clear on his or her responsibility to maintain the confidentiality on the issue you are sharing, but it is still wise for you to reveal only the information necessary to effectively examine the case. Names and other specifics should be avoided.

It may be tempting to speak to your partner, spouse, or best friend when such dilemmas are on your mind. It is human nature in times of trouble to turn to those we know best. You may reason that you value this person's advice or that he or she has a lot of common sense and creative ideas and thus can help you think clearly about your situation. This is a bad idea. Unless this person is in the same field as you are, the questions he or she asks and the advice he or she gives are not going to be grounded in the principles of your profession. Even if he or she is in the same field, that may not translate into having expertise in ethics. And, the person's allegiance to you may color his or her ability to provide an objective sounding board. Beyond this, you are breaching your client's privacy by revealing personal information, even if you feel you've obscured identifying information. Think about it another way—would you want your physician to decide how to manage your care by talking it over with his or her golf pro? Would it bolster your confidence in his professionalism or the quality of her care?

Many agencies today are overworked, and in many cases the quality of supervision has been scaled back to the basics of administrative or paper reviews. Sometimes, supervisors do not share the same professional background as their supervisees or are otherwise ill suited for relevant, competent consultation. Or the people whose primary roles are supervision or administration may have no direct supervision themselves. If any of these scenarios is the case at your workplace, you need to make alternate arrangements to develop a skilled, trustworthy, and consistent resource for consultation. One model may involve purchasing supervision. Another option for seasoned practitioners is peer consultation, one-on-one or in a group format. In developing either of these arrangements, it is wise to create a contract so that there is a common understanding of expectations, including those for maintaining confidentiality (Houston-Vega et al., 1997). Some even suggest going a step further and routinely notifying clients about the arrangement and the qualifications of those who serve as supervisors or consultants (NASW, 1994).

Sometimes the difficulty arises not from a lack of good resources to call on but from having the courage to use them. Whether it is because of fear that we may have erred, professional ego, or personal hubris, it can be difficult to say, "I think I messed up" or "Something happened in my session yesterday and I'm not sure I handled it the right way." Yet unless professionals are willing to confront the issues, there is no way to begin the dialogic process. Without that initiative, all involved are deprived of an opportunity to flex their thinking and generate ideas and alternatives on vexing issues. This goes back to the moral courage issue raised in chapter 1. Being an ethical practitioner means constantly opening yourself to learning and input from others.

Supervisors and colleagues aren't the only resources for consultation. In answering the "Who" question, you may also consult entities designed to assist in ethical dilemmas. These may include formal ethics committees, such as those that are often found at hospitals and other large organizations. Licensure boards, professional organizations, and attorneys who specialize in professional conduct are also resources for consultation. Be aware, though, of two things. You need to take extra care to protect patient identities and avoid revealing excessively personal case information. Second, bear in mind that these entities may

29

have their own agendas or priorities that may influence the nature of the advice they provide. For example, an organization's ethics committee may be more of a risk management device than an opportunity to open up a dilemma for examination. If that's so, the nature of their advice will be oriented toward protecting the organization's interests and liability, not necessarily honoring patient wishes or upholding the highest professional standards. This doesn't mean that you shouldn't consult them, only that you may want to evaluate their advice in light of their stake in the decision.

What Are My Choices and What Will Each Mean for the People Involved?

To effectively examine your options for solving an ethical dilemma, and the wisdom of each choice, you need to get the options on the table. Consulting with others is one way of doing so. Consulting books, articles, or other written resources may also help generate ideas. Brainstorming means generating options without regard to feasibility, probability, or cost. Consider also the option of nonaction. The important part at this stage is to think creatively about an array of possibilities.

Once they are generated, the merits of each option should be examined. What are the pros and cons of each choice? What could they possibly mean for those involved? Let's say you've just found out that your spouse hired one of your clients to do yard work at your home. You doubt your client realized it was your home he'd be working at. Still, it presents a dual relationship, and one that is potentially complicated by the fact that the landscaper is a current, not former, client. Similarly, the fact that you didn't initially know about or create the dual relationship doesn't change the fact that the two relationships exist.

One option is to do nothing. Another is to terminate the client relationship and keep him on as an employee. Another is to tell your spouse and get him or her to rescind the agreement. Another is to speak with your client and explain the complications, hoping he will cancel the agreement with your spouse. If he refuses to withdraw from the landscaping agreement, you might ask your spouse to find a new landscaper, without explaining why. Another option is to discuss the issue with the client and allow him to make the decision to maintain both relationships.

30

Each of these choices presents various merits and difficulties for the people involved:

- Doing nothing might preserve the client's confidentiality in that you need not say anything to your spouse. Perhaps he needs the work and will never find out it's your house. Besides, it's your spouse who hired him, not you. You may prefer not to have to deal with this. Still, your client could feel deceived and exploited if he does find out it's your house and you knew he was being hired. This could lead to a loss of trust. Also the knowledge that he is an employee could affect your ability to treat him fairly in counseling or to take action if there are problems with his performance as a landscaper.
- Assuming the client is not ready for termination, ending your relationship to facilitate his role as landscaper could be considered abandonment. Even if he is ready to terminate, the dual relationship concern remains, as dual relationships can occur subsequent to the helping relationship as well as concurrently with it.
- Telling your spouse and getting him or her to un-hire the landscaper keeps you out of it, but at the expense of the client's confidentiality. And the client/landscaper may want to know why he's being let go. If your spouse tells him, he knows you breached his privacy. If your spouse lies, that's treating him dishonestly.
- Sharing the dilemma with your client is empowering. Explaining the reasoning against dual relationships demonstrates your integrity and your dedication to putting his needs as a patient above your need for a landscaper. A discussion about what to do helps to model effective problem solving. Hopefully, your client will volunteer or agree to withdraw from the landscaping job. In doing so, he need not reveal the reason to your spouse, thus preserving his confidentiality. If he does tell him or her, that is his choice, not yours.
- If your client is not willing to withdraw from the agreement, you should discuss the problems a dual relationship would pose for your work together and consider terminating one or

both of the relationships. This is a variation on informed consent, wherein the client knows the actions you will take if he continues to work at your home (for example, asking your spouse to cancel the agreement with him, without revealing his status as a client). At that point your client will understand the importance of these boundaries and the implications of his choice not to resign from the landscaping job.

- Consulting with the client about the dilemma and allowing the client to decide if a dual relationship is acceptable would be forthright and empowering. However, the decision about how to conduct the helping relationship rests on more than the client's self-determination. It relies as well on the clinician's understanding of his or her responsibilities. The NASW *Code of Ethics* (1999) makes it clear that it is the professional's responsibility to "set clear, appropriate and culturally sensitive boundaries" (1.06c). You may want, for a variety of reasons, to leave the decision to the client, but you are the one who can best foresee the difficulties that can arise from such arrangements. Furthermore, asking him to decide means that he is forced to choose between his financial well-being and his mental well-being. In trying to preserve both (or his relationship with you), he may not act in his long-term interests.

You may be concerned that giving the client this ultimatum could negatively affect the helping relationship. It may, but if discord occurs as a result of you setting a firm boundary around the dual relationship, discord was probably there already. As you are weighing your choices, you should certainly anticipate the risk of disruption and consider the ways to manage it if it occurs. It's doubtful, though, that this tension or conflict is a worse price to pay than the greater disruption that might occur if the client ended up employed at your home on a weekly basis.

Another issue to consider is how quickly you need to act. Some ethical dilemmas are slow-moving targets. They emerge gradually and require (or allow) a thoughtful, planned response. For example, an agency director might need to decide how to deal with a regulation that challenges ethical practice, or a clinician might anticipate receiving a subpoena with a broad request for client information.

Other dilemmas pop up unexpectedly and require a nimble, immediate response (such as going on a home visit to investigate a child abuse complaint and finding that the father, who answers the door, is in your policy class at school). Still other dilemmas *feel* urgent but really aren't. A social worker who is instructed to contact other service providers to determine whether clients followed through with referrals, though no client consent was obtained for such calls, might feel obliged to agree or disagree immediately with that direction. However, he or she may have other choices that can be played out if the worker buys some time by not responding immediately.

You will be best equipped to deal with ethical crises as well as less pressing dilemmas by having a good command of your options and a cadre of resources (supervisory, consultant, written, and experiential) that you draw on whenever dilemmas arise. As to the last feature, the role of experience in resolving dilemmas, this applies to the next decision-making question.

When Have I Faced a Similar Dilemma?

This question calls for examination of precedents in your own experience and critical thinking about how the current dilemma fits or does not fit with those experiences. Its effectiveness relies on your track record in making ethically sound decisions in the past, and on your ability to discriminate between meaningful differences between the situations. Let's say you work in a mental health clinic and a client you've seen off and on for a few months invites you to attend her upcoming wedding. This is the first time you've been invited to a client's wedding, though in your previous work with teens, you were often invited to their graduations and usually attended because this was a significant achievement for your clients and one in which you shared their pride in their success. You were careful, though, only to attend the public, or "performance," portion of their event, not the private or more personal, portions, such as gatherings at their families' homes or at local restaurants. You usually gave them a card with a note of congratulation and a bookmark with a symbolic message rather than a gift for the occasion. And usually their graduations meant that they would soon be terminating treatment with you, their goals having been reached, at least for the time being.

In deciding upon this course of action, you were mindful of confidentiality, which was easier to maintain by avoiding the family gatherings. You avoided the potential for confusing the client or muddying the therapeutic boundaries by giving a gift of recognition rather than a monetary or material gift. Realistically, you also avoided a potentially unmanageable level of expense and the danger of unfair treatment that might arise in buying different gifts for different youths. The decision to attend the graduations seemed clinically and ethically sound, especially as the culmination of the helping relationships.

How does the wedding invitation fit with these past ethical decisions? It might raise confidentiality complications that could be lessened if you attended the ceremony but not the reception. The complications of gift giving might be resolved in the same fashion as the graduation gifts. The sense of affirmation the clients received by your attending might happen in this case, too.

How is this situation different? The event is not as closely related to the goals of the helping relationship. In fact, you don't even know a major player in the wedding—the groom. The client's purpose in inviting you to the wedding may not be as clear as the youths' intentions were in inviting you to graduation. Perhaps the client is just being polite but is not especially comfortable at the thought of you accepting the invitation (or has not really considered the implications of your attending). Or perhaps your approval is important to the client, and your presence will add meaning to the event. A further difference between the wedding and the graduations involves the therapeutic goals and the phase in the helping process. The treatment objectives might be affected positively or negatively by your decision to attend the wedding. Because the relationship is still in process, there may be time to work those issues out, or the wedding attendance could create a distraction in therapy or a shift in the helping relationship. These need to be sorted out in a different fashion from the graduation decision.

Answering the "When" question involves drawing on exemplars and using critical thinking to see how those inform the current situation. Other considerations require the application of theories, laws, regulations, standards, and principles, as demanded in the next question in the decision-making framework.

Where Do Ethical and Clinical Guidelines Lead Me?

Social workers can draw upon an array of resources to provide perspective on ethical dilemmas and to weigh the advisability of different choices. The field of moral philosophy provides historical perspectives through which to determine right actions. Values, standards, and the principles that support them help guide our decision making. Our personal philosophical frameworks are at play here, as well. Laws, regulations, and policies may also shape our choices. The facts of the case, including our knowledge of social work practice and human behavior, help us understand the motivations of people who have a stake in the dilemma, anticipate the effects of our decisions, and craft strategies for effectively carrying out our decision. Let's examine each in turn.

Moral philosophy. The study of ethics is grounded in rich traditions of moral philosophy. From these, two particular schools of thought can be used to assess our options in ethical dilemmas. Utilitarianism, typically associated with the philosophers John Stuart Mill and Jeremy Bentham, evaluates the rightness of a decision based on the outcomes or consequences of that decision. The question "Which choice creates the greatest good for the greatest number?" is frequently associated with utilitarianism. In Mill's words (1861/1967), "The creed which accepts as the foundation of morals 'utility' or the 'greatest happiness principle' holds that actions are right in proportion as they tend to promote happiness; wrong as they tend to produce the reverse of happiness. By happiness is intended pleasure and the absence of pain; by unhappiness, pain and the privation of pleasure" (p. 10).

In this model, there are no absolute directives about what is right and wrong; rather, the outcome of a decision and the relative benefits determine the preferred course of action. Applying utilitarian concepts to practical dilemmas can be challenging in that what is good for the majority may not be right or fair for the minority or for particular individuals involved. And the specification of what is good or preferable can be difficult in that outcomes can be good in different ways. Still, the advantage of viewing our choices through a utilitarian lens is that it forces us to examine the various consequences of our decisions.

35

A contrasting theory to utilitarianism is the deontological perspective. Typically linked to the work of Emmanuel Kant, this model determines rightness by rules rather than outcomes. You may recognize Kant's categorical imperative, which essentially means "Follow only the principle that you want everyone else to follow" (Kidder, 1995, p. 24). Under this theory, ethical decisions are right because they comply with such an imperative, or because the principle that supports the decision is sound. As in utilitarianism, there are challenges in using a deontological perspective in practice. One problem involves the difficulty in achieving consensus about a rule or policy that would hold for all conditions or contexts. Even valued concepts like honesty or loyalty have outer limits where they cease to be useful or where they lead to bad outcomes. Still, while the contextual nature of social work practice makes rule-based thinking tricky, it is still useful in weighing our choices in that it requires us to ask, "Would I want this reasoning of mine to apply to all others' decisions?" and "Is there a rule or principle that would guide my choice in this matter?"

Values, standards, and principles. Values are our beliefs about what is right and wrong, desirable and undesirable, good and bad. Our values guide our individual choices and behaviors. If I value financial security, my decisions about what jobs I take and what expenditures I make will reflect that value. If I value fairness, I will be attuned to situations where people are being disadvantaged and will take action to right those wrongs. Some values are held more strongly than others. That is, while I may care both about fairness and financial security, I would not choose to treat someone deceptively in order to obtain financial benefits. If the values aren't embraced as equally important, a conflict between them is not likely to result in distress. However, when values are held with equal strength but then clash in some way, ethical dilemmas result. For example, if I value honesty and I value loyalty to my friends, which will take precedence if I find out a friend is having an adulterous affair and is using me as an alibi?

Dilemmas can also arise when the individual's values are in conflict with those of other people (clients, supervisors, colleagues) or with other institutions (regulatory boards, legislative bodies, accrediting organizations). A natural first step in ethical decision making thus involves our self-awareness about the values we hold, the origins and implications of those beliefs, and the ways in which they are congruent with or in conflict with those of others around us (Lowenberg et al., 2000).

Like individuals, professions also have core values. In social work, these values are service, social justice, dignity and worth of the person, importance of human relationships, integrity, and competence (NASW, 1999). These values define the profession and serve as the basis for the ethical standards embodied in the *Code of Ethics*, which helps workers enact the profession's values in their daily lives.

Codes of professional conduct date back at least to the physician's Hippocratic Oath, which emerged around 400 BCE (Sinclair, Simon, & Pettifor, 1996). Codes of ethics are usually developed and put forth by professional organizations or associations. These codes generally apply to members of the organization and students who are preparing for professional practice in that field. To the extent that they represent commonly accepted standards for the profession, all members of the profession may subscribe to the code (and may be held accountable to its contents) whether or not they actually belong to the organization that developed the code. For example, social workers are expected to abide by the standards put forward by the NASW *Code of Ethics*, whether they are NASW members or not.

Codes of ethics are also promulgated by licensure or regulatory boards at the state or national level. People who are licensed or certified to practice in those jurisdictions are expected to comply with the code for their discipline, and they are accountable to those standards, such that failing to adhere to them may result in a license revocation or suspension. Because such bodies have the protection of the public as their primary mission, these codes of ethics generally focus on appropriate behaviors in relation to one's clients, rather than the broader range of responsibilities that concern professions' codes of ethics. The standards referred to in this text are all drawn from the NASW *Code of Ethics*. Because they have a great deal in common with the standards for other helping professions and regulatory boards, knowledge of the NASW code provides a solid foundation for ethical practice. However, it is important for professionals to be familiar with all the standards that guide their practice. For any given practitioner, this may include adhering to several codes, as when one is functioning as a licensed professional or within a specialty certification (such as marriage and family therapy or school social work).

NASW's *Code of Ethics* organizes its 155 standards by responsibilities to clients, to colleagues, to practice settings, as professionals, to the profession, and to society at large. Thus, when it discusses a concept such as conflicts of interest, it covers it under each of those sections as it applies to the particular role or responsibility rather than ranking its standards in order of any kind of priority. The code contains standards that are prescriptiive (tenets that tell you what to do) and proscriptive (tenets that caution you *not* to do something). For example, "Social workers who provide services via electronic media (such as computer, telephone, radio, and television) should inform recipients of the limitations and risks associated with such services" (NASW, 1999, 1.03e) is a prescription, and "Social workers should not disclose confidential information to third-party payers unless clients have authorized such disclosure" (NASW, 1999, 1.07h) is a proscription.

To effectively uphold the standards, social workers must be aware of both errors of omission as well as errors of commission. The latter term refers to mistakes that occur when the worker does something that the code says he or she should not do, such as communicating case information to an insurer without patient permission. Errors of omission occur when we fail to do things that our standards say that we should do, for example failing to provide all the elements of informed consent.

The standards in the NASW code are both aspirational and enforceable. Aspirational standards are those that set forth ideals for the profession; unlike enforceable standards, they are not employed as an accountability mechanism for members. While the code does not differentiate between the two, it states, "The extent to which each standard is enforceable is a matter of professional judgment to be exercised by those responsible for reviewing alleged violations of ethical standards" (NASW, 1999, p. 6). In general, aspirational standards are the more abstract items, encompassing issues of social justice and the general welfare, as opposed to those that set forth specific rules that carry an expectation of compliance (Reamer, 1999).

As you review the standards in NASW and other professional codes, you will notice the use of qualifiers, terms such as "appropriate," "undue," "unwarranted," "reasonable steps," and "professional judgment." Here's an example: "Social workers should inform clients, to the extent possible, about the disclosure of confidential information and the potential consequences, when feasible before the disclosure is made" (NASW, 1999, 1.07d). The complexity in interpreting professional standards comes, in part, from the fact that qualifying terms can be fairly elastic, and their meaning open to interpretation. What exactly does "to the extent possible" mean? In what situations would informing the client be appropriately deemed impossible? What if your notion of "possible" differs from your colleagues'? Where is the benchmark in comparing your interpretation of such terms with the interpretations of fellow professionals? Your use of critical thinking, past experience, consultation, and written resources is vital in effectively interpreting these qualifiers for any given case.

Moral principles transcend the helping and health professions, providing overarching guidance for our ethical choices. You can see these virtues reflected in professional values and ethical standards. They can also be used independently to guide our decision making as we weigh our options (Cohen & Cohen, 1999; Kenyon, 1999; Reamer, 2006). Five principles are particularly noteworthy.

- *Autonomy* refers to the helper's responsibility to maximize an individual's right to make his or her own decisions. In examining a choice according to the principle of autonomy, the worker might ask, "Is it client centered? Does it foster the other person's freedom to make decisions about his or her life?"
- *Fidelity* is the duty to keep one's promise or word, or to uphold a trust. In upholding fidelity, the worker should weigh choices by asking, "Is it honest? Is it trustworthy?"
- *Beneficence* is the duty to promote the good or enhance another's well-being. It is contrasted with *nonmaleficence*, or the responsibility to prevent or reduce harm. The test for these principles is reflected in questions such as "Is it beneficial?" or "Is it in the client's best interest?"

- *Justice* refers to fairness, or the duty to treat all equitably, distributing risks and benefits equally. Simply put, this amounts to asking, "Is it fair? If I do this for this client or employee, would I do it for another in the same circumstance?"

***Laws, regulations, and policies*.** Beyond viewing our dilemmas and options through the lens of moral philosophy, values, professional standards, and principles, we must consider the laws, regulations, and policies that may come to bear on the situation. Laws or statutes are developed at the federal, state, and local levels. Case law is shaped by court decisions, not the actions of a legislative body. Regulations and administrative codes are typically issued by agencies with financial or other rule-making authority over an area and are intended to interpret, specify, or codify legislation. For example, the federal McKinney-Vento Homeless Assistance Act (1987) establishes and authorizes fifteen programs to address the welfare of homeless individuals in the United States. Beyond the legislation, however, government agencies such as the U.S. Department of Education (2002) and its state equivalents then promulgated administrative regulations to define terms, clarify processes, and set performance standards on issues such as outreach efforts to enroll homeless children in school and entitlement of homeless children to assistance and services (e.g., meal programs, transportation).

While laws, statutes, and regulations cover geographic jurisdictions, policies are typically formulated at the organizational level. Policies create institutionalized answers to common questions. Policies are developed in the context of a program's unique mission, philosophy, funding, and regulatory environment and therefore usually only influence the practices in that specific organization. For example, the policies of a school that accepts abstinence-only funding for sex education will prevent a social worker from discussing contraception and safe-sex practices, even with a student who asks explicitly for that information. In another district with a different philosophy and funding stream, the social worker will have more latitude for that discussion.

Another example involves the policies used by homeless shelters, the vast majority of which are sex segregated, as guidelines for appropriate placement of transgendered persons. At one shelter, the policy may mandate that transgendered individuals be housed in the facility of their birth gender, whereas another shelter's policies dictate that the individual be housed according to the gender with which the individual currently identifies.

Effective, professional decision making demands that we become conversant with the laws and policies that commonly affect our practice settings or the populations we serve. These include provisions on confidentiality, mandatory reporting, the duty to warn, record keeping, licensure and certification, and parental rights (Corey, Corey, & Callanan, 2003). When faced with novel dilemmas, social workers must be able to identify the array of laws and policies that may impinge on the decision. Sources of information about relevant laws and regulations include texts on social work and the law (Madden, 1998; Saltzman & Furman, 1999), the *U.S. Code* for federal statutes, and the *Code of Federal Regulations* for administrative law (Dickson, 1998). State social work licensure and certification board Web sites often have links to relevant administrative codes for the profession. The U.S. Library of Congress operates several Web sites offering federal, state, and international laws, including the U.S. Law Library of Congress (www.loc.gov/law) and the Global Legal Information Network (www.glin.gov).

It is important to understand the laws and regulations governing your field of practice, but as described in chapter 1, the resolution of ethical dilemmas is far more complex than simply finding and following the law. For one thing, the law may be part of the problem. If the law forbids you to place foster children with "known" homosexuals, and you believe this is discriminatory and deprives children of viable, loving homes, will you not try to find a way to avoid or subvert the law in order to uphold your ethical standards of nondiscrimination and your dedication to the best interests of your clients? If the law states that you can provide information on sexually transmitted diseases to a minor without parent's consent, is that of great comfort when you know the parent and your employer would object to you having such a conversation? Laws are important and provide explicit guidance in some areas, but they do not insulate the worker from ethical conflicts.

Another problem with using the law as a tool for ethical practice is that many things are unethical or improper but not illegal (Josephson, 1991). Asking a client to provide testimonials to your excellence as a counselor would be one example. Failing to report negative research findings would be another. Inviting a client to your birthday party is another. The fact that there's no law against these actions doesn't mean they are the right thing to do.

Even if the issue in question is covered by a law or policy that is helpful to your decision, it still provides no guidance in carrying it out. For example, you may be compelled to report the suspicion of elder abuse to an adult protection agency, but the way in which you handle this with the family and the way in which you make your report require particular skill and clinical acumen.

In answering the "Where" question in this section, we have focused so far on the theories, standards, and principles that constitute ethical guidelines for decision making. Beyond these, our clinical knowledge must also be brought to bear in weighing our choices. Our fundamental understanding of human nature, of culture and gender, of various social and interpersonal difficulties, and of the goals and strategies for social work practice will help us evaluate the efficacy of various choices. Beyond that, the facts of the particular case and the wishes and intentions of the client or others involved must be taken into account. Our clinical acumen comes into play when we generate options and weigh out the likely consequences of a case. They also apply to the strategies we develop for enacting our decisions, as you will see in the following example, which is designed to demonstrate the proper use of the "Where" question.

Applying Ethical and Clinical Guidelines

Let's examine the factors covered in this section by applying them to a case drawn from administrative practice. Let's say Ken is the director of a program in a large agency and a member of a five-person team seeking to fill a leadership position that will ultimately report to him. His good friend Sergio has applied for the position, and Ken very much wants him to get it. Ken thinks he'll do a fine job and that working with someone with whom he communicates well and has a trusting relationship will make his job easier.

When the resumés come in for review by the search committee, Ken notices that Sergio's looks pretty sparse compared to the other applicants'. Maybe he was lazy, or maybe he just underestimated the level of detail required, but Sergio has failed to provide specifics about his relevant past work. Also, his cover letter and resumé have typographical errors and don't list references as applicants were instructed to do.

At the outset of the search, Ken vowed to himself that he would be objective in the process and would not give Sergio unfair advantage, for example, by informing him in advance about interview questions. Ken assumed that he would succeed on his own merits, but now he feels Sergio may not even make it past the first round of review. What's the right thing to do as Sergio's friend, and as the person who must select and supervise the person who gets this position? Can Ken ethically return the resumé to Sergio and tell him to revise and resubmit it?

The utilitarian position would lead Ken to look at the consequences of his choices. Alerting Sergio to the deficiencies in his application might give him an opportunity to revise the materials and present a more competitive portfolio to the committee. It would be a gesture of loyalty between friends. The good that would come of this includes improving Sergio's chances of obtaining the job and perhaps increasing the likelihood that Ken's favored candidate would ultimately get the position. Tipping off Sergio might have the effect of making him more attentive to the requirements of job applications, which would benefit him whether or not he gets this position. On the other hand, it might also lead him to believe that the rules set for others don't apply to him, which could cause problems if he were hired for the position. Should Ken's actions be discovered, his reputation and trustworthiness may be damaged, in ways that go well beyond his role on the committee.

The consequences of telling Sergio go beyond Ken and Sergio themselves. Giving Sergio a chance to revise his materials disadvantages the other candidates, who were not given the opportunity to do so. It violates the standards of fairness on which employment searches rely, and it probably violates implicit or explicit norms within the search committee about confidentiality and the integrity of the process.

On the other hand, if the focus of utilitarianism is on the greatest amount of good for the most people, and Sergio's capabilities and character indicate he would still be a strong candidate for this position compared to the other applicants, one might argue for telling him. In other words, the good that could come from his appointment to the position may far outweigh the significance of any typos in the cover letter. The question is whether it warrants subverting the established hiring process. Perhaps Ken's desire for Sergio's well-being clouds his ability to choose the greatest good, in which case he should recuse himself from the search process.

Failing to tell Sergio might damage the friendship, especially if Sergio was led to believe he would be a shoo-in for the position. If Ken decides not to alert him to the shortcomings in his application, the committee might reject Sergio's application, and another, less-compatible candidate may get the job. Other consequences of this action are that the fairness of the process is preserved, as are Ken's reputation and neutrality, and the integrity of the committee's work. Of the two choices, to tell or not to tell, which choice leads to the greater good? Utilitarianism would appear to support not telling.

What about the deontological perspective? What should be the categorical imperative in this case? Would we want all committee members to feel free to tell their favored candidates about the inner workings of the search process and how their candidacy measures up against the others? Would we want all committee members to agree on a process and then follow that process, ensuring that all applicants are treated equitably? Put this way, the role-based perspective would support not alerting Sergio.

What about values, standards, and principles? Clearly the social work value of integrity would prevent Ken from talking with Sergio about the application. Upholding the dignity and worth of others means treating them in a respectful manner. Telling Sergio is respectful of him, but not the other candidates or the other search committee members, who must rely on Ken's trustworthiness. Similarly, though social workers value human relationships, this does not mean that Ken can ignore his relationship with his colleagues or the other applicants in favor of his bond with Sergio.

The NASW code (1999) has some standards that might apply to this case, among them that social workers will not engage in dishonesty, fraud, or deception (4.04); that they will not "practice, condone, facilitate, or collaborate with any form of discrimination" (4.02); and that they will "act to prevent and eliminate discrimination in the employing organization's . . . employment policies and practices" (4.02). The relevance of some of these passages hinges on the determination of whether the advantage given to Sergio is discriminatory in some fashion toward the other candidates.

The section of the code that addresses confidentiality with colleagues might apply if Ken's discussion with Sergio is seen as a breach of the committee's deliberations. Certainly the concept of conflicts of interest applies in Ken's case, in that his friendship with and loyalty to Sergio are in conflict with his duties as a supervisor and committee member. As the NASW code (1999) states, "Social workers should be alert to and avoid conflicts of interest that interfere with the exercise of professional discretion and impartial judgment" (1.06a). While this standard applies to the social worker's responsibilities to clients, the issues that it addresses can nonetheless be applied to Ken's dilemma.

The moral principles of autonomy, beneficence, nonmaleficence, fidelity, and justice would also seem to weigh against Ken's desire to talk with Sergio about his application. While such a conversation might enhance Sergio's autonomy, it would do so at the expense of the other applicants: while it would be beneficial for Sergio, it would be to the others' detriment. If the decision to allow revised applications is just, it is an option that should be provided to all the candidates, not only the one who is friends with the boss. Ken's desire to talk with Sergio does not uphold the principle of fidelity, while his refusal to do so would demonstrate his trustworthiness as a member of the search committee.

Ken should examine the relevant laws and regulations regarding personnel matters, including nondiscrimination statutes and affirmative action policies. He may find nothing relevant to support him in his desire to give Sergio extra assistance, though special assistance to Sergio may be discriminatory to others, thereby violating agency policy, the law, or both. Were they to find out, the other applicants could pursue redress through a grievance within the organization or an entity such as the Equal Employment Opportunity Commission (Noe, Hollenbeck, Gerhart, & Wright, 2002). The information might prove damaging to the organization's reputation (and to Ken's), even if no formal grievance is filed. The agency's personnel policies and procedures should also have a bearing on Ken's actions, to the extent that they specify the decisions and communications necessary to ensure a fair search process.

Ken's decision may be based on other information beyond his understanding of ethics. One example of the ways clinical knowledge might be used is if Ken looks into why Sergio turned in a shoddy application. Perhaps Sergio doesn't know how to do a proper resumé and cover letter. Perhaps he managed his time poorly and put it together in a rush. Perhaps he assumed the job was "wired" for him, and thus the application itself didn't matter. The particular rationale Ken selects to explain Sergio's behavior may affect his decision about what to do as a result. If Ken feels the errors were made due to ignorance, he might educate Sergio about effective applications, either after the search is concluded or while the deliberations are taking place. Note that deciding to reach out to his friend in this way does not obligate Ken to let Sergio submit a new resumé. If Ken believes Sergio did the application in a rush, he may infer that his friend has poor time management skills, which could be a detriment should he be hired. Or Ken might infer that the rushed application was an anomaly and not an indicator of future performance. What if Ken's knowledge of human behavior (and of his friend in particular) leads him to conclude that Sergio turned in this slipshod application due to certainty that he would get the job regardless of the material submitted? This realization and his experience as a manager and supervisor should serve as a red flag regarding Sergio's suitability for the job and the risk Ken should take to help such a fellow get a job.

The search committee itself is another area where Ken should apply his practice knowledge and case information in making his decision. For example, his knowledge of his colleagues may help him anticipate their actions and reactions if they find out he is biased in favor of Sergio and is providing that particular candidate feedback about the process. Any specific discussions the committee has had about confidentiality, handling internal candidates, and the like, or candidates with whom committee members are acquainted, should also inform his decision.

Answering the "Where" question is a multifaceted task that draws from a variety of ethical, legal, and clinical resources that can help evaluate the options for solving an ethical dilemma. You may feel like you bit off more than you can chew in attempting to balance laws, standards, values, principles, theories, and the like. Don't despair! As in any complex task, it takes a period of practice before this step in the decision-making process becomes second nature. However, it is an essential step for weighing the various options you have generated and in addressing the "it depends." Do the best you can as you gradually incorporate all the elements, and try not to get frustrated if you encounter complexities or contradictions at this stage. As noted earlier, most ethical dilemmas involve weighing competing goods, not just choosing to do the right thing over the wrong thing. Defensible practice involves being able to articulate your choices once you have examined your options, and this is an essential step in assessing those options. As you develop your skills in answering the "Where" question, the resources listed throughout the text will be useful in doing legal research, in finding out more about philosophical traditions in ethics, and in properly incorporating clinical case dimensions.

After considering a dilemma by asking who might provide useful consultation, what the options are, when you have had to make similar decision and where ethical and clinical guidelines lead, you may have narrowed down your choices or settled on a particular course of action. The next question,—"Why?"—asks you to look inside to make sure that the basis for your decision is sound.

Why Am I selecting a Particular Course of Action?

This question is a check on our motivations and asks that we honestly examine our preferences for a particular course of action. Sometimes our own beliefs, biases, and preferences can cloud our ethical judgment. At other times, errors in critical thinking can lead us to the wrong conclusion or diminish our ability to properly consider all the factors in a case. Table 1 offers examples of errors from both categories.

TABLE 1   Errors in Critical Thinking

Error	Thought
Am I acting in self-interest?	"If a client tells me anything upsetting, I *have* to notify the authorities. I won't have any troubling information on *my* conscience."
Am I putting my personal beliefs ahead of the client's needs or the profession's values?	"People shouldn't have more kids than they can afford, so if she needs food stamps, that's her problem."
Do I have an ethical blind spot?	"I would never misappropriate agency funds, but having my secretary work on my daughter's science project makes up for all the extra hours I put into this place."
Am I using all-or-nothing reasoning?	"Selena is working really hard. If I report her for neglecting her kids, she'll lose hope and all that effort will go down the drain."
Am I misapplying otherwise valid concepts?	"In my client's culture, physical punishment is a way of expressing love, so it would be culturally insensitive to report her, even if the discipline is leaving welts on the child."
Is my attraction (or aversion) to people biasing my judgment?	"Kitty is such a sweet and friendly young woman. Maybe I can find her a summer job with one of my friends, even if I'm not doing that for the other girls on my caseload."
Am I playing the odds that a wrong won't be discovered?	"What are the chances this client will find out that I showed a tape of his session in my interviewing class?"
Am I following the crowd?	"Everyone on my unit discusses cases in the lunchroom. It's where we get to let off steam."
Am I caught up in relativism?	"There are no clear answers about accepting gifts from clients, so why shouldn't I accept these World Series tickets? After all, it means a lot to my client to give them to me!"

As you can probably tell from these examples, several problems arise when we fail to adequately examine our motivations. Sometimes these biases and distortions will cause us to overlook valid options. They can also lead us to choose actions that are detrimental to certain clients or to choose actions that unfairly benefit certain persons over others. Over time, bad decisions and uncritical decision-making processes may become habit, creating unfortunate precedents for future decisions.

Another method for rechecking motivations involves applying decision-making tests. As you think about the particular option that appeals to you in solving your ethical dilemma, consider whether it passes the publicity test, the reversibility test, the smell test, and the mom test. The publicity test asks whether our decision can withstand the light of day. If we explained our choice to our colleagues, would they understand our rationale and think we had achieved a reasonable solution? The publicity test doesn't ask whether we are eager to have our dilemmas or decisions broadcast on the nightly news; few of us would be. Rather, it asks us to determine whether our decision is justifiable and within the norms of the profession.

The reversibility test presents a version of the Golden Rule: "Do unto others as you would have others do unto you." That is, would your choice of options be the same if you were in the client's shoes or if your child, friend, or parent were subject to the same decision? In submitting your decision to this test, ask, "Would I want someone to do this (would I think this was a good choice) if the roles were reversed?"

The smell test asks whether the choice we are making lives up to community standards, legal standards, or our own gut instincts about right and wrong (Institute for Global Ethics, 2001). Sometimes this question is reflected in statements such as "It just didn't feel right" or "All the rationalizations in the world can't make this acceptable."

The mom test or mentor test requires us to consider an individual whose integrity we trust, or someone (like mom) who holds us in high regard. How might that person solve this dilemma? How might that person view us in light of the course of action we are choosing? Is the decision one that lives up to the highest ideals of those people we admire and to which we ourselves aspire?

Examining our motivations and subjecting our decisions to these four tests help identify flawed options or flawed decision-making processes. While ruling out or ranking down some of our options, these mechanisms may also help draw attention to better options not previously considered. Or, if our decisions are sound, this process of examination can help ensure that is the case and bolster our rationale for selecting one course of action over another.

It is easy to look at this list of questions and tests and find them to be unreasonably complex for daily ethical decision making. However, paying attention to them helps us all in an initial assessment of our blind spots. Following that, we can work on individual blind spots and patterns, focusing on those particular areas over the others. Having a high level of self-awareness and developing good critical-thinking skills will go a long way in helping us avoid or at least identify distortions in motivation. And having a forthright, reliable resource for supervision and consultation will help to identify patterns of difficulty, comfortably alerting us when we are out of line, when we can't determine that on our own.

How Should I Enact My Decision?

The final question in the decision-making framework addresses the process by which you will carry out the decision, or the way in which you will do whatever you have decided to do. Your professional knowledge base and skill come into play here because often the "How" question involves taking into account the unique features of the client, your history with that person or system, the intended goals of treatment, and the setting in which you work. Let's say that you are a faculty member at a university, and a woman who was your client three years ago appears in one of your courses on the first day of classes. You determine through the *Code of Ethics* that this is an unavoidable dual relationship, but you also believe that it is essential to set clear boundaries to acknowledge the former relationship and distinguish it from the current one. *How* you decide to do this key. Thoughtful, sensitive, and adept handling of the conversation will help to reduce any apprehension the student may have, clarify her options should she be uncomfortable with the dual relationship, and clear the air about the new way that you will relate to each other.

A failure to handle this conversation skillfully could be disruptive for both of you. It could make the student feel singled out, suspicious, or ashamed. Ineffective processes for setting boundaries might include calling her out of class, failing to talk with her in a private setting, acting as if the problems she had when she sought treatment are still in play today, and assuming that trouble will arise from her participation in the class, for example, if she gets unsatisfactory grades. An effective process for setting boundaries might include asking her to meet with you, acknowledging the former relationship, assuring her that you keep your teaching and counseling roles separate, and discussing how you will relate to each other in your new roles as student and teacher.

As you will see when we discuss cases in the following chapters, much attention must be paid to options for addressing the "How" question, because it is my contention that a process that is poorly handled can turn a good decision into a poor one. Be generous in your reading of these options as we go through them. It is hard in a written text to convey vocal tone, body language, and other elements that are essential to sensitively carrying out ethical decisions. As you consider process, think of how to carry out an ethical decision with clinical acumen and with the utmost attention to the needs of the client and others involved.

THE DECISIONS THAT RESULT

Why use this (or any) framework? How does it enhance the decision that results? Why not just go with your gut, have your supervisor tell you what to do, or simply follow the rules without looking for exceptions and complexities? As noted above and in the preceding chapter, good decisions are supported by sound reasoning (Rachels, 1980). Van Hoose and Paradise (1979) contend that a professional "is probably acting in an ethically responsible way concerning a client if (1) he or she has maintained personal and professional honesty, coupled with (2) the best interests of the client, (3) without malice or personal gain, and (4) can justify his or her actions as the best judgment of what should be done based on the current state of the profession" (p. 58). Knowing and using the process consistently will help you to meet those four criteria.

PUTTING IT ALL TOGETHER

Several years ago, my colleague Katie and I wrote an ethics column in which we took questions over the Internet and used them to formulate our topic for the month. The very first question we received was "Is it ethical to pray with a client?" My answer was "It depends," but we figured we should say more than that! Let's run it through the six questions to see where those answers lead us.

Who?

The practitioner faced with this question should consult someone in his or her setting. There are some contexts where prayer may be forbidden (such as public schools) and others where it is allowed, encouraged, or so common that it is almost a norm of the setting (i.e., a faith-based setting, hospital, or hospice).

A supervisor or colleague can help sort out the clinical dimensions of this question and direct the worker to resources to clarify the question. Is the client's request to pray an attempt to distract from or derail the work at hand? Does it convey important information about his or her culture, beliefs, or social supports? Does it require self-disclosure by the worker? Will it be constructive for the client and worker's relationship and treatment goals? Will it blur the focus of the helping relationship? What are the implications of either accepting or declining the request to pray?

A supervisor or colleague can also help us with our own self-awareness. For example, people tend to be less concerned about the use of prayer if it is requested by the client rather than offered by the social worker. If the professional is the one to suggest prayer, a colleague might act as a sounding board on whether that suggestion is appropriate, an abuse of power, or more indicative of the worker's needs than the client's. Similarly, if the worker is reluctant to support a client's request to pray, what is the basis for that? Is the worker placing his or her needs or comfort before that of the client, or is there a legitimate clinical rationale supporting one choice over another?

The supervisor or colleague can also help sort out the balance between being attuned to the role that spirituality might play in the client's life and the actual use of prayer in the provision of social work services. Praying in sessions is not the same as being sensitive to spiritual beliefs. Gaining an understanding of the client's faith tradition, if he or she has one, is an important element in most social work assessments. It aids the worker in understanding how the client makes meaning of adversity, his or her sources of strength, supports and resources that are tied to a particular faith community, and the ways these spiritual beliefs intersect with the problem (Bullis, 1996; Canda & Furman,1999; Carson & Arnold, 1996; Dudley, Smith, & Millison, 1995; Locke, Garrison, & Winship, 1998; Quinlan, 1997). While prayer can be an expression of faith, the act of prayer is not necessary or sufficient to understand the client's spirituality. Consultation can help the worker develop his or her skill and comfort with incorporating spiritual dimensions into social work assessments, and in distinguishing necessary elements of spiritual exploration from expressions of spirituality through prayer.

What?

To pray or not to pray, that is the question. There are several variations on these options, and the choices may depend on the context in which the request for prayer comes up. Table 2 shows some examples. In each, the request for prayer originates with the client.

Some of these requests do not ask for an explicit form of prayer or convey an expectation that the helper will take a leading or even an active role in the prayer. The choices may be; (a) to sit quietly with the clients while they pray, (b) to say; "Yes, I will pray with you or for you," (c) to say something more vague such as "You will be in my thoughts next Thursday morning," (d) to say, "I'm not comfortable with that" or "I'm not able to do that," (e) to say, "Let's talk about that further," or (f) to offer a silent or meditative moment as prayer. Perhaps you have other suggestions as well. It's wise to generate as many options as possible, because while one might seem inappropriate or callous in a given situation (saying "I'm not comfortable with that" to a client's plea for our prayers during surgery), the same option may fit in another case down the road (if a client's prayer is that harm befall another person).

TABLE 2   Requests for Prayer

Setting	Request
A mental health setting	"I'm having surgery on Thursday. I hope you'll pray for me."
A community advocacy group	"Can we ask God to be with us in the work we have ahead?"
A home visit to evaluate parenting skills	"These passages from the Bible give me hope that I can become a better parent. Can we refer to them when we meet? I need God's help to make me a better person."
An emergency room	"We need to pray that God doesn't take Jeremy from us now."
A group for parents of incarcerated youth	"I'd like to pray that that girl drops the charges she made against my son."
In the car, on the way to a meeting with a medical team where a diagnosis of terminal illness may be delivered	"Will you pray with me on this?"

Your options may also vary by how much time you have to make the decision. For the worker transporting the client, or the one whose client is anticipating surgery, the response needs to be made in the moment. For the oncology social worker, requests for prayer may be so common that a response becomes part of the worker's repertoire. For requests that may come as a surprise but have a more lasting impact, the decision made at that moment may be altered in subsequent sessions. So, the decision to go along with a prayer in a community meeting might be examined at the time of the request or revisited subsequently.

When weighing the options, we're always mindful of what each option will mean for the client and for the work we're doing with him or her. Refusing a request for prayer may be devastating to the client or it may be appropriate boundary setting, depending on the contextual factors. This is where the clinical intersects with the ethical. While it would be unethical to push our personal religious beliefs on a client, it might be clinically unsound to assume that our response to the request for prayer will have no impact on the rest of our work with them.

Which of the options is best depends on the worker and the context in which the request is made. Generally, though, an ethically and clinically sound choice involves a response that is focused on the client and that requires a more neutral stance from the worker. In this case, that may be option a, c, or f.

When?

Here the worker should consider if and when he or she has had similar experiences and how he or she responded at the time, as well as the effectiveness of that response. The principle of fairness might arise here: "If I did this for one client, would I not do it for another?" The importance of the dialogic process also comes up. Examining our actions when dilemmas occur helps us evaluate the wisdom of performing the same actions the next time the question arises.

Once when we were discussing the prayer question in a workshop, a participant gave an example much like the terminal diagnosis one above and said, "I didn't have time to weigh out all these choices. I just did what I felt was best (and in fact, my choices about how to pray were limited, since I was driving the car). I didn't have time for all this, 'on one hand, on the other.' "

Of course she didn't. We are often presented with novel problems that we have to resolve right then. But that doesn't mean that the dialogic process is of no use to her. Good ethical practice means we do the best we can in the moment then go back to the office, or to our next supervisory session, and say, "You know, something happened when I was driving Mrs. Jones the other day, and I think I handled it okay, but I'm not sure I would want to do the same in the future." This presents the opportunity to look at the soundness of our choices and to build a repertoire of thoughtful, effective options that we can use even when new situations arise. As noted earlier in this chapter, lots of things get in the way of our willingness to open up those discussions, yet we must do so if we hope to develop ethical habits to draw on throughout our careers.

Where?

Ends-based moral philosophies would have us weigh options by the likely consequences. Among other outcomes, praying with the client may blur worker-client boundaries, obscure the focus of the relationship and the worker's role, set a precedent for prayer in future sessions, help the client feel at ease with the worker, or center and strengthen the client in facing the work ahead. Not praying with the client may put up barriers between the worker and client, create the impression that the worker is insensitive or culturally inept, and divert the conversation away from the work at hand and on to the issue of prayer. It may set needed boundaries, provide an opening to discuss matters of faith, or facilitate referrals to pastoral counselors or assistance in the individual's religious community.

In generating and weighing these possible outcomes, the social worker must make use of his or her clinical expertise and knowledge of the particular case and client. Understanding the basis of the client's request, the importance placed on prayer by the client, and the meaning the client might attach to proceeding with prayer (or refusing to) are all part of weighing consequences and determining which path will carry the greatest benefit.

For a rules-based perspective on the decision, the social worker would look to the existence of policies or guidelines governing such behavior. In the absence of those, the worker might invoke the categorical imperative and consider whether he or she would want all other social workers to choose the same path.

In sorting out this dilemma, the worker must be cognizant of his or her own values regarding prayer, and sensitive to the importance of prayer to the client. If the worker believes strongly in the power of prayer, it is easy to accommodate the client's request, but perhaps this set of values would lead the worker to introduce or agree to prayer in situations where it is inappropriate. A worker who does not believe in prayer might run the risk of imposing these values on the client and being insensitive to the client's needs while giving precedence to his or her own.

Three of the social work profession's values have relevance in this case. The commitment to service means that the worker should put the individual's needs or interests before his or her own, providing services in a client-centered fashion. In upholding the value of competence, the worker should be culturally competent, that is, sensitive to the place that spirituality plays in the life of the client and informed (or willing to learn) about different faith traditions. Competence would also involve having the ability to discern the meaning beneath the client's request and respond to it with skill to preserve and advance the helping relationship. Competence might also mean referring the client elsewhere if his or her request indicates a desire for faith-based services that the worker cannot provide. Whether or not the worker accedes to the client's request, in valuing the dignity and worth of the person, the social worker will be respectful and attuned to the client's individuality.

The NASW *Code of Ethics* does not address the issue of prayer, yet it prohibits the use of professional roles for personal gain. Using the helping relationship to advance one's religious agenda might be interpreted as doing just that.

Insofar as faith is an aspect of a person's culture, the code's standards on cultural competence would apply. Those standards mandate an appreciation for the function of culture in human behavior, an understanding of various cultural groups, and a dedication to continual learning about cultural differences (NASW, 1999). The worker would need to interpret if and how cultural sensitivity impinges on the specific request for prayer.

There are probably no laws that apply here, but the regulations governing various settings might include rulings on the appropriateness of prayer. What about principles? Which choice would be considered beneficial or harmful to the client? Is your decision fair? Is there a legitimate reason why you would (or would not) agree to pray with this client if you haven't (or have) done so with others in the past? Does it meet the standard of fidelity? In praying with the client, or in declining to, are you coming off as a trustworthy individual?

Clinical knowledge and case knowledge are central to this dilemma. As noted earlier, our understanding of the case, the setting, and the client will help us to understand the basis for the client's request, the cultural and biopsychosocial elements involved, the practice norms of the setting or geographic region, and the implications of our decisions. Our communication and assessment skills will help us interpret the meaning the request has for the client and, subsequently, the meaning our response will have. The timing of the request and the specific nature of the request all help shape our response.

Why?

Depending on the context, one might choose not to pray with a client for a number of legitimate reasons: it is inappropriate for the setting, it could exacerbate problems the client is having (such as with religious ideation associated with psychotic disorders), the use of prayer is obscuring the focus of the helping relationship, the prayer is overtly aligned with a particular religious tradition in such a way that the worker is uncomfortable participating, or his or her participation or the need for prayer is best addressed by someone from the client's faith community or a pastoral counselor rather than the particular social worker involved.

There may also be legitimate reasons for choosing to pray with a client: it is congruent with the goals of work, it brings comfort to the client, or praying is a norm of the setting (such as the Serenity Prayer in twelve-step meetings). It is important for workers to be able to articulate the reasons that underlie their ethical choices. However, reasons based primarily on the worker's own needs or agenda would not hold water.

In looking at the decision-making tests, one should ask: "If the client tells others about the prayer, will I be comfortable with my decision? If I explain it to my supervisor, will he or she understand (will it meet the principle of publicity)? Would I be comfortable if others decided to pray with clients in the same circumstances that this client is requesting prayer? Would I want the worker to agree if I were in the client's shoes? Is this a legitimate and legally sound decision? Is it in the client's interests? Or, does it smell bad and look bad? Would people I respect (my mom or mentor) take a similar action? Would they respect me for the actions I am taking?"

How?

How to handle the decision depends on what the decision is. Agreeing to pray, making "space" for meditative or silent prayer, or being with the client in the moment are all relatively straightforward. They are low risk in that they accede to the client's request but require relatively low involvement or exposure by the social worker. The decision to question the request or decline to pray may be more complicated.

Let's say the client's request to review passages from the Bible and pray to enhance her parenting is not an appropriate activity for your visits. You might ask her to talk about what these wishes mean to her in her struggle to become a better parent. If you find her beliefs are sources of strength as she works toward those goals, you might suggest that she review the passages and pray before your visits. You could then begin the session by asking about what she read and how it relates to the issues with which she is struggling. For the client who wants to base sessions on scripture or prayer, the better choice may be to refer him or her to someone in his or her faith community who can offer that, while you provide the assistance appropriate to your professional training. If you were the client, what would you want the worker to do?

The effective process for handling the prayer question depends on your respect for the client's wishes (even if you can't accede to them) and your sensitivity in understanding what the request means to this individual in light of the work that you are doing together.

CONCLUSION

What is the best thing to do when one is presented with an ethical dilemma? It depends. What it depends on and how you generate and weigh options is the crux of thoughtful ethical practice. In this chapter we examined the various considerations for processing ethical dilemmas, and you were introduced to the six-question model that will be used in this book. The key now is to apply that model so that it becomes a natural extension of your decision making. The other key is to increase your comfort with the complexity of ethical decision making. Remember, there are right choices (sometimes several), but which are right depends on contextual factors, which you must uncover and weigh. The remainder of the book is dedicated to just that goal.

Each of the chapters that follow introduces a core ethical concept, standards from the code of ethics that relate to the concept, and examples of cases where the standard is upheld and where it is violated. Building on these cases, each chapter presents a dilemma involving the particular standard and examines it using the "who, what, where, when, why, and how" decision-making model. The goal is to tease out the "it depends" for the case, building your comfort with ethical decision making and your confidence for taking on dilemmas of your own.

Part II

APPLYING STANDARDS FOR
ETHICAL PRACTICE

Chapter 3

SELF-DETERMINATION

The principle of autonomy reflects the individual's fundamental right to have control over the decisions that govern his or her life. Autonomy is linked to constitutional principles of liberty and privacy. Only in exceptional circumstances should professionals, as agents of society, act paternalistically to restrict the individual's freedom or self-determination. Usually, individual autonomy is limited only when the person presents a compelling danger to himself or herself or to others in society. When the client is actively threatening suicide or harm to another, the choice to overrule autonomy is clear. When a person chooses to live on the street or refuses to take medication because of personal desires or religious beliefs, self-determination usually wins out, even if it may cause the helper great discomfort and a sense of foreboding for the future.

The essential social work standard relating to patient autonomy states: "Social workers respect and promote the right of clients to self-determination and assist clients in their efforts to identify and clarify their goals. Social workers may limit clients' right to self-determination when, in the social workers' professional judgment, clients' actions or potential actions pose a serious, foreseeable, and imminent risk to themselves or others" (NASW, 1999, 1.02).

The ideal of self-determination is constrained by societal and individual factors. Laws and cultural norms balance the individual's desires with the safety and well-being of others. Personal options and choices are restricted by resources and capacities, such that a person's career, health-care, or residential preferences are limited by his or her abilities, opportunities, and socioeconomic status. An individual's autonomy may be further restricted when he or she lacks the capacity to make safe decisions. Whether or not a person is competent to exercise autonomous decision making rests on many things: the nature of the decision being made (inconsequential or reversible versus life or death), age and maturity (young children are typically not viewed as capable of making health-care decisions), the capacity to appreciate the consequences of various choices ("What will this mean for me?"), and other factors (Kuther, 2003; Manning & Gaul, 1997; Reamer, 2006).

The determination of competence is an individualized process specific to a particular decision and moment in time, and specific to the individual involved. When a person is deemed incompetent, other individuals act as proxies to carry out the person's wishes. For example, parents make decisions on behalf of their children, spouses are designated to speak for each other, or adult children may speak on behalf of elderly parents.

Individuals can prepare for the possibility of incapacitation by creating living wills and making provisions for a durable power of attorney. These processes specify the person's wishes in health care, finances, and life-extending treatments. In a variation of these processes, psychiatric advanced directives are employed by persons with severe and persistent mental illnesses to specify the steps they wish to have taken in the event that they are incompetent to make choices (Swanson, Swartz, Ferron, Elbogen, & Van Dorn, 2006). For example, a psychiatric advanced directive would alert emergency room personnel that the patient desires a particular form of treatment or prefers a particular type of medication, in line with current medical practices.

Self-determination is a complex philosophical, ethical, legal, and practical issue, with relevance for all domains of service delivery. Helping professionals must be vigilant in protecting the client's wishes against the intrusion of others' beliefs and preferences, expediency, and organizational interests. They must also hold individual will in balance by intervening paternalistically when self-determination puts the client or others in harm's way.

UPHOLDING THE STANDARD

Mrs. Mayberry is an eighty-eight-year-old woman who dislocated her shoulder and broke her elbow after slipping on the ice while walking out to her mailbox. Her hospital discharge plan includes a brief stay at a rehab center to make sure that her arm heals properly and that she does not reinjure it. When Cal, the social worker, met with her to make arrangements for the referral, Mrs. Mayberry flatly refused to agree to placement at the rehab center. Cal did not know Mrs. Mayberry well but wondered if their age, gender, and racial differences might contribute to her distrust of him and this plan. He also wondered if she was resisting because of concerns about her home; sometimes people are reluctant to leave their houses because they are worried about pets, break-ins, or other things. He explored these questions with Mrs. Mayberry.

She said, "It's nothing like that. My mama died in one of those rehab places and if I'm going to die, it'll be at home, not with a bunch of strangers at a place like that." Cal tried to clarify that her condition was not that severe, and that her stay would probably last less than two weeks. He shared his concern that if her arm failed to heal properly, she might ultimately need to be hospitalized or admitted to an assisted living facility anyway. He said that the remote location of her home, and the fact that she lived alone, led the hospital staff, including her doctor, to fear that she would overwork the injured arm and cause more damage.

Mrs. Mayberry replied, "Well, I thank you very much for your concern and for all these folks have done for me here, but I'll be fine on my own."

Cal acknowledged Mrs. Mayberry's decision then asked if they might come up with a compromise. Could a physical therapist visit her home to work on her recovery and check on her progress? Mrs. Mayberry agreed to this option, and Cal began to make the arrangements. He also shared Mrs. Mayberry's decision with the treatment team and his supervisor and documented their conversation in her record.

Tensions in self-determination often arise when helping professionals feel the client is not acting in his or her own best interest. Cal's concern for Mrs. Mayberry's well-being is understandable. While he and the other members of her treatment team understand her desire for independence and her apprehensions about the rehabilitation center, they also believe that her condition will improve best if she is placed there before returning home. While they view it as a brief stay, Mrs. Mayberry's fear that it will be a life sentence fuels her rejection of the placement.

Cal is wise to wonder if the absence of a trusting relationship with Mrs. Mayberry might contribute to her reluctance. In such circumstances, indigenous leaders from the person's cultural community; other professionals; or the client's family, friends, or spiritual leaders might become involved, with the client's permission, to help facilitate communication and negotiate a mutually agreeable outcome. The nature of Mrs. Mayberry's concerns and the vehemence of her response seem to indicate that lack of trust and understanding is not the problem.

Professionals can intervene paternalistically if they believe a client is incompetent to make a health-care decision. Cal was wise not to pursue this course of action. His preliminary interactions with Mrs. Mayberry indicate that she understands her condition and is aware of the risks inherent in her choice to return home. Pursuing further assessments of competence would have been fruitless and would have further alienated the client from the health-care team. Cal or another worker with an ongoing relationship with Mrs. Mayberry might want to have a conversation with her about the point at which she would seek further professional assistance or placement. The treatment team may also discuss the point at which they would deem Mrs. Mayberry's decisions to be so flawed that they warrant intervention to assess competence.

While the offer of in-home services is, to Cal, a less desirable option, it is in keeping with Mrs. Mayberry's wishes. If she is happy and comfortable at home, it ultimately may be a more effective option for healing than a setting she finds foreign and frightening. And Cal has demonstrated respect in honoring her wishes. He has also adhered to informed consent processes in explaining the client's options and documenting her decision.

VIOLATING THE STANDARD

Tonya and Randy are both twenty-eight years old. They both work part-time at a returnable-bottle sorting center in a small town in the upper Midwest. They both were born with Down syndrome. They are in love, have been married for several years, and are eager to start a family. They are aware of their limitations but are confident in their ability, as a

66

team, to successfully raise their children. Vanessa is their caseworker from the developmental disabilities council. During a recent meeting, Tonya confided in Vanessa that they are concerned about their inability to conceive and asked for help in accessing resources to pursue fertility treatments.

Privately, Vanessa cringed. She had been hoping that this notion of parenting would go away over time. While she respected Tonya and Randy's abilities and dedication to each other, her previous work in child protection had left her very discouraged about the capacity of most people, much less those with the limitations Randy and Tonya have, to parent effectively. Her efforts to voice these concerns to them in the past have failed, and she secretly longed for the days when sterilization was routine for certain populations. In responding to Tonya's request for assistance, Vanessa decides to contact a physician who shares her views and who will not actively assist the couple with their quest to have children. She is reluctant to deceive her clients but believes she is acting in their long-term best interest.

Cal's dilemma with Mrs. Mayberry arose from their differing beliefs of what is best for the client. Vanessa's dilemma, while veiled as protecting the clients' interests, stems from the clash of values over her clients' decision to have children. It is not uncommon for social workers and other professionals to struggle with the choices that their clients are making and to have strong feelings about those choices. Vanessa's error is not in her intense reaction to the case but in her failure to address their requests for help and in her surreptitious actions to undermine her clients' rights.

Vanessa's values have been shaped by many experiences, including her upbringing, her education, and her work, for example, in child protective services. It is unclear what preparation she has received for working with the developmentally disabled community and the degree to which she understands the history of oppression and discrimination this group has experienced, particularly around reproductive rights (Buchanan, Brock, Daniels, & Wikler, 2000; Caplan, 2000). It is also not clear how well she understands the capacities of parents with Down syndrome, and this couple in particular. Is she underestimating their abilities and the supports they will draw on in raising a family? Is she placing her judgments ahead of their needs and desires? Supportive and probing supervision is essential in helping social workers address value conflicts and reconcile their beliefs with their professional responsibilities. Vanessa could have benefited from such conversations before the situation reached a point where she felt her only choice was to stonewall or deceive her clients.

Even with ample reflection, knowledge, and understanding, Vanessa may still feel that her clients are making a poor choice and are unworthy of services that will help them have children. If, ultimately, she is unable to assist her clients in exercising their right to services, she must transfer the case to someone who can help them. It is not her role to determine their competence to parent or pursue fertility treatments, and deceiving them by colluding with another professional against their wishes is a violation of her fiduciary responsibilities.

There are situations in which the client's judgment is sufficiently impaired to warrant intervention against the individual's wishes. In cases of reproductive rights, "any restriction or denial of decision-making authority to a disabled woman should be the consequence of an objective procedure, containing proper legal safeguards against every form of abuse. This procedure must be based on an evaluation of the capability of the mentally disabled person by qualified experts, subject to periodic review and to appeal" (Center for Reproductive Rights, 2002). These due process protections are intended to ensure that individual rights are not usurped by family members or representatives of social agencies purporting to know the best interests of others. Vanessa can be assured that Tonya and Randy's competence will be evaluated, as necessary, in a transparent and impartial manner as they progress through the various processes necessary to pursue their goal of parenthood.

RESOLVING DILEMMAS IN SELF-DETERMINATION: HOSTILE IN HOSPICE

Mr. Lee is a fifty-six-year-old in the last stages of lung cancer. His physician has made a referral for hospice services to supplement the care that is being provided by his ex-wife and adult children. When Joan, the hospice social worker, arrives for a first visit, she notes a Confederate flag waving from Mr. Lee's front porch. She finds Mr. Lee in a hospital bed in the living room. His daughter is sitting nearby, and the two are watching the news. Both are smoking cigarettes. In the brief time before the interview starts, Mr. Lee reacts negatively to news stories on immigration and same-sex marriage, using slurs to refer to the people involved and saying loudly to his daughter, "Now that's just plain wrong."

Joan is taken aback by the dense smoke, by Mr. Lee's language, and by his unabashed bigotry. During her one-on-one time with the daughter, she observes, "Your father sure has some strong opinions." The daughter shrugs and says, "Always has. We'll know his days are numbered when he doesn't give a rip anymore." When Joan voices her concern about the smoking, the daughter replies, "Yeah, some others don't like it, either, but if it makes him happy, why not? It's not going to kill him. And if he's going to smoke, why can't I? Don't worry about us blowing the place up, though. We turn off the oxygen when we light up."

In her interview with Mr. Lee, Joan mentions her earlier observation. "Those news reports seemed pretty upsetting to you. What other things do you like to watch?" In response, Mr. Lee springs into an obscenity-laced diatribe about people who are ruining America. Joan is a member of two of the groups he names, lesbians and Native Americans. Her negative reaction to Mr. Lee is so strong that she can't muster a response. Rather, she concludes the interview early and spends the whole ride back to her office thinking of things she wishes she'd said.

Does respect for client self-determination require professionals to endure offensive comments? Does it mean that the social worker should accept troubling behavior? Can professionals carry out their responsibilities in an atmosphere where they are uncomfortable and defensive? In sharing their discomfort with clients, are workers placing their needs and rights above those they are intended to serve? Conversely, in withholding their reactions, are professionals acting dishonestly, doing a disservice to their own humanity, and harming the relationship anyway?

Joan is understandably upset and unnerved by her client's attitudes and his vehemence in expressing them. She is also concerned about his smoking and home environment, in light of his condition. Her responsibility is to help Mr. Lee and his family as they prepare for his impending death, not help him become a more tolerant and open-minded citizen. Nevertheless, how can she overcome her reactions to him and create an environment in which she and others can effectively deliver services? Is she being dishonest in allowing him to condemn groups of which she is a part without alerting him to that fact? Or would such a conversation be in service of her needs instead of her client's?

Who Can Help Joan with Her Decision?

Joan's colleagues will be an important resource in sorting through her reactions to Mr. Lee and determining if she can effectively serve him. They may offer perspectives on his actions and needs in light of his terminal condition. They can help her weigh her options and appropriately balance her needs with his. Those who are also serving the family may be able to assist her in responding to him and will benefit by being prepared in advance for his invectives.

Joan may find that written resources help broaden her understanding of Mr. Lee. Material from social work can help her understand and apply concepts such as honesty, authenticity, and confrontation. Resources in palliative care provide insight into the issues that arise in this area of specialization (Sendor & O'Connor, 1997). Ethics offers insight into the principle of client autonomy and the limits on that when others' rights are being abridged. For example, The NASW National Committee on Racial and Ethnic Diversity (2001) reports that cultural competence "does not imply a universal nor automatic acceptance of all practices of all cultures." The *NASW Standards for Social Work Practice in Palliative and End of Life Care* indicates that social workers are responsible for enhancing the client's quality of life and must adapt their techniques for clients from "different age groups, . . . socioeconomic and educational backgrounds, lifestyles and differing states of mental health and disability" (NASW, 2004, p. 20).

Joan's supervisor should help process her experience at the intake interview. He or she should empathize with Joan about the feelings it engendered and help her depersonalize Mr. Lee's statements or put them in other contexts. The supervisor must also determine if resources exist to transfer the case, should that become necessary.

What Are Joan's Choices?

Joan essentially has four options. She can continue to serve Mr. Lee without addressing his inflammatory comments. The rationale for this choice is that addressing his comments would divert the focus from the intended purpose of her visits and might alienate Mr. Lee. As a second option, Joan can continue to work with him and ask him not to use racial or other kinds of slurs in her presence. This option sets ground rules for their work together and may facilitate Joan's ability to be of help to Mr. Lee. A third choice is to return to his home for the next session and notify him that she is a member of two of the groups he scorns. Doing so treats Mr. Lee with honesty without expecting a change in his behavior. The final option is for Joan to seek a transfer of the case. Given the breadth of Mr. Lee's contempt, it is unlikely that any worker will be immune from his harsh words, but some might be better equipped to deal with them than Joan.

When Has Joan Made a Similar Decision?

Joan has no doubt experienced prejudice against her race and condemnation of her sexual orientation in the past. As a result, she has probably developed strategies for responding to such statements and for inuring herself to their impact. These strategies may include confronting the perpetrator or venting to her social network, colleagues, or others who share her background. The extent to which those strategies are relevant to this situation depends on how well Joan is able to separate her personal reactions from her professional responsibilities. Whether she is typically forthright or passive when confronted with prejudicial comments, her responses to Mr. Lee will represent not only her personal position, but that of her agency and profession. While she may feel victimized by Mr. Lee, she has particular power in this situation in that he and his family need the services she is equipped to deliver. Any comments that she makes or declines to make will carry the weight of her role.

An additional dimension differentiating her past personal responses from her reaction to Mr. Lee is that some past slurs may have occurred outside the context of an ongoing relationship. In those cases, Joan's intent may have been to remedy the immediate situation by removing herself or by putting the offender in his or her place. Different strategies are needed when the intent is to preserve a relationship, in this case, one involving professional services. As such, Joan must take a longer-term view, recognizing that her in-the-moment responses will have long-term consequences.

Joan's experiences with adversity may also play a role in this decision. While she may wish to resign from Mr. Lee's case, will that put her anger at Mr. Lee to rest? Will it perpetuate a pattern where Joan seeks the path of least resistance rather than struggling with and potentially growing from a dilemma? On the other hand, it may not be wise to try to work through Mr. Lee's anger if Joan's pattern is to stay in a toxic situation at the expense of her own health and well-being. Her knowledge of herself and her supervisor's knowledge of the areas on which she needs to work are therefore relevant to the current decision.

In addition to having experienced personal insults, Joan has probably also experienced patients who fail to follow the instructions of their medical team. She has likely encountered clients, like Mr. Lee, who continue the very behaviors that contributed to their current conditions. In a classic struggle with client self-determination, Joan must reconcile her client's insistence on smoking with the other needs he presents. Making too big an issue of his behavior, particularly in light of his terminal status, will probably be fruitless and may alienate him and his family at the very time they should be engaging with the helping network.

Joan's personal and professional experiences shaped her response to Mr. Lee's diatribe, and they can also be marshaled to move purposefully and effectively beyond the difficulties of the first session. Joan should reflect on them in weighing her options, and she should include those insights in her consultations with others about the case.

Where Do Ethical and Clinical Standards Lead Her?

Deontology suggests that right courses of action "are self-evident, can be formulated, and should hold under all circumstances" (Lowenberget et al., 2000, p. 310). What rules might be formulated from Joan's four choices? We will examine each in turn.

The rule embedded in the decision to stay with the case and ignore Mr. Lee's invective might be phrased as "Professionals must rise above their personal distaste for clients' opinions." It would mean putting clients' needs ahead of workers', thus ensuring that people whose habits, appearance, and attitudes are undesirable are not precluded from care. Those are good rules and, in fact, accepted aspects of service delivery. However, there are also legitimate reasons that they are not universal law. The first involves the fair distribution of scarce resources. People who refuse to comply with treatment cannot be forced to conform; however, they may be dropped from treatment so that services can be reallocated to someone who can make better use of them. Another exception to the rule occurs in instances where the client's intentions place the worker's physical and emotional safety at risk. Generally, clients should come first, but there are situations in which the worker's interests and society's should not be subjugated to the client's. Clinical and ethical examination will help tell us if Mr. Lee is one of those cases.

Joan's second option, wherein she would address Mr. Lee's slurs and ask for a moratorium during their sessions, might be translated to a rule stating, "Social workers have a right to work in an environment free of harassment and offensive speech." Again, this is a reasonable rule and one that in the United States is codified into prohibitions against racial and sexual harassment. The twist in universalizing the rule is that there are some conditions where workers must withstand personal affronts in the course of doing their jobs. Clients may become angry at a variety of the worker's actions (involuntary hospitalization, taking custody of neglected children), or their ailments (schizophrenia, Alzheimer's disease, or acute pain) may cause them to lash out at others. Because social work practice is in service to others, there may be times when the worker cannot or should not exercise control over the client's speech and actions.

For Joan's third option, alerting Mr. Lee to her background, the rule might be construed as "Social workers should be honest with their clients" or "Social workers should tell their clients if their background may be objectionable to the client." It is essential that the social worker utilize the principles of honesty and genuineness to convey their desire to help to their clients. Yet like many concepts, there are circumstances where these tools lose their utility. For honesty, those circumstances might include situations that demand excessive self-disclosure by the worker or instances that divert attention from the client to the worker. While candor is good, it is not always good. And the danger of universalizing a rule alerting clients to objectionable characteristics is that clients, for a variety of reasons, may have little choice in service providers. As such, a conversation about backgrounds may perpetuate prejudice and stereotypes, undermine the worker's credibility, divert attention from the problem for work, and suggest client choice where none exists.

The rule embedded in Joan's option to transfer the case might be stated, "Social workers can terminate a client whose thoughts, statements, and behaviors are objectionable." A more positive wording might be "Social workers are not required to continue working with clients whose thoughts, statements, and behaviors are objectionable." As in the first option, the extension of these rules to universal law might mean that clients must conform to workers' expectations in order to receive care, a violation of the service ethic of the profession. Furthermore, it might jeopardize care entirely for clients who are in some way "undesirable."

An examination of the options from the deontological perspective helps to highlight the hazards associated with each of Joan's choices. What consequences are implied by each of her alternatives? If Joan stays with the case but is mute about Mr. Lee's derogatory comments, she may suffer from the abuse, and she may be tempted to shortchange his care because time with him is so repugnant to her. There may also be adverse consequences for the helping relationship if Mr. Lee eventually learns of Joan's background and feels deceived by her silence about it while he went on with his slurs. A positive consequence might occur if Joan learns to handle challenging clients and to effectively manage strongly negative emotional reactions.

What might be the consequences if Joan raises her concerns with Mr. Lee and asks him to tone it down during their visits? He might comply, appreciate her candor, apologize, or explain, thereby facilitating a more positive relationship without requiring Joan to reveal her background. Or he might ridicule her request, question it, and refuse, driving a further wedge between the two. If improperly handled, the request may seem petty, self-centered, or patronizing, and the conversation about it may detract from the original purpose of the visit. That might mean that Mr. Lee and his family are deprived of needed assistance due to the worker's agenda.

In disclosing her background to Mr. Lee, Joan faces some of the same risks and benefits as she does in asking him to cease the comments during her visits. Additional consequences arise from her personalizing the concern by revealing her own background. Mr. Lee might realize that his slurs refer not to faceless groups but to real people, and that those people are hurt by them. At its most ideal, this could be a transformative moment for him. On the other hand, Joan's self-disclosure may mean that he turns his derision on her and refuses to work with someone of her race or sexual orientation. The resulting rift would clarify the future of their relationship but perhaps result in personal damage to Joan.

Transferring the case before the next session would free Joan from having to face Mr. Lee's wrath and would spare him a worker from groups he scorns. The next worker would be better prepared to help him, despite his prejudices, and so service delivery may be more effective. However, transferring the case may set an untenable precedent for the hospice agency, and it would destroy any opportunity Joan might have to overcome challenges with clients such as Mr. Lee. While the greatest potential good appears to come from scenarios where Joan shares her concerns in some way with Mr. Lee, they also appear to be the scenarios that are the most risky for the relationship and Joan personally.

What does an examination of values say? Clearly Joan's values regarding racial and other minority groups are at odds with those of her client. As she strives to reconcile those differences, several social work values are relevant to the case. The value of service is enacted through the principle that states in part, "Social workers' primary goal is to help people in need and to address social problems. Social workers elevate service to others above self-interest." (NASW, 1999, p. 5). The expectation that social workers will value the client's inherent dignity and worth means that "Social workers treat each person in a caring and respectful fashion, mindful of individual differences and cultural and ethnic diversity. Social workers promote clients' socially responsible self-determination" (NASW, 1999, p. 5). Adherence to these values would favor options that keep the focus on Mr. Lee and his needs over Joan's concerns.

The social work value of social justice might suggest contrasting options, encouraging Joan to address Mr. Lee's prejudicial statements. The principle states, "Social workers pursue social change, particularly with and on behalf of vulnerable and oppressed individuals and groups of people. Social workers' social change efforts are focused primarily on issues of poverty, unemployment, discrimination, and other forms of social injustice. These activities seek to promote sensitivity to and knowledge about oppression and cultural and ethnic diversity" (NASW, 1999, p. 5).

A final social work value that emphasizes the importance of human relationships adds yet another dimension to the case. This principle explains, "Social workers understand that relationships between and among people are an important vehicle for change. Social workers engage people as partners in the helping process. Social workers seek to strengthen relationships among people in a purposeful effort to promote, restore, maintain, and enhance the well-being of individuals, families, social groups, organizations, and communities" (NASW, 1999, p. 6). This value would appear to encourage Joan to form an alliance with Mr. Lee to overcome their differences in service of his needs. Alternatively, it may be interpreted as encouraging her to transfer the case to a worker who can better forge a constructive bond with the client.

In addition to the ethical standard on self-determination noted at the outset of the chapter, three other standards might apply to Joan's dilemma:

- "Social workers should terminate services to clients and professional relationships with them when such services and relationships are no longer required or no longer serve the clients' needs or interests" (NASW, 1999, 1.1.6a).
- "Social workers should take reasonable steps to avoid abandoning clients who are still in need of services. Social workers should withdraw services precipitously only under unusual

circumstances, giving careful consideration to all factors in the situation and taking care to minimize possible adverse effects. Social workers should assist in making appropriate arrangements for continuation of services when necessary" (NASW, 1999, 1.1.6b).

- "Social workers should not practice, condone, facilitate, or collaborate with any form of discrimination on the basis of race, ethnicity, national origin, color, sex, sexual orientation, age, marital status, political belief, religion, or mental or physical disability" (NASW, 1999, 4.02c).

The first two standards would structure Joan's actions if she decides to terminate her relationship with Mr. Lee, either before or after sharing her concerns with him. The third would seem to argue for her to raise her concerns rather than tacitly permitting his prejudice through silence.

Practice principles might oblige Joan to narrowly focus her time with Mr. Lee on his needs rather than her personal discomfort. An alternative approach would contend that discussion of these value differences *is* part of the work (Doherty, 1995; Koenig & Spano, 2003). The point of such moral dialogue is not to convert Mr. Lee to her point of view, but rather to foster a discussion of their perspectives in service of the work that they are going to be doing together. "Social workers are not obligated to endorse clients' views blindly, particularly if social workers do not agree with them. Social workers should have confidence in their clients' ability to accept or reject social workers' views. Clients also have the right to know about practitioners' biases that may influence their work in any given case" (Reamer, 2006, p. 107).

In applying ethical principles to Joan's options, we note that the preservation of autonomy is the core issue in the dilemma. While autonomy of beliefs or speech may be less compelling as an ethical issue than autonomy over life-and-death decisions, it is a bedrock concept associated with "Western values of individualism, independence [and] interdependence" (Corey et al., 2003, p. 16). As Mr. Lee exercises his autonomy through his racial vitriol, the effects on others are not significant enough to warrant limiting his autonomy. But do any of Joan's options do that? Even in the options where she might speak with him about her concerns, her intent is to provide for her own comfort, not abridge his rights. Transferring the case (assuming there is a capable worker to receive it) or remaining silent upholds Mr. Lee's autonomy.

None of Joan's choices are overtly deceptive or in violation of the principle of fidelity, but the options where she voices her concerns are the most forthright in honestly and respectfully reacting to Mr. Lee's actions. Those options also appear to best promote positive outcomes in the case and prevent the harm that Mr. Lee's invectives will cause or that Joan will provide substandard services in light of them

The principle of justice calls for Joan to engage in reflection about the nature of her reaction to Mr. Lee. Is she acting out of her own form of prejudice or personal hurt? Or, in contrast, does her reaction occur in defense of a larger principle? Why is Mr. Lee's behavior a particular point of contention compared to that of the myriad other clients she has served? In other words, are her choices to transfer the case or object to his attitudes just? Would she do the same with other clients, or is she unfairly singling him out for his disagreeable comments?

Several laws and regulations stand out in this case. Like other U.S. citizens, Mr. Lee has a constitutional guarantee of free speech. This does not mean that Joan can't exercise her right in expressing her position, but she cannot abridge his rights to services on the basis of his offensive language. The sources that are funding Mr. Lee's care may also have regulations about the provision of services and about the degree to which a provider can decide who to serve and who not to. Joan's agency likely has policies establishing the basis on which cases can be transferred or terminated. They may also have policies for service delivery when clients fail to follow health and safety standards, such as smoking in the presence of an oxygen tank. These policies will provide Joan with guidance and support in her decision making.

Of Joan's four options, the one to transfer the case appears to have the least support in an ethical analysis. Even if it were feasible, it does nothing to remedy the core conflict except move it on to someone else. To continue the case and remain silent also has less merit in that it also fails to address the conflict and runs the risk of taking a toll on Joan and on her care of Mr. Lee. Both options that involve Joan voicing her concerns have multiple benefits. They can be combined if needed, they offer the possibility of reconciliation and understanding, and they do not preclude the option of transferring the case if an impasse is reached.

Why Is Joan Selecting a Particular Course of Action?

Because the conflict arises out of value differences between Joan and her client, she must carefully evaluate her preferred actions in terms of her client's interests. What are her motivations in preferring one choice over another? Whether she is disclosing her reactions to Mr. Lee or her personal background, it must be in service of facilitating their working relationship, rather than selfishness, her own emotional catharsis, or a misplaced dedication to honesty. The decision not to say anything is less compelling if it is made because Joan believes ethics are relative, and she has no right to make her wishes known. Choosing to stay silent or to leave the case demonstrates all-or-nothing reasoning: that she must either capitulate to Mr. Lee's behaviors or retreat.

The principle of reversibility seems to favor Joan's choice to speak up. If she were to put herself in her client's shoes and imagine how she would want to be treated, it is likely that she would prefer to be dealt with forthrightly and respectfully. The first and fourth options (ignoring the comments or transferring the case) give Mr. Lee no capacity to defend his views, explain them, apologize, or rectify them. Those favoring the principle of publicity and mentors would likely suggest that these options are less desirable, at least as a first course of action, for the same reasons.

How Should Joan Carry Out Her Decision?

Attention to process will be essential for the success of this decision. Joan is balancing concerns that are very personal (the slurs about race and sexual orientation) with concerns that are grounded in health and safety (the smoking). Joan must prepare for a conversation about which she has strong emotions. She must manage the risks that Mr. Lee will feel attacked or judged by the conversation. She must be clear about the objective of the conversation and keep that goal in mind, whatever path the actual discussion takes. Joan should prepare carefully for the interaction by considering all the directions the discussion may take and her responses to Mr. Lee's possible reactions. If her intention is simply for the troubling comments to cease during her visits, she can probably achieve this without revealing anything about her own background. However, she will need to decide if and when she would disclose that information, prepare for Mr. Lee's reactions, and determine in advance the point at which she would limit further self-disclosure.

It is possible that Mr. Lee will say, "Oh sure, I can stop. I didn't mean anything by it" or "I didn't mean I wouldn't like you, just those other gays and Indians." Joan should consider whether this is sufficient to achieve her goals and, if it is, thank him for hearing her out and move on to the purpose of her visit.

If, however, Mr. Lee becomes enraged or disgusted by the conversation, Joan must have a simple response and follow-up plan prepared. For example, she might thank him for his honesty and ask whether it is feasible for them to continue working together. If they conclude that it isn't, she should explain the next steps, and the time line for facilitating them. (This is expedited by Joan having sought out the options in advance.)

It may be tempting for Joan to lash out at Mr. Lee if her concerns are rebuffed, and anger would certainly be an authentic response in that circumstance. However, in being mindful of her client's vulnerability, her ethical responsibilities as a social worker, and her role representing the agency, she would need to maintain a calm and focused tone and use other venues to appropriately address her hurt or fury.

CONCLUSION

Self-determination is a reflection of the fundamental right of autonomy. It ensures that individuals are able to make decisions about how they conduct their lives free from the interference of others. The bar for intervening paternalistically is high: when an individual's personal agency seriously impinges on his or her own life and health or that of others. Professionals who are concerned that their patients are making poor and potentially irreversible decisions must utilize available processes to objectively assess their competence for the decision at hand. When the individual involved is judged to be incompetent, professionals can initiate civil commitment procedures, intervene to place the person in a secure setting to prevent suicide, or provide life-saving medical treatments. If the client is judged to be competent, professionals must accept his or her right to make choices, even those that trouble or offend the helper. Exercising paternalism through deception is inappropriate in that it presumes the worker knows what is best for the client, though the worker will never live with the consequences in the same way the client must. And, in addition to being fundamentally dishonest, deception also destroys the trust that is essential in a professional relationship. Social workers and other professionals can, however, be forthright in expressing their concerns to their clients. They can use informed consent procedures to ensure that the client understands his or her options and their likely risks, benefits, and consequences.

Chapter 4

INFORMED CONSENT

The doctrine of informed consent requires that professionals discuss with clients the nature of procedures to be performed and the attendant risks, benefits, and alternatives. Informed consent also addresses the limits of confidentiality, and the procedure is used with research subjects to ensure that they understand the expectations and consequences of the study, should they elect to participate. Informed consent is linked to self-determination, confidentiality, competence, and other standards in that it forms a common basis of understanding from which the worker and client proceed. Equipped with an understanding of their options and the parameters of service, patients then have the right to consent to treatment (or research participation) or to refuse it. The right to informed consent is also embedded in the nature of fiduciary relationships wherein one party has differential power, and thus that party has the inherent responsibility to share necessary information with the other (Kutchins, 1991; Morreim, 1988). Informed consent "is intended to assure the client's freedom, privacy and safety" (Houston-Vega et al., 1997, p. 52).

Effective informed consent is not simply a matter of handing a client a form and asking him or her to sign it. Rather, it requires that the client possess adequate information, have the competence to understand what is being conveyed, have the capacity to give consent, and do so without coercion or deception. Informed consent is an ongoing process, as different steps in the helping process require separate discussions, consent, and documentation of that consent. How much information is enough? The basic standard of informed consent is "what a rational client would reasonably want to know to make an informed decision" (Cohen & Cohen, 1999, p.78). Disclosure includes "a description of the proposed procedures, any possible alternatives, risks and benefits of both, the probability of success, and the implications of no treatment" (Manning & Gaul, 1997, p. 106).

Even under the best of circumstances, obtaining informed consent can be an intricate process, in part due to variations in patients' capacity for understanding and the complexities of the choices they are facing (Manning & Gaul, 1997). Clients in crisis may have difficulty synthesizing and evaluating complex information. The client's diagnosis, culture, and experiences with the health-care system may affect his or her willingness or ability to provide consent. Legal considerations may result in documents that are so dense and lengthy that clients or research subjects simply sign them without appreciating the issues they address. Inconsistent patient-provider bonds and pressures for efficient use of treatment time may erode attention to information sharing and diminish the patient's comfort in providing consent. Scarce resources render the true degree of client choice moot.

Clinicians and researchers may be tempted to shortchange informed consent processes. Perhaps they fear that in describing risks or exceptions to confidentiality, they will frighten the client or subject, bias the results, or lead the individual to drop out of the study or service. Some professionals take the attitude that they know what is best for the other person, and thus the individual's permission is an inconvenient formality. In still other cases, the professionals may reason that the long-term benefits of the study or service provided outweigh the short-term misgivings or discomfort of the participants. Why give them the right to decline if you intend to pursue the project anyway? Unfortunately, such attitudes can lead to grave violations of human rights. A well-known example is the Tuskegee syphilis experiment. From 1932 to 1972, 399 poor black men with syphilis were subjected to painful and risky medical procedures while their disease and associated conditions were allowed to advance unabated. The study participants were not informed of the nature of their disease or the true purpose of the research, nor were they provided with potentially effective treatments (National Center for HIV, STD, and TB Prevention, 2005). "For participating in the study, the men were given free medical exams, free meals and free burials" (National Public Radio, 2002). The institutional review boards and human subject protections we have today may be traced in part to this study. Informed consent procedures are now structured to protect vulnerable, desperate, and poorly educated individuals from abuses of power and position in the name of science.

The NASW *Code of Ethics* has several provisions regarding informed consent for research subjects and clients:

- "Social workers should provide services to clients only in the context of a professional relationship based, when appropriate, on valid informed consent. Social workers should use clear and understandable language to inform clients of the purpose of the services, risks related to the services, limits to services because of the requirements of a third-party payer, relevant costs, reasonable alternatives, clients' right to refuse or withdraw consent, and the time frame covered by the consent. Social workers should provide clients with an opportunity to ask questions" (NASW, 1999, 1.03a).
- "In instances when clients lack the capacity to provide informed consent, social workers should protect clients' interests by seeking permission from an appropriate third party, informing clients consistent with the clients' level of understanding. In such instances social workers should seek to ensure that the third party acts in a manner consistent with clients' wishes and interests. Social workers should take reasonable steps to enhance such clients' ability to give informed consent" (NASW, 1999, 1.03c).
- "In instances when clients are receiving services involuntarily, social workers should provide information about the nature and extent of services and about the extent of clients' right to refuse service" (NASW, 1999, 1.03d).
- "Social workers should obtain clients' informed consent before audio taping or videotaping clients or permitting observation of services to clients by a third party" (NASW, 1999, 1.03f).
- "Social workers engaged in evaluation or research should obtain voluntary and written informed consent from participants, when appropriate, without any implied or actual deprivation or penalty for refusal to participate; without undue inducement to participate; and with due regard for participants' well-being, privacy, and dignity. Informed consent should include information about the nature, extent, and duration of

the participation requested and disclosure of the risks and benefits of participation in the research" (NASW, 1999, 5.02e).

UPHOLDING THE STANDARD

Emma is a child protective worker. Mrs. Lopez had been assigned to her caseload following an investigation that indicated Mrs. Lopez was using forms of punishment that were harmful to her children. Referral to parenting classes is a common element of the case plan for parents in this situation. Involuntary clients such as Mrs. Lopez have no choice about complying with the service plan if they wish to retain custody of their children.

When Emma met with Mrs. Lopez to review the treatment plan, she was cognizant of her client's involuntary status, and the need for informed consent. She described several elements of the case plan then said, "The parenting group we are requiring is an important part of your plan because it will equip you with better alternatives for disciplining your kids. The group I am sending you to is effective for about 50 percent of the people who attend. What we have found is that the participant's attitude is the big difference between those who benefit from it and those who don't. While attending the group is not negotiable if you want to pursue the reunification plan with your kids, you do have a choice about when to start the group and which session you attend."

Establishing the risks and benefits of a particular course of treatment is more familiar, and perhaps easier, in medicine than in social and mental health services. Physicians can say with some certainty what side effects, risks, and benefits a particular medication or procedure will cause. These predictions are less precise in social work, where the dangers and benefits of interventions are less well established and are more reliant on the particular client and the skill of the worker employing them than the treatments themselves. Nevertheless, while social workers strive to establish the evidence base to support or rule out particular interventions, they must likewise work to employ that information in informed consent procedures. To the extent that information on risks and benefits is available, clients have a right to that knowledge.

Involuntary clients and others who are mandated to receive services may have limited latitude in accepting or rejecting the interventions proposed by the social worker. However, like other clients, they are entitled to information about the risks and benefits of the proposed treatment, and the consequences they will face for not participating. In this case, the worker is forthright in describing what she knows abut the efficacy of the parenting classes and the conditions that are related to success.

Some workers might be reluctant to share information about a service with 50-percent effectiveness, fearing that the rate of failure might become a self-fulfilling prophecy for those compelled to attend. Nevertheless, the client has a right to know what is known about the treatment, particularly if she is compelled to participate in order to retain custody of her children. Workers who are reluctant to divulge data for poorly performing interventions might want to consider the rationale for requiring the intervention, given its low success rate.

VIOLATING THE STANDARD

Juan is a counselor in a program for street kids. Because his clients are frequently reluctant to seek services and often distrust professionals, he prefers to work "outside the box," relating to them more casually and skipping some of the formalities of counseling sessions. As such, he usually doesn't discuss confidentiality (and the limits of it) at the outset of service, even though such discussions are considered to be important so that the client knows how information may be used and can judge accordingly what he or she wants to share.

Juan recently began working with Jim, encouraging Jim to find stable housing and a less self-destructive lifestyle. One day, Jim told Juan that he is HIV positive and feels his life is, for all intents and purposes, over. Even though he says he loves his girlfriend, Karen, he refuses to tell her of his status, fearing that he will "scare away the only good thing in my life right now." In the state where Juan practices, professionals are required to report situations such as Jim's to the public health authorities so that the partner at risk can be notified. However, Juan's failure to inform Jim of this possibility means that Jim shared the information with Juan without understanding the potential consequences. How can Juan uphold his legal responsibility so that Jim does not feel betrayed (or worse)?

Juan's failure to engage Jim in a conversation leading to his informed consent for services may now put the helping relationship in peril. A common and important element at the outset of social work services is a discussion of the worker's intention to protect the client's privacy and the situations in which the worker is allowed or compelled to divulge confidential information. Typical situations addressed in this conversation are the need to report suspicions of child abuse, instances where a client is a threat to himself or herself or another, supervisory sessions, parents' rights to information about the services minors are receiving, and statutory obligations, such as the public health disclosure described in Jim's case.

The discussion of these conditions for services can feel awkward and legalistic in a case such as Juan's or in any first session, where the focus should be on the client's presenting problems and relevant history. Nevertheless, the conversation is important because it allows the client to exercise autonomy in determining if he or she wishes to continue services under the conditions set forth by the worker. It also helps alert the client, *in advance*, to the consequences of certain disclosures, so that the worker's actions, in response to a suicide threat, for example, are an expected response rather than a surprise or a betrayal of trust.

Social workers may intentionally avoid or minimize the discussions around informed consent when they have the impression that such warnings will make the client less forthcoming and less comfortable seeking services. While the discussion might inhibit the client's participation, the principle of autonomy grants the client this right. Because people cannot exercise autonomy without full and clear information about their options, it is unfair for persons in power to withhold or distort the information needed to make such a decision.

Juan's approach to informed consent is complicated by his setting and the transient minors he serves. While shelters and other outreach services operate alongside child welfare, public safety, juvenile justice, and traditional social service settings, their responsibility in serving minors is less clear (Staller & Kirk, 1997). Transient and independent clients and an "anti-parent and anti-establishment" tradition (Staller & Kirk, 1997, p. 230) may lead workers to use informal practices around informed consent.

The law in this particular state requires that Juan notify public health authorities about Jim and Karen. Juan may also feel an ethical obligation to protect Karen from harm. At the same time, he has led Jim to believe their conversations were confidential. In breaking this promise, he puts Jim at risk. The helping relationship is already tenuous, and Jim's health and emotional well-being may be compromised by his lifestyle and disease.

How will he react when Juan tells him of his obligation to file a public health report? While the best scenario would be for Jim to be relieved to stop living with his secret, and to be given the opportunity to address Karen forthrightly himself, without the intercession of the authorities, this seems unlikely. More troubling potential outcomes are that he will drop out of service, accelerate his self-injurious activities, or attempt suicide. Even if he makes it through this episode, will his capacity to trust professionals in the future be damaged by this experience? Would he be able to file a grievance against Juan for getting his health information under false pretenses? Could he alert other shelter youths that the staff is untrustworthy, moving this group of kids even further into the margins of the service delivery system? Juan's failure to get Jim's informed consent clearly has serious and reverberating consequences.

Juan and his colleagues must deal honestly and sensitively with the disclosure of Jim's status while trying to help him with his preexisting problems. They must also examine their institutional and individual approaches to informed consent and develop protocols so that clients of the shelter understand the constraints on service and on confidentiality before problematic disclosures are made.

RESOLVING DILEMMAS IN INFORMED CONSENT: ADVERTISING FOR ADOPTIONS

New Beginnings is a private child welfare agency that contracts with a state department of social services to facilitate adoptions for hard-to-place youth. Kathy, a new worker at the agency, has raised questions about two of the strategies New Beginnings uses to reach out to potential adoptive families. In particular, she is troubled by advertisements placed in the local paper that provide pictures of the youths, their first names, ages, and profiles including their interests and special needs. She has also raised concerns about open houses or "fairs" at which adoptive couples are introduced to and mingle with children who have been placed for adoption. After attending her first open house, Kathy voiced her objections at a staff meeting, equating the experience to a "meat market where vulnerable children were being given a high-stakes once-over in hopes of adoption." The staff assured Kathy that New Beginnings was not unique in using these strategies, and that they were ultimately in the best interest of the children. She replied, "They may be common, but does that make them ethical?"

Kathy's complaints may be grounded in a number of ethical issues: concerns about the dignity and worth of vulnerable clients, questions of conflict of interest in the agency's goals for placements and the best interests of the clients involved, and matters of confidentiality and the amount of information newspaper readers and pre-adoptive families should have about at-risk youth. For the purposes of this chapter, we will examine her case through the lens of informed consent. That is, what rights should minor clients have about their involvement in these strategies on their behalf? Do the older children in the hard-to-place adoptee group have different rights from those of the younger children served by the same agency? If Kathy's colleagues are correct that theirs are standard practices, what are her chances, as a new worker, of overturning a widespread, if troubling, practice?

Who Can Be a Resource to Kathy?

Kathy's search for consultation might begin with her supervisor and agency colleagues; she should make an earnest and open-minded effort to learn the history of the fairs and advertisements, the criteria by which youth are selected for the programs, and the information the clients receive about the process. Are all children required to participate if their case worker or guardian approves it? How are the children prepared for the ads and fairs? Are emotionally fragile children exempt from the fairs and open houses? What other efforts to enhance placements have been tried? How effective are the advertising and open house strategies? Does the funding system in any way encourage New Beginnings to shortchange the children's rights to privacy in order to secure placements and advance the agency's well-being?

It would be helpful to know what the youth themselves think. Has there been research on advertising for adoptions? Have first-person accounts been published about the experience? Does Kathy have access to individuals who have participated in the recruitment process (such as adoptive parents, social workers, or adoptees) who can provide their perspectives on the practice? Kathy should be mindful of her professional role and responsibilities in engaging current clients at New Beginnings in such conversations. That is, her research and advocacy on the fairs should not be allowed to interfere with her attention to her clients at New Beginnings and their needs. She should not triangulate the youth against the agency or the advertising practice in her zeal for change. However, her agency might support focus groups on the topic, and she may personally know individuals who can provide feedback from their own experiences.

Kathy might go on to compare New Beginnings' practices with those of other adoption organizations. Are the agencies' practices consistent? Are there state regulations or national standards that support this practice? Are there recommendations for enhancing the youths' rights while using innovative methods to secure placements? And what does the research show? Is there any indication that youth are harmed by the advertising and fairs? Is there a meaningful distinction between the fairs and the ads—that is, is one recruitment strategy more problematic than the other? Where do online registries fit with the tactics New Beginnings uses? Have others raised concerns similar to Kathy's? If not, why is it troubling to her, but not to her colleagues or employer? Are people working on this issue on a large scale? Each of these questions may indeed lead to more questions, but they are all a requisite part of the information that Kathy should gather to clarify her concerns and understand the efforts that have already been made to address them.

What Are Her Options?

Through the ethical decision-making process, Kathy must determine what rights, if any, children have in deciding to participate in adoption advertisements or fairs. If she determines they have a right that is now being abridged, she must decide what procedural changes are called for. Her choices may include ceasing the practices that concern her or building in acceptable measures of consent and competence for the children involved. Regardless of the change to be pursued, Kathy will need to decide if she is equipped to alter the practice and what strategies she might employ to create change.

When Might She Have Made Similar Decisions?

What experiences and lessons can Kathy draw upon in considering her current dilemma? Perhaps she has expertise in adoptions or in children's services that can help her understand the limits of informed consent for minors, particularly those in state custody? Maybe she has had experience bucking the status quo? Has she been able to effectively communicate her concerns and advocate for alternative, more ethical ways of doing things? Does she have a passion for social justice that allows her to take unpopular stances and adopt strategies for long-term change? Is she able to forge strategic alliances with people who share her concerns about issues such as this? Even if Kathy has been unsuccessful in past change efforts, she may draw lessons from those experiences that can be applied to this case.

Where Do Ethical and Clinical Guidelines Lead Her?

In essence, Kathy is investigating three possibilities: (a) Advertising children for adoption is unethical and should be halted; (b) Adults who are acting in the children's interests have the right to make decisions about their care, and therefore the youths' consent is not required for adoption publicity; or (c) Minors have an ethical right to informed consent that can be exercised within the practice of adoption publicity efforts.

How would the deontological perspective view each of these? Most broadly, should it become law that humans, and particularly children, can be unknowingly (and perhaps knowingly) marketed? This conjures distressing, yet real, images of the public bidding and selling of slaves, sexual trafficking, and "mail order" brides. While these practices are all different, each treats humans as products to be packaged and sold (or adopted). More narrowly, would we want the advertisement of potential adoptees to become a universal law? Aren't there any circumstances (a child's safety, emotional fragility, or potential for humiliation) where even discreet advertisements should be deemed inappropriate? Should adults be given the universal right to act on behalf of minors without their consent? Clearly there is some discomfort in rendering this a universal law, in that there are already a variety of exceptions to parental rights (Dickson, 1998; Koocher & Keith-Spiegel, 1990).

What about a rule that minors have the right to informed consent in adoption advertising? Were that to become a universal law, there might be situations in which the minor's youth or immaturity would lead him or her to make poor decisions. Similarly, the withholding of consent might prove damaging to the child's prospects for permanency and lead to a backlog in the service system if foster homes are filled with youth who are eligible but unadvertised for adoption.

Clearly, a rule-based examination of Kathy's options renders all of them wanting in one way or another. However, the process of examination also reveals the risks and challenges in each in the options. This may be helpful to Kathy because some risks may be more desirable than others. The deontological perspective, then, helps her decide what rules she might be willing to live with.

What are the consequences of each of Kathy's options? Ceasing public listings of children available for adoption would vastly diminish the pool of interested families and thus the number of children who could be placed in permanent homes. It would also close off a popular avenue for informing the public about the crisis of children in need of placement (Freundlich, Gerstenzang, & Blair, n.d., p. 11). On the other hand, cessation of such practices might result in more innovative and less potentially exploitive recruitment procedures. It might also protect some children from harm or humiliation at the hands of classmates or others who do not have the youths' best interests at heart.

The second option, not allowing the youth themselves to consent to the service, might be construed as further victimizing an already fragile and powerless population. Such disempowerment might result in poor mental health outcomes for these youth and resentment toward the system and workers who have forced the publicity. Proceeding with the photo listings despite the child's reservations might expose him or her to embarrassment as others come to learn the child's history and status as a foster child.

Possible outcomes must also be considered for the option of allowing youths to consent to publicity. Creating and implementing consent procedures may be cumbersome and time consuming, particularly for an already overburdened child welfare system. Workers might need training to assess the child's developmental capacity for consent. Another likely consequence is that some children may refuse consent. How would this affect the efforts to secure them a home?

Many individual and institutional values are at play in the issue of advertising children for adoption. Foster families, adoptive families, and social workers in the child welfare field value permanent and loving homes. Their agencies value efficiency and resourcefulness in successfully matching children with adoptive families. The children themselves likely value placement with a family, but they also value safety and anonymity, particularly following traumatic events and bureaucratic processes that have violated that safety and anonymity. The practice of photo listing is congruent with the value placed on prompt and effective placements. Prohibitions on how much information is shared through those processes help to honor the children's safety and privacy. However, questions remain about the extent to which photo listing promotes the value of client empowerment if youth do not have the right to object to the practice.

Social work values related to the dignity and worth of individuals expect that social workers will "promote clients' socially responsible self-determination . . . [and] seek to enhance clients' capacity and opportunity to change and to address their own needs" (NASW, 1999, pp. 5-6). In sustaining the importance of human relationships, "social workers engage people as partners in the helping process. Social workers seek to strengthen relationships among people in a purposeful effort to promote, restore, maintain, and enhance the well-being of individuals, families, social groups, organizations, and communities" (NASW, 1999, p. 6). These values make no distinction for the age or custody of the clients involved. As such, they may be construed to support any of Kathy's three choices. Upholding clients' dignity and worth may be achieved through the cessation of the adoption advertising or if informed consent procedures are built in. Giving precedence to human relationships might support the use of advertising practices in service of the good of securing an adoptive family.

The ethical standards on informed consent cited at the beginning of this chapter have relevance for this case. Social workers should allow for informed consent. In cases where clients are not legally or clinically competent to render consent, social workers should ensure that their guardians and others are acting in the clients' best interests and include the clients themselves in the process to the extent possible.

Ethical standards on confidentiality also apply to this case since the essence of the adoption advertising controversy involves how much information should be shared without the consent of the youths involved. Key provisions include the following:

- "Social workers may disclose confidential information when appropriate with valid consent from a client or a person legally authorized to consent on behalf of a client" (NASW, 1999, 1.07b).
- "Social workers should inform clients, to the extent possible, about the disclosure of confidential information and the potential consequences, when feasible before the disclosure is made. This applies whether social workers disclose confidential information on the basis of a legal requirement or client consent" (NASW, 1999, 1.07d).
- "Social workers should discuss with clients and other interested parties the nature of confidentiality and limitations of clients' right to confidentiality. Social workers should review with clients circumstances where confidential information may be requested and where disclosure of confidential information may be legally required. This discussion should occur as soon as possible in the social worker-client relationship and as needed throughout the course of the relationship" (NASW, 1999, 1.07e).

How might these ethical standards influence Kathy's decision? While they make no distinction between adult and child clients, the standards clearly favor the right of the client to be informed about his or her rights and options, and the actions being taken on his or her behalf. In most cases, minors are not considered competent to render consent for medical and social services, and therefore an adult's permission is required for receipt of care or participation in research. Nevertheless, the execution of the legal right to act on behalf of minors is strengthened when youth are afforded an ethical right to participate in the decision making. The standards would therefore seem to uphold the use of adoption fairs and photos with the consent of the child's guardians, but they would also encourage the youth's involvement to the extent possible.

This involvement might be expressed in one of two ways. Assent "recognizes that minors may not, as a function of their developmental level, be capable of giving fully reasoned consent but may still be capable of reaching and expressing a preference" (Koocher & Keith-Spiegel, 1990, p. 10). A second mechanism for involving youth in the decision about photo listing would be to provide each individual with the right to decline inclusion in the list. While only a legal guardian could provide consent for inclusion, allowing the youth to opt out of the service would empower the client and provide maximum protection and respect for the child's concerns. In addressing minors and health care, the American Academy of Pediatrics (1995) suggests that "A patient's reluctance or refusal to assent should also carry considerable weight when the proposed intervention is not essential to his or her welfare and/or can be deferred without substantial risk" (p. 316).

In Kathy's case, the negative effects of such a provision would be that the child's likelihood of placement would be limited and the provision of services in an impermanent setting would be prolonged. As in other cases involving competence and informed consent, an assessment would be required to determine whether the child was capable of comprehending the risks and benefits in order to make a reasoned decision (Devettere, 2000; Gustafson & McNamara, 1987; Richards, 2003). Manning and Gaul (1997) suggest that "The touchstone of assessing competency is to look for a 'thoughtful' decision making process, taking into account reversible versus irreversible conditions, and the level of preparedness for the decision versus impulsiveness that affects the quality of the decision" (p. 109). Assent and dissent effectively broaden Kathy's original three choices by elaborating on the different forms that clients' consent might take.

The concern for the principle of autonomy is at the core of Kathy's dilemma. On one hand, individuals should have the maximum degree of choice in the matters that affect them. The third option (allowing consent) would provide the greatest autonomy for the minor clients. However, in the United States, minors are accorded limited rights. Furthermore, the child welfare system, having intervened paternalistically to rescue youth from abuse and neglect, is charged with their care and well-being. As such, the system considers the long-term advantages of permanent homes to outweigh the short-term challenges inherent in finding such homes for individual children.

All of Kathy's choices are in keeping with the principle of fidelity, assuming that whatever privileges New Beginnings and other agencies afford minor clients, they are forthright about what the specific options and processes will be. Kathy's choices are consistent with the principle of justice as well. That is, whichever option is chosen, there is no indication that it will be implemented unevenly, except as is necessitated by differences in a child's decision-making capacity. However, the element of justice that is concerned with the fair distribution of scarce resources might be detrimentally affected by Kathy's third choice, that of offering the youth consent, if the refusal to render consent means that a log jam occurs with foster homes occupied by those kids who are ready for another form of placement.

How the options sort out on the basis of beneficence and nonmaleficence will depend on one's evaluations of what is "good" in the case. That is, each option offers some kind of benefit for the clients: a stronger possibility of placement in a secure home, the right to exercise self-determination, the opportunity to protect the privacy and dignity of youth in the child welfare system. Each offers potential harms, too: diminishing the pool of families interested in adoption, increasing the difficulty of finding homes for hard-to-place children, putting vulnerable youth in positions that might be embarrassing or hurtful, paternalistically overriding children's wishes about photo listing or fairs. Like the utilitarian analysis, the principles of beneficence and nonmaleficence help weigh these outcomes. They may also help Kathy craft an option that preserves the practice of advertising for adoption matches while ensuring that young children are provided the opportunity for assent, and older ones, consent.

Photo listing has a fifty-year history, and the practice has evolved as information-sharing technologies have become more sophisticated and the needs of children for placement have continued unabated (Freundlich et al., n.d., pp. 6–8). The practice is endorsed and financed by child advocacy groups such as the Child Welfare League of America and by governmental entities such as the federal Children's Bureau (Freundlich et al., n.d., pp. 7–8). The North American Council on Adoptable Children recommends caution in selecting and preparing children for individualized promotion activities, though it endorses those practices as worthwhile (Schuerger, 2002). Those entities help to shape the rules and procedures governing adoptions. However, Kathy is not alone in the concerns she has about the process (Scarth, 2004).

Federal and state laws on confidentiality regulate the information that can be shared during child-specific recruitment. Such laws prohibit disclosure of information about HIV status, substance abuse treatment, and other conditions until later in the adoption process. HIPAA, the Health Insurance Portability and Accountability Act, regulates the use of health information but has not resulted in uniform state practices with regard to adoption advertising (Freundlich et al., n.d., p. 14).

Each state has its own regulations about the use of advertising for adoptions. Some prohibit advertising by those seeking to adopt or by their representatives, such as physicians or attorneys. Other states restrict the right to advertise to state agencies or those with licensed or contractual arrangements to provide adoption services in the state (National Adoption Information Clearinghouse, 2004). Each of those statutes is intended to protect participants in the adoption triad from unscrupulous practices. It appears that no state statute addresses Kathy's concern about the rights of children in state custody to consent to advertisements or participation in recruitment activities.

Specific state agencies may have policies or procedures that address Kathy's concerns. Kathy would need to investigate those that apply to her state and consult with other jurisdictions to learn about models her state might adopt. While arduous, this process might help her to learn more about the regulatory personnel and processes in her state. These contacts will enable her to craft a more effective strategy for change, should she decide that informed consent provisions are required in the photo listing system.

In addition to legal and policy considerations, standards of practice for photo listings must also be taken into account. For example, the disclosure of personal and potentially harmful information must be considered in light of the entire adoption process. For example, limited and generally positive information is shared at the recruitment phase, while comprehensive information is disclosed about the child as the process unfolds, based on a family's intent to pursue adoption (Freundlich & Gerstenzang, 2004). The children involved should be included to the extent possible and should be given the opportunity to express concerns and provide input on their postings. For example, Freundlich et al. (n.d.) suggest

- Discussing the purpose of photo listing with the child and showing the child examples. This might involve talking about what the child likes and dislikes about different forms of photo listings and what he or she wants to include or exclude in his or her own description or having the child review the photo listing and pick the photo to be used.
- Considering the information to be shared in light of the worker's own family. Workers should ask themselves, "Would I want such information posted about my child?"
- Being prepared to address a child's reluctance. This may include exploring the nature of his or her apprehensions, answering questions, acknowledging fears, and adjusting the process to address the child's concerns (for example, by using pseudonyms).
- Demonstrating restraint in the portrayal of the child. Even though information *could* be shared, sometimes it should not be. Imagine how the child would react if certain facts or characteristics were available through the Internet, newspaper, or public service programming on TV. Even if the child is too young to appreciate the consequences, how might he or she feel about such disclosures later in life? (pp. 19–21, 33).

Kathy may find additional practice standards helpful. For example, the *NASW Standards for the Practice of Social Work with Adolescents* addresses confidentiality and client empowerment (NASW, 2003, pp.

12, 15). Practice standards in individual social service departments may stipulate how children should be selected, screened, and prepared for photo listing or adoption fairs. The National Resource Center for Foster Care and Permanency Planning (n.d.) recommends that the children chosen for child-specific recruitment be representative of the larger population of available children and be available for adoption (rather than in line for a kinship placement). An individual child's safety must be ensured, so that publicity does not put him or her at risk at the hands of angry relatives. Furthermore, recruitment publicity is premature and possibly damaging if the child's caretaker opposes it or the child is not ready for placement (Schuerger, 2002).

Why Would Kathy Select a Particular Course of Action?

If Kathy's exploration of the ethical, legal, and clinical advisability of the choices leads her to conclude that youth deserve the right to provide assent or dissent for photo listing and adoption fairs, she must still examine her own motivations in pursuing that path. For example, does her personal history predispose her to advocate inappropriately for the youth involved? In other words, does she care about it more than they do? Is she appropriately applying the concept of informed consent in such a way that youth are protected and empowered, in keeping with their developmental capacities?

Does her plan treat the youths in the way that she would want to be treated? Are the basis of her concerns and the rationale for her plan understandable to others? Is she comfortable asking others to work with her on this issue? Is she behaving in a way that reflects the best standards of the profession? Are her decisions and actions in line with her beliefs and those of people she respects?

How Should She Carry It Out?

As a new employee at the agency, Kathy is probably not strategically poised to bring about the organizational change she desires. As she conducts the research suggested here, she should build social capital in the organization, forge relationships with people who share her concern or have decision-making power, and educate others about the options for reconciling client rights and agency practices.

The change needed will depend on how divergent the agency's current practices are from her ideal. If youth are already carefully screened and prepared for in-person recruitment events, and if they are actively involved in the photo listing process, then instituting an assent-dissent provision should be a relatively minor change in both policies and practices. The process of effecting change will take longer and require more steps and strategies if the agency tends to act on behalf of, rather than with, the clients, particularly if they do so with the approval of the state child welfare agency. The work of authors such as Frey (1990) and Brager and Holloway (1983) may prove influential as Kathy considers the special challenges of changing organizational processes and policies.

CONCLUSION

Informed consent processes are essential for personal autonomy. People cannot exercise self-determination in the absence of honest information about their choices and the related risks and benefits. True informed consent requires that the information be presented to the person in an understandable fashion, that consent be rendered voluntarily and without coercion, and that the individual be competent to provide consent. The assessment of competence is a highly individualized process. It depends on the state of the client (age, cognitive capacity, ability to weigh alternatives and compare outcomes) and the nature of the decision.

When clients are not competent to provide consent, others may be legally or ethically empowered to do so on their behalf. Even under these conditions, however, social workers should be mindful of the client's stake in the decisions, ensuring that the third party is acting in the client's interests. In some clinical and research settings, clients have the opportunity to give assent, that is, informed agreement with the consent that has provided for them, or dissent, the right to refuse or withdraw from the service suggested. Many resources are available to help clinicians and researchers institute the proper protocols for protecting clients and human research subjects (Appelbaum, Lidz, & Meisel, 1987; Richards, 2003; U.S. Department of Health and Human Services, 2003a).

It is essential that informed consent be obtained at the outset of service, as it provides the ground rules about confidentiality, treatment criteria, and other policies that lay the foundation for the helping relationship. Informed consent is then employed throughout the duration of the therapeutic process as changing circumstances require new decisions and as the client's understanding and interests evolve.

Chapter 5

CONFLICTS OF INTEREST

Conflicts of interest occur when a worker's needs or interests threaten to take precedence over those of the client or otherwise impede the practitioner's ability to carry out his or her professional responsibilities. For instance, a worker who is hired to develop housing for ex-convicts returning to the community may experience a conflict of interest when one of the homes is targeted for her neighborhood. Conflicts can also occur when the worker's loyalties to clients are split in such a way that upholding the interests of one client would disadvantage another. Difficult situations arise in family therapy when the interests of the children may be at odds with those of the parents, and the worker owes loyalty to the entire family.

Conflicts of interest can give rise to a loss of professional objectivity and compromises in professional judgment (Fisher, 2003). As discussed in chapter 2, accepting a gift from a client may be clinically and ethically sound, depending on contextual factors, or it may create a conflict for the social worker, who is now reluctant to make appropriate therapeutic demands of the client or reinforce agency rules, because accepting the gift has undermined the worker's ability to carry out his or her responsibilities. When there are personal or financial stakes for the worker, other conflicts of interest can occur such as receiving commissions from the sale of books or vitamin supplements that are recommended to clients, or when a researcher has a stake in a treatment that is being investigated and skews findings to obscure the treatments shortcomings. Conflicts can also occur when loyalty to one's employer (and the need for a job) conflicts with the best interests of the client, with one's professional expertise, or with one's ethical obligations.

Examples of ethical tenets on conflicts of interest include

- "Social workers should not take unfair advantage of any professional relationship or exploit others to further their personal, religious, political, or business interests" (NASW, 1999, 1.06a).

- "Social workers should be alert to and avoid conflicts of interest that interfere with the exercise of professional discretion and impartial judgment. Social workers should inform clients when a real or potential conflict of interest arises and take reasonable steps to resolve the issue in a manner that makes the clients' interests primary and protects clients' interests to the greatest extent possible. In some cases, protecting clients' interests may require termination of the professional relationship with proper referral of the client" (NASW, 1999, 1.06a).

The code clearly describes the variety of ways the worker's interests can intersect with the client's interests and places responsibility on the professional to detect and address potentially compromising situations. Recent political scandals have called attention to the ethical imperative of avoiding conflicts of interest. Even if it is legal for politicians to accept contributions or sports tickets from groups they regulate, these are ethically troubling practices. The rejoinder "I would have supported that legislation anyway" doesn't remove the cloud of suspicion that the support was facilitated by the gift. The cumulative result of such practices is an erosion of public trust in the individuals involved and the professions they represent.

UPHOLDING THE STANDARD

Mountain Vista Assisted Living is run by a for-profit corporation that is intent on generating goodwill and referrals for its programs. Iris works on the geriatric unit at the local hospital and thus does extensive business with the area nursing homes. She is impressed with Mountain Vista's services. Though its fees are much higher than those of other facilities in the region, she suggests it to patients and their families as one of several options to consider.

Last year at Christmastime, Mountain Vista sent her a large fruit basket with a note thanking her for her referrals. Iris is accustomed to getting office supplies, lunches, and coffee breaks from the various pharmaceutical companies that do business with the hospital, so she thought nothing of accepting the basket and sharing it with the workers on her unit. This year, when the holidays rolled around, Mountain Vista sent Iris a gift certificate for $100 to the local mall. Iris did not want Mountain

Vista, her colleagues, her patients, or staff at other nursing homes to think that she practiced favoritism toward Mountain Vista because of its generous rewards. Nor did she want the gift from them to put her in a bind if for some reason she needed to stop her referrals or confront them in some way in the future. She returned the gift card to Mountain Vista with a note thanking them for their thoughtfulness, but noting that giving clients referrals is part of her job and that it would be improper to take gifts for doing so.

Iris exercised a good deal of self-restraint in returning the facility's gift. It would have been easy to rationalize that her hard work and insufficient pay warrant a little extra recognition now and then. She might be confident in her ability to resist any influence Mountain Vista seeks to exert with its gift and argue that as long as her practices are sound she shouldn't care what others think. Or she may assume that no one will find out about the gift and take it, reasoning that it is easier to ask forgiveness than permission.

However, taking it might not pass the smell and publicity tests with her colleagues and patients. Not being transparent about the gift further raises suspicions that Iris knew that it was wrong to accept it. And perceptions matter. Iris is in a position of authority, and she is a representative of her profession and her organization. The acceptance of a gift from a community agency reflects on those entities as well as Iris herself.

Some might question drawing the line at the gift certificate. Because she had accepted a fruit basket in the past, perhaps Mountain Vista believed Iris was comfortable with such transactions. Why does a gift certificate create a conflict of interest when a fruit basket doesn't? Depending on the fruit basket, price may be a differentiating factor. However, this might cause Iris to rethink her habit of accepting the fruit baskets. Even though she shared it with the unit rather than keeping it for her personal use, Mountain Vista probably does not know that, hence the current gift. It would be wise for her to discuss the various gifts in supervision to determine any explicit policy or guidelines that might help to differentiate among the various gifts that unit personnel receive. It also puts on the record the fact that the gift was received and returned.

Iris's attention to process in declining the gift is also noteworthy. In returning the gift, she expressed appreciation for the gesture and avoided condemning Mountain Vista or impugning their motives. However, she set a clear boundary regarding the appropriateness of such gifts in the future.

VIOLATING THE STANDARD

Andrew is the administrator at a pioneering multiservice center that receives state funds to provide a continuum of services to children with emotional and behavioral problems. Because of the funding structure, any resources Andrew saves by moving a child to a less intensive, less expensive service create additional funds for services for those who need them (and for the agency's reserves). Having done a good deal of research in personnel management and staff retention, Andrew has come to believe that innovative compensation systems lead to better employee morale and greater efficiency and productivity. Therefore he has instituted a compensation system whereby any staff member who places a child in a less restrictive setting in less than three days receives a $200 gift certificate to the local mall or the restaurant of his or her choice. Some high performers under this system receive such a bonus for almost all of their cases.

Andrew's fellow agency directors question this system. They are concerned that it provides an incentive for premature discharges and shoddy placements. They suspect that some workers encourage hospitalizations on the front end so they can get credit for more discharges, and that others avoid high-need clients, because their conditions preclude successful attainment of the bonus. Andrew notes that the gift certificates cost a fraction of the money saved by reduced hospitalizations and that less restrictive settings are healthier for the clients themselves.

The premises underlying Andrew's compensation system are not unusual or inherently unethical. Performance-based compensation is a common feature of many workplaces. Bonuses, commissions, and profit- or gain-sharing arrangements base varying proportions of workers' pay on efficiency or productivity targets. Managed care systems are predicated on rewarding providers and users of care for the judicious use of services. Cost reductions resulting from the elimination of unnecessary service usage can conserve scarce resources for other uses. Such incentive systems can help encourage productivity and reward excellence in meeting organization expectations.

The danger, as Andrew's critics note, is in the behaviors that are rewarded. The incentive system must be aligned with the agency's mission and goals so that the proper activities are reinforced. If the agency's goal is to provide the best possible care for children, then that should be the standard by which workers are rewarded. To distribute rewards based on expediency, or to give it improper weight, is to depart from the primary mission of caring for children.

Improper specification of expectations can lead workers to cut corners in order to meet performance targets to qualify for financial rewards. Sometimes these systems can lead to fraudulent practices, as Sears learned when it rewarded its auto mechanics for their automotive parts sales. The unintended consequence was that thousands of customers purchased parts they did not need (Halverson, 1992). In Andrew's case, the consequences of a poorly conceived reward structure will be played out in the lives of children who are already vulnerable. While Andrew may believe he can rely on the integrity of his workforce, money, even in the form of gift certificates, can motivate inappropriate behavior as well as desired behavior.

It does not appear that Andrew has built into his system the necessary checks and balances to ensure that it is not compromised by financial conflicts of interest. Utilization reviews would help identify troubling patterns of admissions and discharges. Quality assurance reviews could examine randomly selected cases to ensure that their discharges were appropriate and made to suitable settings. A system of penalties could be instituted for adverse findings. Additional rewards could be employed for work on complex cases or hard-to-place clients, so that the level of difficulty is factored into the compensation schema.

If the revamped compensation system seems difficult or costly to administer, that is because it is. A simple single-outcome system cannot take into account the complex tasks of social work in the same way it might effectively reward car sales. A more sophisticated system is fairer for employees and safer for clients. Perhaps simply having it in place will deter workers who are inclined to put their well-being ahead of their clients'.

RESOLVING DILEMMAS IN CONFLICTS OF INTEREST: THE CASE OF THE ANGRY PARENT

Ann and Alex Rawlings sought counseling from Joanne Williams for two years as they tried to work on their marital discord and their disagreements about how best to discipline their two sons. During treatment, Joanne perceived that Alex's parenting style was unnecessarily harsh, especially when contrasted with Ann's nurturing, supportive style. Despite their best efforts, the couple recently decided to divorce and ceased sessions with Joanne, refusing to attend a termination session. Today Joanne received a subpoena from Ann's attorney requesting her records and testimony for the child custody proceedings, particularly those concerning Ann's suitability over Alex as the custodial parent.

As noted earlier in the chapter, some ethical dilemmas arise when the interests of clients are at odds with those of the worker. In other cases, dilemmas pit the interests of clients against each other. Such is the case with the Rawlings, who both began service as Joanne's clients. Now Ann's request puts Joanne in the position of acting in favor of one client at the expense of the other. Without a waiver of confidentiality from Alex, Joanne would be violating his privacy, ostensibly for Ann's benefit. A complicating factor is Joanne's opinion that Ann's case has merit. If she declines to take a partisan role in their dispute, it will mean remaining silent about her substantive concerns in the case.

Who Can Be a Resource to Joanne?

Triangulation of the therapist between parties in custody disputes represents a growing area of malpractice risk for psychologists and social workers ("Practice Basics," 2005). Therefore one of Joanne's first calls should be to her attorney for advice about how to proceed. This consultation should not only help her weigh her choices but also offer procedural guidance so that whatever course she chooses is done in the proper manner. For example, should she communicate with Ann or Ann's attorney about the subpoena, explaining the problem it presents and her responsibilities to Alex as her client? What notification, if any, should Joanne provide to Alex?

With or without legal counsel, there are several other steps Joanne should take. She should consult the privilege statutes in her state, which may expressly prohibit disclosure of confidential material in divorces and related actions unless compelled by a judge. Joanne could cite the statute in refusing to comply with the subpoena.

As in other cases in this book, Joanne will find consultation with colleagues and ethical and practice standards helpful in sorting out her options and generating alternatives (Smith, 2003). She should also review the informed consent procedures and documents she used at the outset of the Rawlings' treatment. What was their understanding about confidentiality and the stance she would take in any actions they might take against each other? A clearly specified policy will provide Joanne guidance in responding to Ann's demand for information. For example, some clinicians state at the outset of conjoint work that the focus of service is on the relationship and on the couple, not the pair as two individuals. The clinician then clarifies his or her intent as bipartisan, in that he or she will address the issues observed rather than taking sides in the couple's disputes. Some practitioners may go further and specify that they will not serve in an adversarial capacity for or against either partner. Informed consent procedures also address information sharing, for example, stating that the clinician will not keep secrets from one party on behalf of the other. Thus, individual communications with the therapist can be shared freely with the other member of the client system. If Joanne had a well-founded informed consent procedure and followed it in her treatment of the Rawlings, she can reference it and provide documentation about it in her communications with Ann and her attorney.

What Are Joanne's Options?

Joanne essentially has two options. She can comply with the subpoena, or she can refuse to comply. Within these two contrasting alternatives there are several variations in substance and process. For example, if she decides to comply, she must decide whether she will seek to limit the disclosure required (to records over verbal testimony, for example). She must also decide what she will tell Alex about her decision and what her stance will be if his legal team subpoenas her for their cause.

If she decides not to comply, will she urge Ann and the attorney to rescind the subpoena, or will she take other steps resist it? What basis will she use for declining? Will she simply refuse to participate, citing legal, ethical, or informed consent provisions, or will she try to broker a middle ground, for example, encouraging the court to assign a custody evaluation to an impartial clinician hired for that specific task?

When Has Joanne Faced Similar Dilemmas?

Two issues are central to this dilemma. One involves neutrality in serving multiperson systems such as groups, couples, and families. The second involves containment when the clinician possesses troubling or unsettling information. Even if Joanne has never before been subpoenaed in a client dispute, she has likely faced the underlying issues in the case, and her position on those will shape her response this time. Let's examine them each in turn.

A crucial element of professional development involves addressing the reality of the worker's partiality for some clients over others. While affinity for particular clients may create difficulties in a caseload, it leads to particular tension when differential connections exist within a client system. Partiality can come from a variety of sources. Countertransference can lead the clinician to identify more strongly with some individuals over others, or to have negative reactions to particular clients. The research on clinician attraction to clients indicates an array of sources, including the client's physical attractiveness, intellectual stimulation, similarity in life experiences and interests, and motivation for treatment (Fisher, 2004; Ladany, O'Brien, Hill, Melincoff, Knox, & Petersen, 1997; Nickell, Hecker, Ray, & Berkick, 1995). One's affinity for particular clients may be linked to positive therapeutic attributes such as enthusiasm, warmth, and increased empathy. The clinician may be more invested, caring, and attentive to the client, and more willing to go the extra mile for the client's success. On the other hand, such partiality may blind the worker to the client's needs and difficulties and may hinder the worker from carrying out his or her professional responsibilities. Taken to the extreme, affinity may lead to boundary transgressions, including harmful dual relationships and sexual impropriety. Within client systems, partiality may lead to feelings of rejection, anger, and confusion on the part of the nonfavored client(s). It may exacerbate existing fissures within families and couples, and it may irreparably undermine the clinician's effectiveness in the treatment process.

Joanne should reflect on her work with the Rawlings and her sense that Ann is the more suitable parent of the two. On what does she base that conclusion? Is Alex an ineffective or harmful parent, or simply one whose style is different from the type Joanne favors? In taking stock of her treatment of them, Joanne should consider whether her partiality may have played a role in their decision to discontinue treatment and in Ann's belief that Joanne will support her bid for custody. This reflection will require Joanne to examine her assumptions about their suitability as parents and her responsibility for testifying about the custody matter. The reflections will also help Joanne to refine her practices in the future, should she find that partiality played a negative role in their care.

Beyond reexamining the Rawlings' case, Joanne should consider other cases where she has felt an affinity for one member of a client system over others. How has she managed the helping relationship in light of that connection? Has it led her to make decisions that favor the client she preferred, or conversely, to rule in favor of the less favored client in an attempt to compensate for the slight? In that our decisions build on our past history, these past experiences will increase Joanne's understanding of her inclinations in the current dilemma.

The second issue in this dilemma involves her sense that Alex is the less desirable parent. Joanne is being asked to share her assessment of Alex's suitability as a parent when that was not the focus of treatment. Is it fair or appropriate to testify as to her impressions of his parenting when she has received that information secondarily in the context of her work with the couple on their relationship? Has she seen Ann and Alex in interactions with their children? When parenting issues were discussed in therapy, were the clients aware that Joanne might ultimately be passing judgment on their respective fitness as parents? These questions are intended to assess the soundness of Joanne's assessment that Ann's parenting is preferable to Alex's.

In addition to examining the rationale for this conclusion, Joanne must also look at situations in the past where she has had to contain information or opinions that she is not at liberty to share. This is a common phenomenon in clinical practice. Clients may, for example, disclose troubling fantasies; reveal past crimes or describe disturbing behaviors, such as driving while intoxicated; or report taking jobs or positions for which the clinician feels they are patently ill suited. In these and similar scenarios, the social worker may wish that he or she could speak up, and tell someone, when practicalities, ethics, and roles require that the worker share his or her concerns only with the client or in the confidence of supervision, and not with an outside party. Joanne's temptation to comply with the subpoena stems in part from her sense that Ann's claim has merit. However, as in other situations requiring containment, that apprehension is not an adequate justification for breaking Alex's confidentiality. Joanne may find, in reflecting on other disquieting experiences, that the tools she used to manage those dilemmas are appropriate for this case as well.

Where Do Ethical and Clinical Guidelines Fit with Joanne's Decision Making?

At least two rules are embedded in the option to comply with the subpoena to testify for Ann in the custody dispute: that professionals are obligated to render assessments in cases affecting their clients, even if those opinions are based on confidential information and may be detrimental to the client, and that social workers should comply with subpoenas. Two rules are also reflected in the option to resist the subpoena: that professionals should always maintain the privacy of material received in confidence, and that professionals should not violate the trust of their clients.

In a deontological framework, what would be the implication of transforming these rules into universal laws? Clearly, social workers should behave lawfully and comply with subpoenas, maintain privacy, and be trustworthy, though in ethical practice, professionals may find exceptions to these rules in upholding other goods, such as public safety or client well-being. We might be comfortable with them as guiding principles, but not without exceptions.

In contrast, the rule permitting social workers to speak up, even against the client's interests, is problematic as a universal principle, though there may be times when the social worker might rightfully do so. To create a universal law that would allow professionals to freely share their impressions without the affected client's permission would undermine the basis on which the helping relationship is grounded. For that reason, professional ethics permit such disclosures only in extreme circumstances to avoid greater harms, such as injury or death. If Joanne believed Alex to be a harmful parent, she should have used mechanisms such as a child protective service report and/or referral for services to address the problem. If he is not harmful, but merely less appealing to Joanne as a parent than Ann, she has little basis on which to enter into the custody dispute.

Using a utilitarian position, we might envision numerous consequences of Joanne's two choices. Should she comply with the subpoena, she might influence the custody process in favor of Ann, which *might* ultimately be a favorable outcome for the children if her assessment is well founded. If she is wrong in her impressions of Ann and Alex's relative abilities as parents, her involvement might result in poor outcomes for the children and the parents. Her testimony would probably distress Alex, and we can envision numerous deleterious consequences from that, including distrust in the therapeutic process, a sense of betrayal, and perhaps even a lawsuit or licensure action for breach of privacy. Another result of Joanne taking a partisan role in the case is that her participation adds to the fissures in the family rather than helping to create a constructive outcome for all concerned.

If Joanne fails to respond to the subpoena, she could be held in contempt of court. If she responds but refuses to testify, the result may be that her clinical observations are kept out of the custody decision-making process when they might have had bearing on the case. Her refusal to participate might anger Ann, resulting in attempts to compel her testimony or retaliation in the form of negative comments or a complaint to Joanne's regulatory board. If Joanne argues for an independent clinician to do a custody evaluation and that process is in some way flawed, the children may be harmed by a poor placement or parenting arrangement.

Of these outcomes, which is the most troubling? While either party in conjoint treatment or a custody matter may lash out against the professional, Joanne is on safer ethical ground protecting her clients' confidentiality than breaching it. This is not to say that a complaint may not be filed, only that Joanne's actions in maintaining Alex's privacy are in keeping with the standards of the profession, and abridging it is not. Joanne's apprehensions about Alex as a parent have to take a backseat to her fiduciary responsibility to him and other clients who must trust her discretion. Likewise, Joanne must trust that an impartial evaluation focused specifically on the question of custody may yield a more thorough and accurate appraisal of both parents than her impressions gleaned secondarily from couple's treatment.

Both personal and professional values are at play in this case. The social work value of integrity speaks to Joanne's responsibility to treat both members of this client system in an honest, fair, and trustworthy manner. In practice, that would mean adhering to commitments she made about confidentiality, impartiality, and her intentions in the treatment process. The value would also seem to require her to be forthright about her intentions, and inform Ann and Alex about her response to the subpoena.

Joanne's personal values and life experiences no doubt play a role in the case. Among other things, those may lead her to favor a warmer, more maternal style of parenting over a more aloof, directive style. They may bias her in favor of granting custody to mothers. Her values may also make her responsive to authority in such a way that she'd be unlikely to question the validity of the subpoena. Hopefully, supervision and self-awareness have sensitized Joanne to these preferences and qualities, and as a result she has developed strategies to manage their impact on her work. While these values may have a useful place in some activities, such as follow-through and client advocacy, in this case they may lead her to reach poorly founded conclusions in the custody matter and disadvantage her client Alex as a result of her biases.

The standards in the NASW *Code of Ethics* provide guidance on avoiding conflicts of interest throughout the helping process.

- "When social workers provide services to two or more people who have a relationship with each other (for example, couples, family members), social workers should clarify with all parties which individuals will be considered clients and the nature of social workers' professional obligations to the various individuals who are receiving services. Social workers who anticipate a conflict of interest among the individuals receiving services or who anticipate having to perform in potentially conflicting roles (for example, when a social worker is asked to testify in a child custody dispute or divorce proceedings involving clients) should clarify their role with the parties involved and take appropriate action to minimize any conflict of interest" (NASW, 1999, 1.06d).

- "Social workers should inform clients involved in family, couples, marital, or group counseling of the social worker's, employer's, and agency's policy concerning the social worker's disclosure of confidential information among the parties involved in the counseling" (NASW, 1999, 1.07g).

- "Social workers should protect the confidentiality of clients during legal proceedings to the extent permitted by law. When a court of law or other legally authorized body orders social workers to disclose confidential or privileged information without a client's consent and such disclosure could cause harm to the client, social workers should request that the court withdraw the order or limit the order as narrowly as possible or maintain the records under seal, unavailable for public inspection" (NASW, 1999, 1.07j).

In light of the code's provisions, Joanne should have explicitly addressed issues of confidentiality and loyalty at the outset of treatment. For example, she may have stated that she viewed information shared as open for disclosure within the entire client system. Similarly, it would have been ethically sound to clarify her intention to avoid triangulation between the clients in disputes in sessions or following treatment. The code would suggest that Joanne seek to have the subpoena withdrawn or require a court order for her testimony, in that complying with the subpoena without Alex's permission is a violation of his privacy.

How do ethical principles align with Joanne's choices? Three have particular relevance for her decisions in this matter. The principle of fidelity, and the related concepts of honesty and trustworthiness, would encourage her to act in congruence with the understandings set forth at the outset of her service in the case. That is, which decision regarding the subpoena is consistent with the informed consent agreements made with the Rawlings? If the informed consent promised privacy and neutrality, it would be proper to resist the subpoena and keep the promises made to her clients.

Which choice leads to the well-being of the parties or avoids harm to them? The principles of beneficence and nonmalfeasance appear to support not testifying. While Ann and potentially the children are helped by Joanne's testimony, Alex is harmed by it. If Joanne fails to testify, she is neither harming nor helping Alex: his case and Ann's will be judged on their merits. Failing to testify would not necessarily harm Ann and the children, unless Joanne has a powerful perspective on the case that no other testimony would equal.

Justice, the duty to treat all equally, would also align with a decision not to testify for Ann. Theoretically, justice might be served if Joanne shared her impressions of *both* Ann's and Alex's parenting. However, being even handed is not the only principle at stake in this case. It would still be inappropriate for Joanne to testify if her assessment of the parenting was not central to her work with the couple. Furthermore, testifying about the strengths and weaknesses of both parents doesn't negate the fact that one parent has not permitted such disclosure. Put another way, it is not fair to work with the couple on one issue then testify about other things learned in the course of that treatment, nor is it fair to breach a client's privacy without compelling professional reasons.

Laws and regulations are also germane to this case. The Health Insurance Privacy and Portability Act of 1996 established federal standards to protect the personal health information in all forms, including paper records, electronic data and communications, and verbal communications (HIPAA Medical Privacy Rule, 2003; "Protecting the Privacy of Patients' Health Information," 2003). These provisions would appear to restrict Joanne's ability to share information in the custody suit without both clients' permission. As noted earlier, state laws may specifically address disclosures in divorce and custody matters. Even if they do not, state confidentiality provisions, if more stringent than HIPAA, would apply to Joanne's dilemma. There are no apparent statutes that would support Joanne in choosing to testify for Ann and against Alex in this dispute.

Like legal standards, there is also a robust body of clinical wisdom about managing confidentiality and conflicts of interest in conjoint and family therapies. Many point to the initial sessions and informed consent processes as the foundation for clear expectations about the clinician's loyalties and responsibilities. Whether the clinician treats each member of the system as individual clients or sees them only as a system, focusing on the interactions and relationship, the chosen perspective should be explicit from the outset and revisited throughout treatment as possible conflicts of interest emerge (Gottlieb, 1996).

Why Is Joanne Selecting a Particular Course of Action?

The temptation to abridge a client's privacy often arises from a sense of duty, notions of the greater good, or the clinician's belief that he or she is averting harm. While there is nothing inherently bad in any of these motivations, the intentions are often misguided. Too often, the urge to break confidentiality reflects distortions in a professional's sense of self-importance ("Only I can stop this disaster from happening") or in the risk involved ("What if there's *any* chance of harm coming from my silence about what I know?"). Social workers and other helping professionals are privileged by society and the clients they serve to enter peoples' lives, learn their deepest secrets, and address their most profound concerns. Because of this power, ethical and legal protections are in place to ensure that these intimacies are not violated. This is not simply to preserve the client's privacy, but to reinforce the sanctity of the work with which the profession is entrusted. Therefore, the contracts such as those established though informed consent notify the client about the nature of the work, the ways that information will be used, and the worker's intent to protect information (Smith, 2003). Occasionally, professionals may need to break that agreement to avert a serious, imminent, and foreseeable harm, but by and large they must exercise fidelity to the agreement and refrain from sharing information. If this threshold for breaking confidentiality seems high, that is because it is!

In the Rawlings' case, Joanne may well feel that Ann is the preferable parent, and she may feel torn in withholding information that would help Ann obtain custody. However, her professional responsibilities are greater than her desires in the case. She must ask herself if she is in a position to objectively and competently assess appropriate parenting, what specific harms she wishes to avert by testifying, and whether that disclosure is worth the betrayal of Alex and the legal and ethical repercussions of a breach of privacy. Is Alex's parenting detrimental, or simply not Joanne's preferred style? If it is detrimental, are there other mechanisms for introducing those findings into court? Could a custody evaluation by a neutral party better address those than Joanne could, given the nature of her contact with the parents and the therapeutic privilege barriers to testimony?

Would Joanne be comfortable subjecting her choices to review by her colleagues via the principle of publicity? In fact, her efforts to seek consultation on the case would help her measure this, and it is likely that most would support her in not testifying, thereby upholding the ethical and legal standards in the case. Otherwise, she would have to make the case to them that the information she has to share is so compelling as to justify breaking the law and her promise to her client.

In contrast, the principle of reversibility may be of little help in resolving this dilemma, in that Joanne's sympathies may shift depending on whose perspective she takes in the case. That is, if she puts herself in Ann's shoes, she might want to testify, but if she looks at the situation from Alex's point of view, she would refrain from doing so.

How Should Joanne Carry Out Her Decision?

If Joanne decides that her testimony would undermine the interests of one of her clients, she must contest the subpoena. A first step would involve contacting both clients to notify them of the request for information in his case. Ann, of course, may have already approved of the release in writing. Theoretically, Alex could also permit Joanne to share the information in compliance with the subpoena, but it is more likely that he will refuse to waive his privilege of confidentiality. If that is the case, Joanne could, with her clients' permission, contact the attorney who issued the subpoena and describe the privacy concerns and the inappropriateness of testifying about custody given the nature of her services. If Joanne's knowledge is deemed to be irrelevant for the custody proceedings, the attorney could withdraw the subpoena.

Failing that, Joanne or her legal representative should contact the court in writing, specifying the legal and ethical grounds for her refusal to appear. This communication should be made in writing and copied to the attorneys in the case (Houston-Vega et al., 1997; Madden, 1998). Alternatively, Joanne's attorney could file a motion to quash the subpoena, voiding the order to appear. In this, the judge may determine that the goals of Joanne's testimony can be met by other means (evaluations or testimony by others without privilege exceptions). If the judge affirms the subpoena and determines Joanne's testimony or records would be relevant, legal representation would help her in depositions, court testimony, and other matters. If Joanne is compelled to testify, representation will ensure that her responses are legally sound and that any refusals to answer are made on solid legal grounds.

CONCLUSION

Many situations can give rise to conflicts of interest, including tensions between the client's needs and the worker's financial, or personal interests, and cases where the worker experiences divided loyalties within a client system. Conflicts of interest are often linked to other ethical issues. Professionals are expected to address potential conflicts of interest as part of informed consent procedures. Dual or sexual relationships or other therapeutic boundary crossings inherently create conflicts of interest as the worker strives to reconcile the social, business, or other sorts of ties to the client with his or her professional responsibilities. In an attempt to manage conflicting roles and responsibilities, workers may breach other ethical standards such as those on confidentiality, competence, or professionalism.

Helping professionals are expected to be alert to conflicts of interest and take steps to avoid or mitigate their effects. Sometimes conflicts are apparent because of roles or relationships. An employee declines to serve as a supervisor for his son, who works in the same setting. Or a worker, in reading a referral, recognizes the client as her son's bus driver. She declines to take the case based on the possibility that the work may reveal information that is difficult for her to contain or keep separate from her interests as a mother. In both of these cases, the worker can divert the conflict by declining a role that creates conflict.

In other cases, conflicts are internal and less easily managed. A worker with a history of sexual abuse finds herself berating a client whom she believes to be sexual offender. The hallmark of the conflict is in the worker's own emotional reactions and difficulties in achieving objectivity. These may reveal themselves in supervisory or consultative conversations, but if they do not, it is the worker who must be aware of the conflict and take steps to ensure that the client's interests are given priority.

Beyond self-awareness and supervision, legal, ethical, and collegial resources are beneficial in identifying and managing conflicts of interest. Solving dilemmas of this type does not require that social workers ignore or negate their own interests, only that they ensure that the interests of clients are protected and preserved.

Chapter 6

PROFESSIONAL BOUNDARIES

A particular type of conflict of interest occurs when clinicians engage in dual relationships with their clients. Sexual relationships are one type of dual relationship. Dual or multiple relationships occur any time a helping professional has an attachment or affiliation with the client beyond the therapeutic or helping relationship. The other relationship may be social, financial, sexual, or professional in nature. The other relationship may occur at the same time as the helping process or before or after the client-worker relationship. As such, dual relationships may involve accepting a former supervisor as a client, hiring a client to do bookkeeping for one's practice, accepting a student as a therapy client, going out to lunch with a client after referring him or her to another agency, inviting a former client to join a Bible study group, selling a former client a franchise in an office cleaning business, having sexual relations with a client during sessions, or inviting a client and his wife to join you and your partner for a night at the theater.

As you can probably see from this list, some dual relationships are more troubling than others, in that they have a differential potential to diminish one's professional objectivity and to lead to client confusion and exploitation. Dual relationships are not mere instances of inadvertently running into a client in the community or at a social gathering. Such events are usually unanticipated, "temporary, and most likely, manageable" (Reamer, 1998, p. 50), and while they may be uncomfortable and require attention to proper boundaries, they do not constitute dual relationships (Reamer, 2001).

The NASW *Code of Ethics* (1999) stipulates: "Social workers should not engage in dual or multiple relationships with clients or former clients in which there is a risk of exploitation or potential harm to the client. In instances when dual or multiple relationships are unavoidable, social workers should take steps to protect clients and are responsible for setting clear, appropriate, and culturally sensitive boundaries. (Dual or multiple relationships occur when social workers relate to clients in more than one relationship, whether professional, social, or business. Dual or multiple relationships can occur simultaneously or consecutively.)" (1.06c).

Clearly, when dual relationships can be avoided, the social worker should do so. This may mean declining to join a team, club, or committee of which a client is a member. It may mean transferring a client who lives in the worker's neighborhood, belongs to the worker's church, or serves as the worker's accountant if these associations might unnecessarily complicate the helping relationship or otherwise affect the worker's ability to act in the client's best interests. Sometimes workers recommend such a referral in order to preserve their own privacy or to keep their personal and professional lives separate.

Not all dual relationships are avoidable. A client and his therapist may both be elected to the local school board. A student may be assigned to a class taught by his former caseworker. The building inspector assigned to appraise your house may have attended your support group for grieving parents. The parent of a child hospitalized on your ward may turn out to be the same person who sold you your car (complete with unreported engine problems). A social worker's promotion may mean that he is now supervising his friends and former peers on the direct-services staff. If these relationships can't be avoided, they must be managed in such a way that the other relationships don't present conflicts of interest for carrying out the professional relationship. This involves careful evaluation of the options and appropriate boundary setting by the worker.

Even if the working relationship is in the past, the professional must be alert to and address any ways in which the new relationship may detrimentally affect the gains made in the earlier one. For example, having a former client as a student in class might raise concerns about objectivity in grading or unfair treatment in the class that could undermine successful earlier therapeutic efforts to set "clear, appropriate and culturally sensitive boundaries" (NASW, 1999, 1.06c). The professor might talk privately with the student about the new relationship as distinct from the past one, assure the student of his or her objectivity and of the confidentiality of their therapeutic relationship, and offer to make alternative arrangements if the two determine that the professor's instruction or grading might be influenced by the prior relationship. As part of boundary setting, the instructor may alert his or her superior to the fact that a former client is enrolled in class, so that the supervisor can inform the teacher of any policies or options that relate to such situations. For example, the school may recommend using unique identifiers rather than names on papers to ensure anonymity in grading. Or the supervisor might offer to be available for consultation should the student or teacher experience difficulties during the class.

Sexual relationships are a particularly damaging form of dual relationship and are never advisable. Because sexual relationships are a common area of difficulty for helping professionals ("Legal Issues," 2003; Strom-Gottfried, 1999), codes of ethics, such as NASW's, address them with very explicit standards:

- "Social workers should under no circumstances engage in sexual activities or sexual contact with current clients, whether such contact is consensual or forced" (NASW, 1999, 1.09a).
- "Social workers should not take unfair advantage of any professional relationship or exploit others to further their personal, religious, political, or business interests" (NASW, 1999, 1.06b).
- "Social workers who function as supervisors or educators should not engage in sexual activities or contact with supervisees, students, trainees, or other colleagues over whom they exercise professional authority" (NASW, 1999, 2.07a).
- "Social workers should avoid engaging in sexual relationships with colleagues when there is potential for a conflict of interest. Social workers who become involved in, or anticipate becoming involved in, a sexual relationship with a colleague have a duty to transfer professional responsibilities, when necessary, to avoid a conflict of interest" (NASW, 1999, 2.07b).

Sexual improprieties are generally believed to be among the final acts in a slippery slope of boundary transgressions that can include excessive disclosure by the worker about himself or herself, seeking contact with clients outside of appointments, seeking favors or influence from clients, sexualizing elements of the clinical interaction, and comparing the client favorably to the worker's loved ones (Gabbard, 1996).While sexual misconduct is generally construed as a phenomenon between male workers and female clients, research indicates the emergence of other patterns, particularly female client–female worker transgressions (Gartrell & Sanderson, 1994; Strom-Gottfried, 1999).

Social workers are sometimes perplexed at the prohibition on sexual relationships with former clients, noting that many state regulatory boards and some other helping professions set a clear ban on sexual involvement within two years (American Psychological Association, 2002) or five years (American Counseling Association, 2005) of termination.They contrast this with NASW's more ambiguous standard that "Social workers should not engage in sexual activities or sexual contact with former clients because of the potential for harm to the client. If social workers engage in conduct contrary to this prohibition or claim that an exception to this prohibition is warranted because of extraordinary circumstances, it is social workers—not their clients—who assume the full burden of demonstrating that the former client has not been exploited, coerced, or manipulated, intentionally or unintentionally" (NASW, 1999, 1.09c).

Implicit in NASW's lifetime ban on sexual involvement with former clients is the notion that once a person is a client, he or she is always a client, and that all clients must be treated the same.Therefore, a social worker who facilitates an educational group for heart attack survivors would be held to the same standard vis-à-vis her former clients that an outpatient therapist would be with his. The social worker who decides to pursue an intimate relationship with a former client would have to demonstrate, if questioned, that the context of the relationship (the timing and circumstances under which it evolved) and the nature of the original helping relationship indicate that the sexual relationship is not predatory or exploitive.

Upon close examination, NASW's standard does not differ greatly in substance from those that set specific time limits. All discourage sexual involvement with former clients (even after the two-year or five-year moratoriums) and emphasize the worker's responsibility to demonstrate that he or she did not misuse power in pursuing a relationship with the client. Clearly, the message to workers is "Proceed with caution!" Even relationships built on the best of foundations may come to an end. One built on an earlier client-worker relationship places the professional at particular and ongoing jeopardy for ensuring, even retrospectively, that no harm was done to the former client.

UPHOLDING THE STANDARD

Tim is a social worker in private practice. Several weeks ago, his friend Dean's daughter died in a car accident. Tim and his wife have been spending a great deal of time supporting and comforting Dean's family in the wake of their tragic loss.

Today, Tim got a call from Dean, who asked to come see him on a professional basis. "You've been such a champion for us these last few weeks, but I know I need extra help to deal with this."

Tim sympathized with his situation and commended him for reaching out for help but said, "I'm happy to help you any way I can as your friend, but I think it would be better for you to see someone else to take it further than that."

"Don't you do this kind of work in your practice?"

"Yes, sure, but because I value our friendship, I can't see you in my practice. I may not be objective enough to help you."

"But that's just it! I don't want to have to dredge all this up with someone new. I want to see you because you already know all about us and what we've been through."

"Dean, you have to trust me when I say it's not in your best interest to see me professionally. There are a lot of great clinicians out there who work on just the kinds of things you are struggling with. I'm happy to suggest some and even go with you on a first visit to see someone, but I can't take on the counseling myself. We're just too close."

It may seem paradoxical to refuse to accept a friend as a client, when the two people involved already have a close and trusting relationship and the worker already knows a great deal about the potential client. Some might argue that rather than causing harm, such an arrangement could allow for efficient and effective service. Even professionals who are conversant with the notion of professional boundaries might share the lay person's confusion as to why such an arrangement is unwise.

Tim addresses one core reason for boundaries when he notes that he may not be objective enough to help with Dean's care (Epstein & Simon, 1990). He, too, is grieving the young girl's death. How can he distinguish his own reactions from the needs of his client? Even if he had no prior relationship with Dean's daughter, due to his friendship with Dean he knows a great deal about his life and past. If he changes hats to become his clinician, what is he to do with that information? Can he put it in the proper clinical perspective? Similarly, what is he to do, as a friend, with the information he will learn as Dean's counselor? How can he ignore what he learns in the therapeutic relationship when they are interacting as friends? Even if the chances are small that he will learn something troubling about Dean and his family, is that a price he wants to pay for taking on his friend's case?

Beyond addressing objectivity and how information is received and viewed, boundaries help regulate the roles and rules that are part of the therapeutic interaction (Reamer, 2001). Can Tim ask questions, provide guidance, push for self-examination, and utilize confrontation in clinical work with Dean as he would with any other client in the same circumstance, or are his techniques and decisions limited because of his friendship and history with the client? Will Dean view Tim with the same authority with which he would view another worker he knows less well? After the counseling, how will their relationship be construed? Will they relate to each other in the future as friends or as client and worker? As Dean reveals himself in the safety of therapy, will he be comfortable resuming his friendship with Tim, or will he eventually seek to put distance between them following his self-exposure in therapy? Is having Tim as a worker worth the potential price of losing him as a friend and as a supporter through the grief process?

Those advocating for the dual role might suggest that in his grief, Dean has already poured his heart out to his friend. And no doubt Tim's responses to his friend's loss are influenced by his therapeutic training and his professional knowledge base. But giving and receiving that information in the context of a friendship is still not the same as the process of disclosure in therapy. Advocates for taking the case might argue that the risk of harm to Dean is slight, and therefore therapy would not constitute a dual relationship as described in the NASW code. As the social worker, it is up to Tim to assess the risk, taking into account such factors as the power differential, the length and intensity of the two relationships, the client's strength and clarity, the likelihood of challenges to his own objectivity, and the message the relationship might send to others (Ebert, 1997; Gottleib, 1994; Kitchener, 1988). He should also appraise the reasons for taking the case. His assessment that others can better help Dean with his grief is important here: an abundance of competent resources makes it less compelling for Tim himself to take the case. Ultimately, he is making the selfless and safest choice in supporting his friend's pursuit of counseling with someone else while preserving his role as friend and protecting the friendship.

VIOLATING THE STANDARD

Amelia works in a community program designed to help persons with a history of psychiatric hospitalization develop vocational skills, with the ultimate goal that clients will attain full employment. Her client Honey had worked as a seamstress prior to the onset of her illness, and she hoped eventually to return to that field. One day Honey overheard Amelia talking to a colleague about her search for a wedding dress, and Honey mentioned wistfully, "Those were my favorite pieces to do when I was working—so much creativity, and always for a happy occasion."

It occurred to Amelia that she could develop a win-win scenario if she hired Honey to sew her dress. It would help boost Honey's confidence, and give her some extra money and a chance to feel useful again. She suggested it to Honey, who eagerly agreed, and the two settled upon on a price; selected a pattern, fabric, and trim; and talked often about their ideas for the gown. Amelia felt that her employer might disapprove of her paying Honey under the table and might question Amelia's objectivity for taking Honey under her wing in such a fashion, so she also suggested that they reserve their activities and discussions of the gown for "non-work" time.

Eight weeks before the wedding, however, Honey's attendance at the vocational program began to drop off. When her worker Diane called to check on her, she screamed, "Just stop pressuring me!" Amelia became increasingly concerned about the status of the dress, and as the date neared, unable to reach Honey by phone, she went to her home.

The apartment was in total disarray, the misshapen bodice of a wedding gown was laid across the back of a sofa, and a pile of tattered fabric lay nearby. Upon seeing Amelia, Honey burst into furious sobs. "This is very bad fabric!" she shrieked. "I couldn't get it to come out right, so I had to keep recutting it and starting over. Now there's not enough left to finish the bottom!"

Amelia was dumbfounded. She had expected to find a finished garment, and she, too, was furious. She gathered her composure and said, "It's okay, Honey. Just give me what you have, and I'll pay someone else to do it."

Honey sobbed, "What about my pay? I've put a lot of time into this—much more than I agreed to. Plus, I've had to miss time at my sheltered job to work on your project!"

When Amelia resisted and tried to explain the additional costs and delays that Honey's errors had incurred, Honey concluded the conversation, shouting tearfully, "That's not fair to just use me like that! I'm telling Diane!"

In entering into a business arrangement with Honey, Amelia created a dual relationship that conflicts with her role as the woman's social worker. While she may have originally rationalized the purchase of Honey's services as congruent with her treatment goals of employment, Amelia could have met that goal more appropriately by helping Honey to find a job or start a business rather than becoming her first and only customer. And Amelia's reluctance for other workers to learn about the arrangement is a sign that she knows the agreement with Honey was inappropriate, however she might try to justify it as therapeutic.

As in this case, a common danger of dual relationships is the exploitation of clients (Epstein & Simon, 1990). Did Amelia's authority as Honey's worker lead Honey to take on a task she might have otherwise declined? Did it lead her to do the task for less money than she might ordinarily get, and did it constrain her from speaking up when the project did not go as planned? Did the pressure of doing the project for her social worker create additional countertherapeutic strain on Honey? Did it create other harm as she withdrew from the treatment center and decompensated due to the pressure?

A second effect of dual relationships is erosion in the social worker's capacity to carry out his or her professional responsibilities because of the conflict created by the other relationship (Epstein & Simon, 1990). We have no evidence that Amelia's treatment of Honey was different because Honey had control of the wedding dress, but one can imagine Amelia treating Honey favorably or overlooking problems because of their business relationship. Furthermore, because of her responsibilities as Honey's social worker, Amelia is constrained from treating Honey as she would any other seamstress who botched the wedding dress and failed to deliver on time. How can she help Honey develop her vocational skills while reporting her to the Better Business Bureau or taking her to small claims court to recoup the dress costs? The boundaries that protect the client in the helping process also protect the worker who upholds the distinctions between those she serves as a professional and those she befriends or hires.

RESOLVING DILEMMAS IN BOUNDARY MAINTENANCE: THE SLEEPLESS SLEEPOVER

Gary is a social worker at a child guidance clinic who is assigned to provide consultation for a chain of group homes for severely emotionally disturbed children and adolescents. Gary returned home from work one night to find that a friend of his eleven-year-old daughter, Sally, would be sleeping over. When he met Sally's new friend, Gail, he realized she was a former resident of one of the group homes where he is a consultant.

Is Gary on the verge of a dual relationship with Gail? His role at the group home where she was placed was that of consultant, so it is unclear whether his contact with her there might be construed as a client-worker relationship. Even if that might be considered a professional relationship, does her friendship with his daughter constitute a social relationship with him? If there is a dual relationship, is it potentially harmful to Gail as a former client? While we may question whether this case fits the criteria for a dual relationship, most parents can identify with Gary's unease about the surprise guest and his desire to set proper, professional boundaries. The question here is less about avoiding a dual relationship and more about the nature of Gary's concerns and the boundaries he must set as a result.

What concerns might prompt Gary to set boundaries in this case? Perhaps his knowledge of Gail's history makes him concerned that she is an unsuitable companion for his daughter. Perhaps his knowledge of her history makes it difficult for him to maintain her confidentiality during her visits or in conversations with his family. Perhaps he is uncomfortable at the thought of a former client, however remote the relationship, having such intimate involvement with his family, and staying at his home. Perhaps he is concerned that others will take this the wrong way and see the relationship as inappropriate or exploitive of Gail.

Who Will Be Helpful?

What experiences and resources can Gary draw upon to respond in the moment to the dilemma that greeted him at home? It may be possible to call a colleague or supervisor for advice. It will be helpful if it is someone who knows his role at the group home and the challenges of parenting in a community where there are likely to be overlapping relationships between the worker's children and those he serves.

Gary may also consider calling Gail's parents or guardians. They may not know that the sleepover is with the family of someone affiliated with the group home. If they are comfortable with the arrangement, it may alleviate some of Gary's concerns, in that they have consented to the arrangement. If they are uncomfortable with it (or are responsive to Gary's discomfort), they may call Gail home from the sleepover or discourage future play dates.

A trickier question is whether or not Gary should consult his wife, who arranged the sleepover. On one hand, saying, "Gail used to be at the group home, so it puts me in an awkward spot to have her stay here," alerts his wife to the difficulty and involves her as an ally in problem solving. On the other hand, it reveals information about Gail's status as a client that his wife has no right to know, and it may open a deluge of other questions about Gail that he is unprepared and unauthorized to answer.

What Are Gary's Choices?

As noted earlier, Gary's choices vary depending upon the nature of his concerns and the goals he wishes to achieve. If he is concerned about mixing the two roles (counselor and dad), he can withdraw from the role of dad for the night, allowing his wife to supervise the sleep-over and deal with the two girls as she would with any other overnight guest. Alternatively, he could speak privately with Gail or her parents and explain that because of their past relationship, having her spend the night in his home would be uncomfortable and ethically question-able. Should he pursue this course of action, he would hope that the child or her parents would end the sleepover and explain to Sally and her mother their reasons so that he doesn't have to. A third solution would combine these two choices, allowing the sleepover that has already commenced, but ensuring that no overnight visits take place in the future.

Different choices would arise if Gary is concerned that Gail is somehow unstable and a risk to his daughter and his family. First, Gary should be very certain that his concerns are well founded and not a judgmental, knee-jerk reaction based on some distant case history. He must also consider that in taking steps to insulate his family from her as an overnight guest, he may be stigmatizing Gail and providing only limited protection from her in that she and Sally may continue to be friends and schoolmates with or without his approval. If he determines that she cannot spend the night because of his safety concerns, his options are to end the sleepover without explaining why or to speak with her and her parents about ending it, using the ethics rationale described earlier.

If Gary is simply uncomfortable having a former client in his home, he must weigh the risks and benefits of somehow ending the sleepover for his own well-being with the risks and benefits of allowing it to con-tinue for the well-being of his daughter and her friend. This requires Gary to forthrightly examine the basis for his apprehensions. Does set-ting boundaries mean that Gail must be sent home or banished as a friend of his daughter's simply for his convenience? Can he set bound-aries about the ways in which he interacts with Gail and demonstrate restraint in what he says about her, in order to let the girls' friendship move forward and run its normal course without his interference?

When Has Gary Faced a Similar Dilemma?

Practice in small communities often requires that professionals develop family norms to help maintain boundaries between their work, social lives, and business dealings (Schank & Skovholt, 1997). For example, family and friends learn not to ask, "Who was that?" when strangers approach the social worker at the supermarket and say, "I'm doing a lot better now." Partners and spouses ask first, before hiring a babysitter, landscaper, mechanic, and so forth, "Is there any reason I shouldn't get so-and-so to do such-and-such?" This allows the social worker to approve or decline the hire without divulging why such a decision would be unwise. The spouse may assume that an answer in the affirmative is tantamount to identifying the person as a client, but there may be other reasons and relationships that would influence a yes or no answer in this case. This helps couples set proper boundaries without requiring them to inappropriately seek or divulge information. In trying to understand the nature of their parent's work, children may also ask about clients and thus learn the norms of confidentiality and boundary setting. As a result of these conversations, children may develop particular compassion and understanding about human troubles (Boisen & Bosch, 2005; Burkemper, 2005; Gumpert & Black, 2005; Manning & Van Pelt, 2005; Strom-Gottfried, 2005).

Against this backdrop, we might wonder what the understandings are in Gary's family. Might the awkwardness of the sleepover have been avoided with better communication? How have similar incidents been handled in this family or in this professional community? Is Sally's friendship with Gail an artifact of her sensitivity and concern for others? Would she interpret boundary setting as a message not to be kind, not to reach out to others? The precedents in the family for managing overlapping relationships and for the way that the members of the family relate to each other would help shed light on effective strategies for the sleepover.

Other factors that may help the decision-making process include Gary's past experiences with setting limits. Has he had other interactions with youth from the group home, in the community, as classmates of his children, or as direct clients? Have he and his wife regulated Sally's friends and houseguests before? If there are other friends whom they perceive as a poor influence or an unwelcome guest, how have those situations been handled? Is Sally mature enough to set limits or communicate with her parents if a friend demonstrates disturbing behavior or proposes inappropriate activities? How might those experiences be brought to bear on this situation?

Where Do Ethical and Clinical Guidelines Lead Him?

We start our examination of Gary's choices with two traditions of moral philosophy. Looking at Gary's case through a deontological lens, we can ask, "What rules are embedded in Gary's choices, and what choice would he want to adopt as a universal rule?" This case helps demonstrate the complexities of applying theory to practice, in that we could reasonably derive several conflicting principles for any one of Gary's choices. Deciding to tell Gail she can't sleep over might embody rules ranging from "No one I knew as a client can be friends with my daughter" to "No one I knew as a client can spend the night at my house" to "No one who troubles me can stay overnight." Which principle is at stake here?

Deciding to let the sleepover go on may reflect various principles from "My daughter has to be the judge of her own friends. I can't regulate that for her" to "I could never say anything that might hurt Gail's feelings." Both are valid principles, but neither would likely be favored as a universal rule. The advantage of the deontological perspective for Gary is that it requires him to define the basis on which he is making any given choice. What principle is being upheld in a particular decision? Taking the choice out of the context for a moment and examining it through the larger principle at stake helps give substance to the choice. In using a rule-based lens, Gary and other decision makers are asking, "What's really going on underneath each of my particular options?"

From a utilitarian perspective, we would look at the consequences of Gary's choices for those involved. For example, ceasing the sleepover might bring Gary short-term and long-term peace of mind. Its consequences for Sally and Gail depend greatly on how it is handled and interpreted. If the girls experience it as appropriate and discrete boundary setting, perhaps it will help assure Gail that Gary, in putting her need for protection before his own family's interests, wants to protect her from harmful dual relationships. It may send a message to Sally that her father has integrity and the best interests of her and her friend at heart. Alternatively, his actions could breach Gail's privacy and stigmatize her with Sally and with others Sally may tell about Gail's history at the group home. It could make her feel ashamed, unwelcome in their home, and unworthy of the kinds of activities many youth her age take for granted.

Rather than feeling protected, Sally may feel embarrassed and disgusted at her father's intervention. As a result, she might cling more tightly to the friendship than she would have had he let the friendship progress naturally. Sally might take away the message that being the recipient of mental health services is something to be ashamed of. For better or for worse, it may affect her selection of friends or her willingness to invite them home in the future.

Several social work values apply in this case. In the name of social justice, social workers pledge to work to end discrimination and "promote sensitivity to and knowledge about oppression" (NASW, 1999, p. 2). In valuing the dignity and worth of the person, social workers "treat each person in a caring and respectful fashion, mindful of individual differences and cultural and ethnic diversity" (NASW, 1999, p. 2). In acknowledging the importance of human relationships, "social workers seek to strengthen relationships among people in a purposeful effort to promote, restore, maintain, and enhance the well-being of individuals, families, social groups, organizations, and communities" (NASW, 1999, p. 2).

All of these would seem to encourage Gary to be very careful in ensuring he is not treating Gail in a pejorative or stigmatizing fashion because of her prior status as a group home client. They might be interpreted as supporting Gary in giving latitude to Gail's friendship with his daughter, even allowing the sleepover if that is a common element of such friendships, assuming it does not exploit or harm Gail. Of course if Gary is concerned about Gail's history or instability, his values may place priority on protecting his family over his professional values. He may argue that it is all well and good to foster a client's relationships, but that doesn't require that it be done with the worker's own family.

NASW ethical standards are less germane to this case, in that Gary's role at the group home and Gail's former residence there seem not to fit the criteria for dual relationships. Similarly, there are no apparent laws or policies governing decisions such as Gary's, with the exception of those specific to his agency or the group home. We can, however, examine the case through the principles of autonomy, fidelity, beneficence, and justice. How can Gary encourage the maximum level of autonomy for Gail in this case? On one hand, allowing her to visit unfettered would seem to be in keeping with her wishes to befriend his daughter and enjoy her company. On the other hand, as a minor, her judgment in the matter may be limited. As such, her parents' or guardian's wishes are part of the principle of autonomy, since they are empowered legally to act in her best interests. That is not to say Gail has no voice in the matter. The adults in this situation can enhance her autonomy by seeking her input, or by honestly informing her of the difficulty Gary is experiencing and the rationale for his decision.

Since Gail appears to be unaware of Gary's role at the group home or of his knowledge of her past, her trust relationship with him is linked more to his role as an adult figure and the father of her friend. However, because of his professional role, he has a responsibility to behave in a trustworthy manner, irrespective of her relationship with him. He can uphold the principle of fidelity if he does not misuse his role by divulging confidential information about her and by treating her with honesty and integrity. The principle of fidelity would rule out acting deceptively to bring an end to the sleepover or using clinical information to dissuade his wife or daughter from allowing Gail to visit their home.

Gary upholds the principles of beneficence and nonmaleficence by choosing the course of action that is in Gail's best interests and that avoids causing her harm. These principles would favor those options that do not taint the friendship (irrespective of allowing the sleepover to continue) and those that support Gail's privacy.

How is justice served in this case? How would Gary handle any situation in which he was uncomfortable with Sally's friends or overnight guests? Is it fair for him to intervene in this friendship, based solely on his knowledge of Gail's treatment history, if he has not done so in others? Is it fair to send Gail home without spending time with her to learn more about her current circumstances and behaviors? (On the other hand, is it fair to assess her if Gary never does so with Sally's other friends?)

The literature on practice in rural areas provides some ideas about practice norms that may apply in Gary's case (Boisen & Bosch, 2005; Burkemper, 2005; Gumpert & Black, 2005; Manning & Van Pelt, 2005; Schank & Skovholt, 1997; Strom-Gottfried, 2005). Essentially, they say the same thing: it is easier for professionals to set boundaries around their own choices than around those of their offspring. Depending on the facts of the case and the appraisal of risk, practitioners should let the friendship, with all the activities normally associated with such friendships, continue or set limits on what activities the friendship can entail (no sleepovers at either home, for example) while revealing as little information about the rationale as possible (Schank & Skovholt, 1997).

Why Is a Particular Course of Action Preferable?

As alluded to in earlier sections, a theme in this case is whether Gary is acting in self-interest or in the interest of others (Gail, his daughter, his family). Self-awareness will be essential in determining his motivations and whether they are leading to a constructive outcome. Is he overly averse to risk? Is he making unfair assumptions about Gail? Is she being unfairly exiled because he knows more about her than he does Sally's other friends, who might be equally worrisome? Does he trust his daughter's judgment in her selection of friends, and his wife's in arranging get-togethers among those friends? Or is he naive about Gail's motivations and capacity for harm? Is he putting his family and career in harm's way because he is too timid to set limits around the friendship? These questions help Gary put his decision to the smell, reversibility, mentor, and publicity tests described in chapter 2.

Whatever Gary decides to do in the moment, this case is ripe for discussion in supervision or consultation. Professionals who know Gary, his work, and his community can help him sort through the answers to these questions, not just for the case of Gail, but for all the future overlapping relationships that will occur as his family participates in their community over time.

How Shall He Enact His Decision?

A common complaint about professional boundaries is that they convey an elitist attitude and create a unidirectional relationship in

135

which the worker has the power to set the terms of the relationship in a fashion that marginalizes the service recipient (Lazarus, 1994). Such criticisms construe boundaries as protecting the worker from the client rather than grounding and guiding the professional relationship in the client's interests.

Regardless of the merit of these criticisms, social workers must take care to implement boundaries in a respectful and sensitive manner. Even in his shock at seeing Gail at his house, it is important for Gary to take time to collect himself and examine his options and motivations rather than acting in a rash and fear-based manner. If, after deliberation, he decides that the best course of action is to end the sleepover, he must summon his therapeutic skills in order to employ them to discuss the situation with Gail and her family. Whether he is the one to talk with Gail, or her parents or guardians are, Gary should be alert to her responses, take steps to address any untoward reactions, and document the experience so that he is prepared to discuss it with his supervisor when they debrief about the decision.

Even if he decides to do nothing, Gary would be wise to pay attention to the situation, in case the circumstances change in such a way that he or his wife might want to intervene to set limits on the friendship. Again, it will be helpful to talk to colleagues to review his decision making and prepare for the conversation with his daughter and his wife, as well as Gail or her family.

CONCLUSION

Boundaries provide structure to the helping relationship, dictating the ways professionals and clients interact. Boundaries establish norms and set limits so that the professional roles of supervisor, teacher, or therapist aren't confused with those of friend, business associate, or lover. They protect clients from abuses of power and place primacy on the professional relationship over all others. Sexual relationships between those in power (supervisors, instructors, counselors) and those who may be exploited by such relationships (supervisees, students, clients) are clearly unethical. In many jurisdictions, sexual contact between workers and clients is a criminal offense. Dual relationships arise when social or business relationships are mixed simultaneously or in succession with helping relationships. While not all dual relationships are harmful, they should be avoided, if possible, since they have the capacity to confound the helping relationship. If the dual relationship cannot be avoided, it is the worker's responsibility to establish therapeutic boundaries to ensure that the client's needs and the working relationship are given priority.

Some authors have developed guidelines for weighing the risks of dual relationships (Ebert, 1997; Erickson, 2001; Gottleib, 1994; Kitchener, 1988), and numerous resources exist to help clinicians maintain proper boundaries in complex situations (Boisen & Bosch, 2005; Burkemper, 2005; Gartrell & Sanderson, 1994; Gumpert & Black, 2005; Manning & Van Pelt, 2005; Reamer, 2001; Schank & Skovholt, 1997; Strom-Gottfried, 2005). While workers in different communities and service settings may draw limits in different ways, all must be mindful of the purpose of professional boundaries and set them respectfully, forthrightly, and consistently so that the best interests of clients are maintained.

Chapter 7

CONFIDENTIALITY

The assurance that personal information will be held in the strictest confidence is essential for the helping process. Few of us would be open with our physicians, attorneys, or clergy if we feared that those persons could not be relied upon to protect the information we entrust to them (Corey et al., 2003). Thus, our codes of ethics place a high premium on maintaining patient privacy and on requiring clinician discretion (Cohen & Cohen, 1999). Discretion refers to expectations that the helper will not engage in fishing expeditions, seeking extraneous or tantalizing information that is beyond the bounds of the particular helping relationship. Discretion means that staff won't seek out information or try to access records on cases for which they have no professional responsibility. Because ethical codes and individual integrity may be insufficient to protect case information from prying eyes, technology to protect records and alert administrators when access is sought by unauthorized persons is now available. These "snoop alerts" serve as a line of protection from workers in large systems who may seek information on their relatives, friends, and neighbors. They also protect data in sensational or high-profile cases from the curious.

Respect for privacy goes beyond what information is sought to include what information is shared. It implies restraint on the part of the worker—not gossiping about clients, not sharing information about clients with our families or friends, and not pointing to a TV or news item and saying, "I know about that case." Confidentiality requires restraint about where we discuss cases; we must ensure that conversations, even for professional purposes, do not take place in public or semiprivate places. This can be a difficult standard to uphold in some circumstances. It is challenging to create an atmosphere of privacy when offices are configured into cubicles or services are provided in shared hospital rooms or in clients' homes. Nevertheless, respect for confidentiality requires the worker to endeavor to maintain clients' privacy, even under difficult circumstances. Even if it is more efficient to discuss a case in the hall or elevator on the way to a meeting, it is not ethically sound to do so.

A third feature of discretion in confidentiality is self-discipline—the notion that helpers will divulge information only for compelling professional reasons and will be vigilant in protecting written and electronic communications about clients, and cautious in responding to attempts by others to seek information, whether in the form of a subpoena, an insurance authorization form, a child custody report, or a request for case information from a fellow professional. This does not mean that helping professionals always withhold information in these cases, only that they ensure that proper consent has been obtained and that information shared doesn't exceed the purpose for which it was sought.

Sometimes, the respect for privacy means that we must receive and hold information that brings us discomfort. Absent information that leads us to believe risk of harm is likely, hearing a client's abusive fantasies (or other troubling material) is a necessary prerequisite to helping him or her work on them. Helping professionals don't have the freedom to mention these experiences to our friends or family or coworkers, or to the client's friends or family or coworkers. Professionals *do* have the freedom to discuss them, in confidence, with their supervisors or consultants, based on the understanding that that person will maintain the client's privacy and that the information sharing is intended to ensure competent service to the client. It is not at all easy to be the repository of disturbing information about our fellow citizens. But managing this discomfort appropriately comes with the territory of being a helping professional.

As mentioned above, there are situations in which social workers are encouraged, and at times compelled, to break confidentiality (Houston-Vega et al., 1997). For example, sharing case information in supervision or consultation is intended to ensure high-quality services for the benefit of the client. If a client presents a danger to himself or herself or another person, we are empowered to intercede because safety takes precedence over privacy in such circumstances. State mandatory reporting laws require that suspicions of child or elder abuse be reported to the relevant protection agencies so that they can investigate and intercede if necessary. Some referral sources, such as employee assistance programs, or payers, such as managed care companies, may require that case information be conveyed to them as a condition of treatment. Even in these situations, though, there are limits on what we can share and with whom we can share it. For example, if a worker suspects a child is being abused, he or she is not empowered to share that suspicion with the child's teacher, grandmother, or neighbor; the worker is required to report it to the local child welfare agency. Likewise, in reporting it to Child Protective Services, the worker is not obliged to share all that he or she knows about the case, only that material necessary to carry out the responsibility for child protection.

The duty to warn, established in *Tarasoff v. Regents of the University of California*, obliges professionals to alert the intended victim of a serious threat against him or her or to otherwise assist that person in protecting himself or herself (Dickson, 1998). However, it does not allow workers to talk to the media about their concerns or reveal the confidences the client has shared throughout the course of treatment.

Confidentiality is a highly charged and relatively complex area of ethics. It is influenced by laws set by various legislative bodies, by the results of civil litigation, and by regulations and policies. For example, the court cases in other jurisdictions subsequent to *Tarasoff* have shaped its applications and limitations. The federal Health Insurance Portability and Accountability Act has stipulations about the storage and sharing of patient records, and about verbal and other communications about clients (HIPAA Medical Privacy Rule, 2003; U.S. Department of Health and Human Services, 2003b). In *Jaffee v. Redmond,* the U.S. Supreme Court held client communications to be privileged and explicitly extended that privilege to licensed social workers ("Social Workers and Psychotherapist-Patient Privilege," 2005). Disclosures about substance abuse treatment are strictly regulated by 42 C.F.R. (Confidentiality of Alcohol and Drug Abuse Patient Records, n.d.). These guidelines pertain to records "maintained in connection with the performance of any program or activity relating to substance abuse education, prevention, training, treatment, rehabilitation, or research that is conducted, regulated or directly or indirectly assisted by any federal department or agency" (Reamer, 2006, p. 161).

Confidentiality standards are also shaped by expectations that vary by client population and practice setting. For example, parents of minor clients have the legal right to know when their children appear for service and the nature of those services. However, minors' rights are protected according to setting and state in cases of emergency care, and when mental health services, treatment for sexually transmitted diseases, contraception, and prenatal care are sought. Settings that take a team approach to service or involve a network of providers (such as Multisystemic Therapy) would enlarge the network of helpers with an interest in case information and a right to be party to consultations about case progress (Franklin & Jordan, 2002).

The principle of maintaining client privacy is strongly linked to the principle of informed consent. In addition to ensuring that patients understand the pros and cons, and options and limitations of various aspects of treatment, professionals must also discuss confidentiality, and inform clients about the intent to keep information private *and* the limitations of that intent. Patients have the right to understand up front the conditions under which their information must be shared, and they should agree to those conditions in writing. Thus, for example, a client would understand at the outset of care that using health insurance for mental health services will result in the appearance of information on services provided on the Explanation of Benefits form that will be sent to the policy holder following treatment. Or a client who, during the course of service, describes parenting practices that raise the concern of abuse would have been aware from the beginning of services what the result of such a disclosure would be.

In contemporary practice, confidentiality is also complicated by the ascendance of technology intended to lead to more efficient practice. Fax machines, electronic records, e-mail, voice mail, miniaturized recorders, and other tools can be used to enhance practice but can also jeopardize confidentiality by making records and other forms of stored information easier to access and disperse (Freeny, 1998). Therefore, upholding the principle of confidentiality goes beyond exercising discretion. It requires vigilance so that the tools of practice are not vulnerable to misuse or misappropriation by others. It also requires new methods of tracking and destroying data when the required period for maintaining the record has lapsed.

Ethical standards for maintaining client privacy include the following:

- "Social workers should protect the confidentiality of all information obtained in the course of professional service, except for compelling professional reasons. The general expectation that social workers will keep information confidential does not apply when disclosure is necessary to prevent serious, foreseeable, and imminent harm to a client or other identifiable person. In all instances, social workers should disclose the least amount of confidential information necessary to achieve the desired purpose; only information that is directly relevant to the purpose for which the disclosure is made should be revealed" (NASW, 1999, 1.07c).
- "Social workers should protect the confidentiality of clients during legal proceedings to the extent permitted by law. When a court of law or other legally authorized body orders social workers to disclose confidential or privileged information without a client's consent and such disclosure could cause harm to the client, social workers should request that the court withdraw the order or limit the order as narrowly as possible or maintain the records under seal, unavailable for public inspection" (NASW, 1999, 1.07j).
- "Social workers should inform clients involved in family, couples, marital, or group counseling of the social worker's, employer's, and agency's policy concerning the social worker's disclosure of confidential information among the parties involved in the counseling" (NASW, 1999, 1.07g).
- "Social workers should not disclose confidential information to third-party payers unless clients have authorized such disclosure" (NASW, 1999, 1.07h).
- "Social workers should transfer or dispose of clients' records in a manner that protects clients' confidentiality and is consistent with state statutes governing records and social work licensure" (NASW, 1999, 1.07n).
- "Social workers should take reasonable precautions to protect client confidentiality in the event of the social worker's termination of practice, incapacitation, or death" (NASW, 1999, 1.07o).

- "Social workers should not disclose identifying information when discussing clients for teaching or training purposes unless the client has consented to disclosure of confidential information" (NASW, 1999, 1.07p).
- "Social workers should not disclose identifying information when discussing clients with consultants unless the client has consented to disclosure of confidential information or there is a compelling need for such disclosure" (NASW, 1999, 1.07r).

UPHOLDING THE STANDARD

Ella is a school social worker who serves in several elementary schools. She has been collaborating with Child Protective Services to offer support to Kareem, a seven-year-old who recently moved to the district. Kareem and his younger siblings came to the attention of Child Protective Services after their mother contracted AIDS and was unable to sufficiently care for them. Ella has been helping Kareem adjust to his new classroom and build a social network with his peers. His teacher, Ms. Lancaster, has been asking Ella for information about Kareem and his family so that she can understand him better and help him out.

While Ms. Lancaster is a fellow professional and a potential collaborator in Kareem's care, Ella is cautious of how much information to share with her and how she will use it. In particular, she is concerned that Ms. Lancaster and some of the other teachers gossip about the families of their students. She is not comfortable with how information she might share about his case or his mother's condition will be used. Beyond these concerns, Ella has no permission from CPS or the family to share information with other professionals at the school.

After taking all this into account, Ella thanked Ms. Lancaster for her concern for Kareem. She shared with the teacher the goals they are working on, and the two discussed ways that his progress might be assisted or reinforced in the classroom. She did not share his family history or the reasons for his referral, but the two did discuss their perceptions of his strengths and struggles since arriving at the school.

Ella effectively balanced two competing priorities—to collaborate with fellow professionals who are essential members of Kareem's environment while protecting sensitive information about his case from misuse. While Ella may have concerns about the faculty's commitment to students' privacy, Ms. Lancaster must be regarded as an important member of Kareem's service system. As Berman-Rossi and Rossi (1990) note, "The social worker is called upon to help the child to make use of the school as well as to enable the school to become useful to the child" (p. 196). Ella's decision opens the lines of communication with Kareem's teacher while keeping the focus on service goals rather than his personal history.

Ella's actions appear consistent with standards of the School Social Work Association of America. Their position statement on confidentiality notes that "Information should be shared with other school personnel only on a need-to-know basis and only for compelling professional reasons. Prior to sharing confidential information, school social workers should evaluate the responsibility to and the welfare of the student. The responsibility to maintain confidentiality also must be weighed against the responsibility to the family and the school community. However, the focus should always be on what is best for the student" (School Social Work Association of America, 2001).

It appears that Ella did not discuss the teacher's request with Kareem's other service providers, and it is not clear whether she consulted her own supervisor or colleagues, though these discussions could have been useful in shaping her decision and developing a consistent plan for communications with school personnel. Ella might also have spoken with Kareem's parents or guardians to obtain informed consent for the information she intended to share. And, had Kareem been older, she might also have discussed with him what information he wanted the school to have or she could have directed Ms. Lancaster to him to find out more.

Depending on her concerns and her responsibilities in relation to the school, Ella might consider taking action on her observation that faculty members treat student information in an inappropriate and disrespectful manner. A school culture dominated by gossip about students not only impedes important communications but may reflect deeper problems concerning the way Kareem and others are viewed and treated in the classroom.

VIOLATING THE STANDARD

Jeffrey is a thirty-something single professional. He met Elise at a cocktail party and in the course of conversation told her he was a therapist. "Wow," she said, "that must be fascinating ... listening to people's private stories all day long!"

Eager to make an impression, he replied, "It is. Sometimes it's a burden, and sometimes it's amazing how messed up people are—even people who seem so put together on the outside. Sometimes I wish I didn't know so much about people I should respect. You'd be surprised."

"Like what?" she said.

Jeffrey knew better, but he was quite caught up in displaying his importance, so he forged on. "Well, you know Jones, the candidate for governor? He's been seeing me off and on for years. He's got a real thing for Internet porn, but he figures he's safe as long as he can talk to me and keep those demons under control."

Jeffrey's is a particularly egregious violation of client privacy in that he disclosed highly sensitive information about a well-known person for his own self-aggrandizement. Not only does it represent a violation of confidentiality, but it may also signal other vulnerabilities in Jeffrey's professionalism and respect for clients. In their work on client exploitation, Epstein and Simon (1990) note that such disclosures are a form of exhibitionism, akin to excessive self-disclosure or seeking celebrity from a famous client. As such, it may serve as a marker for other steps along the path to boundary and other violations.

At the very least, Jeffrey's disclosure is a failure of containment, or the ability to keep to ourselves information that we know others might find scintillating. Should Jeffrey try to rationalize his disclosure by contending that the candidate's habits render him unsuitable for office, the method he chose to share the information undermines his argument. In other words, if he had legitimate concerns that the candidate's addiction was placing others at risk, his first steps would be to discuss the concerns with the client and with a consultant who would also respect the client's confidentiality, not with a cocktail party acquaintance. Such conversations would help determine whom the candidate's behavior put at risk, and Jeffrey's responsibility, if any, to alert those at risk.

Passing along information that was received in the sanctity of the helping relationship is a disturbing violation of trust. And, once the information is out, Jeffrey is powerless to call it back, as Elise may now share it with others until it takes on a life of its own. In doing so, Jeffrey has opened himself up to severe professional and civil sanctions should the disclosed information be made public.

Perhaps there are already rumors circulating about the candidate's Internet porn addiction. This does not legitimize Jeffrey's actions. The source of the information differentiates confidentiality breaches from mere gossip. That is, the manner in which a helping professional comes to possess information places regulations on what he or she is permitted to do with it. Information that is shared by clients or collateral contacts in the context of a professional relationship has special protections. Personal communications with a friend, colleague, or family member may carry the presumption of privacy, but that is mutual (expected of both parties) and less formally articulated than the presumption of privacy in a helping relationship. Violations of a friend's privacy may cost the friendship, but they don't carry legal or ethical penalties.

Information derived from public sources such as the Internet, Web logs, news reports, or magazines is already in the public sphere. Sharing it at a cocktail party qualifies as a conversation or gossip rather than a breach of trust. Therefore, Jeffrey would be less vulnerable if he had learned of the candidate's secrets through a personal relationship with him or through the media. But having learned of them under the veil of privacy as a professional, he is forbidden to pass them on, even by confirming or denouncing the suspicions of others.

RESOLVING DILEMMAS IN UPHOLDING CONFIDENTIALITY: SUICIDE AND SECRETS

Marci, age sixteen, had been a client in Rebecca's private practice for approximately a month when she died in an apparent suicide from an overdose of several prescription drugs. Marci had been referred to Rebecca by her parents, who were concerned with her declining grades and sour disposition. During the few sessions they had together, Rebecca learned that Marci was preoccupied with her body image and sense of worth. In part this seemed to be driven by her boyfriend Mark's criticisms of her appearance and his warnings that she shouldn't let herself "go" like her mother and sister. Marci had tentatively divulged that Mark had been physically aggressive toward her, and that there had been one episode of forced sexual activity. When Rebecca pressed her for details, Marci downplayed the incident, saying, "He was just trying to encourage me to be less uptight." At the time of Marci's death, Rebecca was still trying to build trust with her client and formulate an assessment, but she suspected elements of depression, an eating disorder, and substance use, perhaps in an effort to self-medicate or lose weight.

Marci's parents are tormented by their daughter's death and have contacted Rebecca to ask about their daughter's state of mind so that they can better understand what happened.

The death of a child is among life's most traumatic and unnatural experiences. Losses from suicide are even more challenging in that the deaths are sudden and intentional, and often violent. Suicide touches all those involved with the deceased, as peers, family, neighbors, teachers, coworkers, and others struggle to make sense of a seemingly senseless loss.

Marci's tragic death creates a multidimensional dilemma for her therapist. On one hand, her grieving parents are seeking information ostensibly as part of their bereavement process. Because Marci was a minor, they may have legal rights to case information. However, the ethical standards of Rebecca's profession protect a client's confidentiality, even in death. And if Rebecca shares information with the intent of bringing Marci's parents comfort and understanding, where should she stop in revealing the girl's confidences? Finally, what role might any perceptions of culpability or liability play in Rebecca's decision to share information about the case or withhold it?

Who Can Be Helpful to Rebecca?

Rebecca needs several forms of assistance: interpersonal support to deal with the sudden and traumatic loss of her client, assistance in anticipating and preparing for requests for information and other examinations of her practices prior to Marci's death, and legal and ethical advice in responding to Marci's parents' request for information and other inquiries. Rebecca may want to turn to different resources for each of these issues.

Patient deaths are less common in mental health, child welfare, and school settings than they are in fields of practice such as nursing homes or health and hospice settings. When deaths do occur in mental health and similar settings, they tend to be traumatic and unanticipated—the result of suicide, accidents, or interpersonal violence (Strom-Gottfried & Mowbray, 2006). Deaths by suicide have a distinct impact on the professionals involved (Halligan & Corcoran, 2001; Maltsberger, 1992). An assortment of quantitative, qualitative, and case studies indicates significant professional and personal effects following the death of a client by suicide including shock, fear of another incident, guilt, distrust, intrusive thoughts, a sense of betrayal, depression, helplessness, loss of confidence, fear, hypomania, anger, and avoidance of triggering stimuli (Chemtob, Hamada, Bauer, Kinney, & Torigoe, 1988; Cooper, 1995; Menninger, 1991).

Dealing with the emotional impact of her client's death will help Rebecca's own psychosocial well-being and will ensure that she doesn't confound her ethical decision making with her grief processes. For support during this time, Rebecca may turn to her colleagues, her personal support system, her faith community, or therapeutic resources. As she processes her grief with people who are not entitled to information about the case, Rebecca should be certain that the focus of this assistance is on her and her sense of loss, rather than on Marci or the facts of her life and death.

For the purposes of debriefing about her work on the case, conducting a psychological autopsy, and preparing for inquiries into the case, Rebecca should turn to her fellow professionals. Hopefully she has an established system for supervision or peer consultation that she can mobilize following the death and in anticipation of the dilemmas that will likely follow. Had she sought feedback when Marci revealed troubling information during treatment, this consultation would be a natural extension of assistance in an already complex case. If she did not, she will need to pull together people who can provide clearheaded advice in a time of crisis, and ensure that she makes sound decisions in the aftermath of Marci's case and in services to her current caseload.

Rebecca should also seek legal consultation. An attorney can advise her on Marci's parents' rights to case information, the processes they must use to obtain access, and the legal risks and benefits in withholding case information from them. Legal consultation will also be wise should Rebecca have concerns about her liability in Marci's death. If there is a possibility that she might face accusations of negligence in not detecting warning signs of suicide, insufficiently assessing the risk of lethality, or failing to notify Marci's parents about risks she faced from her possible drug use and her boyfriend's abusive behavior, it would be best to know her legal rights and alternatives up front.

What Are Rebecca's Options?

At two extremes, Rebecca's choices include declining to share any information with Marci's parents or making all case information available to them. The latter may include verbal discussions about Marci's care and/or the surrender of the treatment records from her services. An intermediate choice would involve sharing a limited amount of information about the case, such as Rebecca's knowledge of and response to any suicide threats or the status of treatment goals at the time of Marci's death. Families who have experienced suicide are often plagued with the question "Why?" and by feelings of responsibility for the suicide. If Rebecca believes that the parents' queries originated in these areas, she could target her response to share what she has observed or concluded in relation to these questions. The distinction here is that Rebecca is emphasizing her own impressions while sharing limited information about the case itself.

When Has Rebecca Made Similar Decisions?

While Rebecca may have never before faced the sudden death of a client or a request by survivors for case information, she has undoubtedly seen minors in her practice prior to treating Marci. Therefore, a starting place in her decision making about what to share following Marci's death would be what information she would ordinarily share with the parents about the teen's case. Related to this is what understanding she had with Marci and her parents about privacy in the case. That is, while Marci's parents may have the legal right to data on their child's care, the informed consent processes at the outset of treatment would have established the ethical limits on confidentiality.

Clinicians treating adolescent clients commonly seek agreement with the child and parents about the information to be disclosed between the two parties. This conversation helps to inform all parties about the boundaries and conditions for information sharing. It provides comfort to parents, who are rightfully concerned about their child's well-being, and it provides security to the client, who may wish to disclose troubling or painful material in therapy. One common standard is that the worker should share any information that would raise the parents' concerns about the safety of their child, and the informed consent process elaborates on what type of information this would include in practice. If the agreement is that the youth and clinician will give periodic updates to the parents on progress toward treatment goals, without specific information on the issues under discussion, that, too, would need to be articulated at the outset of service. The nature of Rebecca's specific understanding with Marci and her parents would help to shape her decision in this matter. If the agreement was that information would be shared freely, Rebecca might feel entitled to share information now. If the agreement was that only a limited scope of information would be revealed, that might apply, too.

Rebecca's decision might be shaped by her actions during the course of treatment. That is, if she was faithful to the informed consent agreement in disclosing information to Marci's parents, she would likely be less reluctant to do so now. However, if she failed to notify the parents about information they might have expected to learn, she may be uncomfortable disclosing it after the client's death. Any discomfort at lapses in the treatment process should be addressed separately from Rebecca's current dilemma. In other words, Rebecca's failure to follow the informed consent agreement during service is not a sufficient reason to continue withholding information or to share it freely now to compensate for her error.

Another precedent on which Rebecca might rely is her handling of cases where questions have been raised about the appropriateness of services rendered. If she believes that the parents' query arises out of their suspicion of malpractice or their intent to sue, and Rebecca has had similar experiences, she should consider how they would apply in this situation. Since malpractice litigation is an adversarial process, that might mean that Rebecca would be very circumspect in her communications about the case and refuse to volunteer information unless compelled to do so.

Where Will Ethical and Clinical Standards Lead Her?

How would the deontological perspective view Rebecca's choices? For the option to strictly maintain Marci's privacy, the implied rule is that the social worker should never disclose information unless the client agrees to it through informed consent, or more broadly, that no one should share another's confidences without that person's permission. This seems like a good rule for lay people and professionals. It is reflected in ethical standards and in professional practice. Following the deontological perspective would thus refer Rebecca back to the original understanding with Marci and her parents about sharing information in the case. Marci's original informed consent would then form the basis of Rebecca's decision about what she could ethically share (or not share) following the client's death.

What rules are embedded in the decision to share information with the parents? Depending on the parents' motivations in seeking the information, the rules might include "It is acceptable to share information if it will help bring the family comfort" or "It is acceptable to share case information once a client is deceased" or "Parents have a right to know about the services provided to minors, so the social worker should surrender the data." While each of these may have merit in some cases, it is unlikely we would accept any of them as universal laws. For the first, it may be hard to discern what will bring comfort, and the risk of revelation is that it may bring either comfort or distress at the expense of the client's privacy. The second rule would essentially overturn the promise of privacy, undermining the hallmark of the helping process. While some may argue that privacy rights are moot if the client is deceased, clients live on in the memories and relationships they leave behind. These can be irretrievably damaged if secrets are revealed without the client's consent. Last, while the third rule on parents' rights may be supported in law for many services, procedures, and jurisdictions, there are circumstances where parents are asked not to exercise that right in deference to the trust necessary for the therapeutic relationship (Corey et al., 2003).

The ethical merit of Rebecca's other choice, releasing information that is limited in some way, would depend on the basis for her decision on what to reveal. For example, disclosing information within the bounds of the informed consent agreement would be a defensible rule. Revealing information on her impressions, rather than Marci's secrets, might also be defensible. Disseminating information solely to appease the parents and forestall litigation would not be.

How would a utilitarian perspective view Rebecca's choices? The consequences of withholding all case information include upholding the principle of confidentiality while protecting Marci's privacy and taking a stand for the same on behalf of other clients. It would mean not revealing Marci's secrets and avoiding any damage they might cause to her memory. Withholding the information would place the good of the deceased person ahead of that of her living parents. A refusal to share case information might very well be troubling to Marci's parents. It might exacerbate their distress and make them suspicious of Rebecca's motives. It might encourage them to pursue legal action for access.

Conversing about the case and sharing records would have inverse consequences. It would jeopardize the principle of confidentiality, reveal Marci's secrets, and perhaps lead to mistrust among current and future clients. While it might placate Marci's parents, there is no guarantee that would be the case. A further consequence for Rebecca is that it could be construed as a violation of her ethical responsibilities. As such, it might result in a complaint to her licensure board or professional association. If the breach were deemed to have violated HIPAA, there might be additional financial penalties.

The primary social work value at play in this case is that of integrity—behaving in a trustworthy fashion. Embracing that value would mean declining to release unauthorized case information to Marci's parents. Because social workers also value service to others and supporting relationships, it may be difficult for Rebecca to refuse the parents' request. However, Rebecca's greatest responsibility is to her client and to acting in accord with Marci's expectations when they commenced treatment.

The ethical standards in this case are fairly straightforward. As noted at the outset of this chapter, NASW standards permit communications for compelling professional reasons and to prevent harmful acts. However, the NASW code also explicitly states that "Social workers should protect the confidentiality of deceased clients consistent with the preceding standards" (NASW, 1999, 1.07r).

The ethical principles of autonomy, fidelity, and nonmaleficence are all relevant to the case. Of Rebecca's choices, the decision to withhold case information best honors Marci's right to make her own decisions about what she wanted others to know or not know about her life. That option also demonstrates Rebecca's honesty in that she would be acting in good faith to see that Marci's privacy is protected. Discretion in information sharing also meets the principle of nonmaleficence if it best protects Marci's legacy. Some might argue that Marci's legacy is not the "real" Marci unless people better understand the struggles and events she experienced when she was alive. While authenticity and honesty are valid concepts, the principle of autonomy grants every person the right to keep his or her thoughts and experiences private. If Marci chose to present a different face to the world than the one she was experiencing in her innermost thoughts, it is not Rebecca's duty or right to undermine that.

Seeking legal consultation would be essential for Rebecca to weigh her choices in light of the relevant laws. State laws specify the parents' rights to information during the course of treatment and following the minor's death. They also specify the penalties Rebecca might face for unauthorized disclosure of client records. HIPAA might also be relevant in this decision, as would the confidentiality provisions in various states, if they are more stringent than HIPAA itself. Because the language in these statutes presumes the client is living, the applicability to Marci's case may be open to interpretation. For example some states may forbid disclosure of minors' protected health information including information concerning past treatment. In states that permit or require disclosure, or those that have no law, the professional may release information *unless* it is deemed that such disclosure would be an invasion of the minor's privacy, endanger or cause harm to the client, or otherwise not be in the best interest of the client (Stephan, n.d.).

The practice standards concerning confidentiality are congruent with the ethical standards. Clinicians go to great lengths to protect the privacy of their clients, revealing information in only a narrow range of circumstances, typically with the client's permission or when compelled to do so to prevent harm such as child maltreatment. This case offers no potential for prevention and no capacity by which Rebecca can obtain her client's guidance or permission. She may use previous conversations around informed consent as a guide to the client's wishes, but those will provide only an approximation of permission, since neither Rebecca nor Marci likely anticipated the issues that would arise at the outset of therapy.

Entities that wish to compel clinicians to surrender case information have processes at their disposal to do so. Agencies and individuals can issue subpoenas for testimony or records regarding a case. Should the professional object to the disclosure, the court can review the merits of the request and the refusal and issue an order for compliance if it so chooses. If the disclosure is ordered by the court but the client refuses, the worker faces a double bind where sanctions may arise from honoring either party over the other. However, in Rebecca's dilemma, those who are likely to petition for the information are probably the same people representing the client's estate. As a result, if presented with a court order to surrender information in the case, Rebecca might feel disloyal to Marci, but she should be secure in the knowledge that she did not surrender her client's confidences carelessly and without due process.

The discussion of subpoenas and court orders reminds us that ethical decision making involves consideration of the facts of the case. We do not know the nature of Marci's despair or suicidal ideation prior to her death. We do not know Rebecca's liability in the case, and we do not know Marci's parents' intentions in seeking information. If there was no indication of suicidal intent during treatment, if Rebecca's clinical practices were sound, and if Marci's parents simply want assurance that they were not at fault for her death, Rebecca could probably respond to their queries without violating the confidentiality her client had been led to expect. If the parents simply want an opportunity to talk about their daughter and her struggles with a safe person outside the family, that too would require little revelation on Rebecca's part. Shifts in the facts of the case, however, might lead in another direction, as the decision-making schema clearly supports Rebecca in withholding information on the case unless she is compelled to release it.

Why Is Rebecca Selecting a Particular Course of Action?

Any given resolution to an ethical dilemma can be rendered inappropriate if it is selected for the wrong reasons. Therefore, it is vital for helping professionals to examine their motivations in favoring one resolution strategy over another.

Earlier in this chapter we alluded to possible errors in the course of treatment that can take on greater significance in light of the client's sudden death. Failing to establish clear guidelines for sharing information with the minor's parents, failing to follow through on information-sharing agreements that were made, or negligently addressing the client's risks to herself or others are just some examples. In the event that she did make errors in practice, Rebecca may be tempted to withhold information from the parents because of her own liability. In fact, she may even receive legal advice to do so. While there may be valid reasons to withhold information in the case, from an ethical perspective, doing so to obscure her own errors would place Rebecca's interests over the interests of the parents, and potentially Marci's interests. It might also be strategically unwise, in that attempts to hide errors can exasperate the other parties and exacerbate the errors themselves.

Rebecca may also perceive confidentiality as an all-or-nothing proposition. This stance would push her to the tell-or-don't tell extremes among her options. In doing so, she may overlook valid options of limited, discrete disclosures that could contribute to the parents' peace of mind without revealing information that would taint the memory of their daughter or indict those, like Mark, who are still living.

The principle of publicity might favor any of the choices, depending on Rebecca's rationale for employing them. Fellow professionals and other teen clients would likely understand and respect Rebecca's strict adherence to patient privacy to support the sanctity of the therapeutic relationship. However, other parents and the court of public opinion might find the stance irrelevant in light of the patient's death, and heartless in light of the parents' despair. Should she decide to share information, the positions would probably be reversed. Withholding information only to serve her own interests or to stonewall investigation of the case would probably be condemned by a variety of observers and violate the smell test.

What happens when Rebecca puts herself in others' shoes? If she were the parent, Rebecca would no doubt have the same questions and expectations as Marci's parents. What if she were Marci? Based on her knowledge of the teen, what does Rebecca believe she would want? Perhaps she would wish to keep her relationship with Mark and her substance use concealed. But would she permit certain information to be shared if it brought comfort to her parents and facilitated their mourning? Reversibility always requires speculation as the social worker endeavors to view the choices from another's stance. In this case it may help Rebecca to be faithful to her client's wishes and the spirit of patient privacy while protecting the parents (and Marci's memory) from hurtful and unhelpful information.

In meeting the mom or mentor test, Rebecca need not rely on her imagination about what people she respects might do in this situation. As part of her decision making in the case, she can call on her mentors for input about her choices. Like all consultation, these conversations may lead her to different conclusions, but in doing so they will ensure that she has evaluated the case from a variety of angles.

How Should Rebecca Carry Out Her Decision?

While some risk management practices would suggest that professionals avoid contact with the aggrieved and bereaved family of a client who has committed suicide, clinical wisdom and practical experiences seem to suggest otherwise (Pearlman, 1992; Schacht, 1992). That is, while social workers may be reluctant to reach out to a family and express their sadness at the death for fear that it will open them up to questions and condemnation, such an authentic expression of shared loss is usually viewed positively by the family as a sign of caring (Kleepsies, Penk, & Forsyth, 1993). Conversely, avoiding such contact or staying away from the funeral or visiting hours may be interpreted as cold and heartless and may exacerbate the family's distrust and anger at the worker.

The conversations Rebecca has with the parents immediately following the loss will set the stage for her approach to them at a later point. Those encounters will be an opportunity for Rebecca to demonstrate sensitivity and professionalism and gauge the parents' concern. Substantive discussions about Marci's state of mind or requests for information should be deferred to another time and setting. In addition to allowing them to find a more appropriate venue and context for the conversation, addressing their concerns at a later point will allow Rebecca to plan her strategy and allow all parties to meet when they are no longer experiencing the disorientation that immediately follows a traumatic loss.

When the meeting is arranged, Rebecca should establish the scope of the conversation so that the parents do not arrive with unrealistic expectations. Rebecca must manage several tensions in the meeting. She must be sensitive to the parents' pain and allow them to express their grief without taking an ongoing role as their therapist. She must also be clear about the confidentiality limits she will follow and the rationale behind them, while being sensitive to their needs and sympathetic to their request.

Rebecca should expect an emotional and delicate conversation. She should be well prepared for it in advance, anticipating what she wants to say and the ways in which she will address various rejoinders, pleas, or queries from the parents. She should also anticipate her own feelings that may come up in the session and use her consultation to prepare for them. She should make use of her professional support system to debrief after the meeting and prepare for next steps as needed. Rebecca should have kept a record of her actions throughout the duration of the case, and she must be certain to document the content, flow, and conclusions reached in the meeting with Marci's parents as well.

CONCLUSION

Confidentiality is the cornerstone of the helping process. The assurance of privacy creates a climate in which an individual's most intimate acts, thoughts, and emotions can be revealed and addressed. Requests for case information can be fulfilled with waivers signed by the client or duly issued subpoenas or court orders. While there are many legal and ethical protections for privacy, the right is limited for certain populations (minors), and certain acts (child abuse) and actions (danger to oneself or others). It may also be limited as a condition of treatment. For example, clients in involuntary or correctional settings may have to agree to certain forms of information sharing, and clients who use insurance for services will find that some information is shared with the payer in order to secure reimbursement. Ethical standards about confidentiality require that clients be informed up front about the limits on privacy. Such informed consent protects both the worker and the client should circumstances arise that require disclosures to be made.

Even with proper informed consent and permission to make disclosures, professionals are expected to exercise discretion in the amount of information they seek and in the amount they share. They must safeguard data by treating records and electronic communications with care and avoid discussing cases in nonsecure settings, such as lobbies or restaurants. Communications about cases should be in the clients' interests, not for the aggrandizement of the worker, the amusement of friends, or the satisfaction of family members.

Chapter 8

COMPETENCE

According to the principle of competence, those we are serving must be able to trust that we are qualified to care for them and will do so to the best of our abilities. This means that a social worker has the knowledge and experience necessary to address clients' needs, uses resources such as supervision or consultation to ensure effective practice, and is free of impairments that may diminish effective delivery of care. Competence also implies that professionals will be self-regulating—that practitioners will refer cases when they do not have the requisite abilities, that they will seek help if personal problems or addictions impair their work, and that they will pursue additional knowledge, training, or consultation to maintain and advance their skills. Competent practice means professionals know their limits and take action *themselves* to address these limits, instead of waiting for someone else to tell them they are in over their heads.

Competence is related to the principles of beneficence and non-maleficence in that competent practice involves doing good and not doing harm. It is also related to other standards such as informed consent, in that clients have a right to know about the worker's ability to help them with the needs that they present. In situations where the worker's competence may not meet minimal standards (for example, in areas with scarce resources, emerging fields of practice, or innovative treatments), good practice demands that clients understand the relative risks and benefits of seeking treatment under these circumstances and that clinicians do whatever they can to bolster their competence, including getting extra training, reviewing available literature, seeking specialized supervision, and carefully evaluating the services rendered.

The NASW standards related to competence state:

- "Social workers should provide services and represent themselves as competent only within the boundaries of their education, training, license, certification, consultation received, supervised experience, or other relevant professional experience" (NASW, 1999, 1.04a).

- "Social workers should provide services in substantive areas or use intervention techniques or approaches that are new to them only after engaging in appropriate study, training, consultation, and supervision from people who are competent in those interventions or techniques" (NASW, 1999, 1.04b).
- "When generally recognized standards do not exist with respect to an emerging area of practice, social workers should exercise careful judgment and take responsible steps (including appropriate education, research, training, consultation, and supervision) to ensure the competence of their work and to protect clients from harm" (NASW, 1999, 1.04c).
- "Social workers should seek the advice and counsel of colleagues whenever such consultation is in the best interests of clients" (NASW, 1999, 2.05a).
- "Social workers who provide supervision or consultation should have the necessary knowledge and skill to supervise or consult appropriately and should do so only within their areas of knowledge and competence" (NASW, 1999, 3.01a).
- "Social workers who function as educators, field instructors for students, or trainers should provide instruction only within their areas of knowledge and competence and should provide instruction based on the most current information and knowledge available in the profession" (NASW, 1999, 3.02a).
- "Social workers should accept responsibility or employment only on the basis of existing competence or the intention to acquire the necessary competence" (NASW, 1999, 4.01).

UPHOLDING THE STANDARD

Liu has recently opened a full-time private practice after five years in an agency setting. She is awaiting designation as an approved provider for several insurance companies and in the meantime is finding it difficult to sustain her cash flow with self-paid clients.

Today Liu received a call from a woman whom she had seen in counseling for several months the year before. The woman and her husband recently adopted a baby from China and are concerned about the child's development and capacity for attachment. Because she had been happy with Liu's care in the past, she felt confident in Liu's ability to help with this new issue.

Liu was in a quandary. As a Chinese woman, she might be well positioned to help the client and her husband understand the child and the issues she presents. She had already forged a trusting relationship with the parents and might be of further help to them. On the other hand, Liu had never worked with children, had no expertise in adoption, and was not familiar with the literature on bonding and attachment. While she desperately wanted to take the case, she decided that she did not have the requisite expertise to help with such a crucial issue.

Liu met with the couple once to observe the child and talk with the parents about their needs, observations, and expectations. She then facilitated a referral to colleagues at her former workplace with expertise in early childhood disorders. She offered to be available to the couple and the receiving therapist if her cultural and family therapy expertise would be beneficial to the case.

Liu's decision represents professional maturity and ethical sophistication in putting the clients' best interests before her own financial needs. While she could have rationalized agreeing to work with the family, her understanding of the dynamic issues in the case led her to exercise restraint and refer the family to someone better prepared to help. Liu's actions were in keeping with standards in the NASW *Code of Ethics*.

Social workers should refer clients to other professionals when the other professionals' specialized knowledge or expertise is needed to serve clients fully or when social workers believe that they are not being effective or making reasonable progress with clients and that additional service is required (NASW, 1999, 2.06a).

In exercising self-awareness and self-restraint, Liu shows that she is practicing within her area of competence and upholds her fiduciary responsibility to her clients, who must rely on her ability and judgments. In declining the case, Liu furthers the respect and trust that were built in the previous episode of treatment. In the long run, her demonstrated concern for their well-being and her strong sense of self may encourage the couple to return to her in the future should they have needs in areas where she can be of help.

VIOLATING THE STANDARD

Jeb has worked at a mental health center for over twenty years. After his wife left him last year, Jeb poured himself into his work. He takes on the most difficult cases, works long hours, and is bereft when clients struggle or withdraw from treatment. Kerry, the administrative assistant in his unit, has observed other changes in Jeb's behavior. He disappears from the office during the day for hours at a time and appears giddy and incoherent when he returns. His paperwork is months behind, and he is often forgetful, missing meetings and repeating himself in conversations.

Kerry raised her concerns with Jeb's supervisor, Nancy, who suggested she mind her own business. "Jeb's going through a rough time right now. I don't want to make him feel worse when work is all he has these days. I'm not going to confront him with such vague accusations when he's carrying half the cases for the unit."

Kerry's willingness to speak up about her observations of Jeb's behavior demonstrates moral courage. In contrast, Nancy's decision to overlook Jeb's impairment is a disservice to him and to his clients. It also puts her at risk for enabling his negligent practice. While his coworkers may be uncomfortable suggesting that he is drinking while out of the office or hypothesizing that his erratic behavior is due to depression, intoxication, or some other unhealthy cause, for the purposes of action the cause is less relevant than the effects. Kerry, Nancy, and other workers can substantiate a pattern of problematic behavior including, at the very least, errant paperwork, extreme reactions to client difficulties, and missed appointments. The NASW code has two standards that speak to this situation:

162

- "Social workers who have direct knowledge of a social work colleague's impairment that is due to personal problems, psychosocial distress, substance abuse, or mental health difficulties and that interferes with practice effectiveness should consult with that colleague when feasible and assist the colleague in taking remedial action" (NASW, 1999, 2.09a).
- "Social workers who believe that a social work colleague's impairment interferes with practice effectiveness and that the colleague has not taken adequate steps to address the impairment should take action through appropriate channels established by employers, agencies, NASW, licensing and regulatory bodies, and other professional organizations" (NASW, 1999, 2.09b).

In keeping with the NASW code, Jeb's social work colleagues should speak with him to share their concerns and their willingness to assist him to get the help he needs. The organization's human resource department will be an important resource for such a meeting, particularly if it is conducted as a supervisory intervention. Koocher and Keith-Spiegel (1995) suggest that workers prep carefully for such a meeting, holding it in a private and business-like environment, alerting the worker to the purpose of the session when arranging the meeting time ("I want to share some concerns with you"), remaining calm and confident in the session, staying mindful of the personal and organizational interests at play in the conversation, and approaching the individual as an ally in solving a problem of mutual concern.

Role and goal clarity are important here. The person raising the concerns, whether a supervisor, subordinate, or colleague, should avoid the roles of detective, confessor, or therapist and focus instead on helping the impaired worker to develop a mutually satisfactory plan for change. That agreement may include a self-referral for counseling, referral to an employee assistance program or other service, notification of other individuals or entities about the concerns, and/or a corrective action plan with specific consequences for future transgressions.

Clearly this is not an easy conversation for either party. Empathy for the impaired worker and the skillful application of communication strategies are essential for successfully navigating this "crucial conversation" (Patterson, Grenny, McMillan, & Switzler, 2002, p. 1). Koocher and Keith-Spiegel (1995) recommend that the person raising the issue debrief with a colleague, and mentally organize the information that comes up in the conversation before documenting the discussion. Organizational policies may, of course, structure the worker's options by dictating the type of follow-up that must take place.

Kerry should not be deterred by Nancy's reluctance to intervene. She or others with direct knowledge of Jeb's problem areas should seek support from others in the agency administration, making the case that rather than being disloyal to Jeb, a confrontation may be an overture to the help he needs to stop a dangerous, destructive spiral. Clearly these individuals have ethics on their side. They may have organizational and personnel policies on their side as well. And, for some workers, intervening to stop professional impairment or incompetence may be a condition of their license, such that in acting to limit a coworker's liability, they are also mitigating their own.

RESOLVING DILEMMAS IN COMPETENCE: THE CASE OF THE SHIRKING VIOLET

> Violet is a new employee at a mental health center in a rural area. Her employer recently received a contract to provide mental health services to children in the area who have been victims of sexual abuse. Violet took courses in child psychopathology and family violence in her graduate program, but she has never provided therapy to children and knows very little about sexual abuse. She has been asked by the agency's director to lead the treatment team for this new program, and she protested that she felt unprepared to do so. The director replied, "Violet, I thought you were a generalist practitioner. In small towns like ours, we all have to stretch ourselves a bit. Now, I expect you to develop a can-do attitude and take on this project, or I'll find someone who will."

Who Can Help Violet?

Violet needs two types of assistance with her dilemma: someone who can assist her with the pressures she is experiencing to practice outside her scope of ability, and someone who can help enhance those abilities. It would be appropriate for Violet first to approach her supervisor with both concerns. While she may be concerned that the supervisor is already on the side of the director on this issue, approaching the supervisor first serves several functions. It clarifies the supervisor's stance and allows Violet a chance to articulate her concerns and learn what plans, if any, exist to help her develop the skills necessary to take on the new project. Does the supervisor understand and appreciate Violet's apprehensions? Can the supervisor envision the risks involved if the agency embarks on an ambitious new initiative with someone unprepared at the helm?

If the supervisor agrees with Violet's concerns, does he or she have the expertise necessary to prepare and guide Violet in her new role? Can he or she intercede with the director to set a less ambitious time line to ensure that the agency can properly meet its obligations to the funding source? Can a learning plan be developed that will prove satisfactory to the director and to Violet?

Consulting with the supervisor will also provide a valuable check for Violet about the validity of her concerns. For example, if she is perennially timid about taking on new assignments, resistant to change, or inclined to underestimate her skills, her supervisor will need to address these issues as part of a larger pattern of behavior. If the proposed new role is primarily one of coordination rather than clinical services, has she had experiences that may help prepare her for this next level of practice? Are there areas of her current work that transfer more readily to these new services? A person who has been providing good supervision can help Violet examine her concerns and her competence for the new position.

On the other hand, Violet's agency may not be competent. It could be characterized by rash administrative decisions, lax supervision, high turnover, and laissez faire employees. Who can Violet turn to if this is the case? One hopes that in her professional preparation she had faculty or field instructors whose opinions she values. Alternatively, perhaps she has colleagues inside or outside her current agency to whom she can turn. The key is to seek out those people who can hear her concerns, provide feedback, and help her weigh her options. Sometimes people in situations like Violet's are reluctant to pursue consultation, perhaps because they are ashamed of their situation, or reluctant to air the agency's dirty laundry to the community. Violet should keep in mind that her purpose in talking with others has a constructive intent. It is not to demean the agency or reveal her vulnerabilities, but rather, to ensure that she has the skills needed to respond to the demands of her workplace and adequately serve her clientele. Outside consultants may also help Violet strategize about how to respond effectively to the director's orders. Violet may also use these resources as a sounding board to determine if the situation is so untenable that she should resign.

If Violet decides that she should take on the new role, she should seek assistance in evaluating what knowledge and skills it will demand that she doesn't currently possess. Then, with the help of her supervisor, a mentor, or peer consultant, she should develop a plan to address those areas of weakness. Following the plan, Violet can enhance her competence through readings, case discussions, online classes or continuing education programs, and sessions with an expert in that subject area.

What Are Violet's Options?

In examining the options, let us assume that Violet is accurate in her appraisal that she is not competent to take on the new role, and that her supervisor is not able or willing to intercede with the director on Violet's behalf. Under these conditions, three options remain. Violet can take the position, she can decline it and attempt to stay at the agency, or she can resign.

When Has She Made Similar Decisions?

In considering the experiences Violet can draw upon in this dilemma, it would be helpful for us to know her history in dealing with authority figures and in successfully advocating for herself and others. Is it her pattern to leave when adversity arises? Is she known for her complaints and inflexibility? Or has she been able to seek constructive solutions to disputes in the past? Does she have allies at the agency who might share her concerns about their readiness for the new program? Despite her short tenure at the agency, she may have a reservoir of personal or professional experiences that are relevant for addressing the pressures placed on her by the director.

What about experiences in practicing in areas of low competence? In her experiences as a student intern and as a new employee, how has she been able to achieve a level of comfort with the demands of her position? How might those experiences apply to this case? If observation has been a useful learning method, can she strive to build that into her request for staff development in children's services?

Violet must decide if she can develop a proper level of competence in keeping with the agency's changes, slow or stop those changes, or remove herself from the agency. We hope that Violet brings to this decision a history of successful decisions and actions that can serve as a foundation for her choice in the current dilemma. A history of poor, deferred, or unexamined decisions will mean a weaker set of precedents from which she can draw.

Where Do Ethical and Clinical Guidelines Lead Her?

What are the rules embedded in Violet's choices? In choosing to leave or resist the pressure to take on a role for which she is unqualified, the rule might be "Refuse to accept roles for which you are incompetent." The same rule might also be embedded in the choice to accommodate the director's plan and develop competence. An alternative rule for that choice might be "In some circumstances (few resources, demanding boss, plan to improve skills), it is okay to practice outside one's competence." Would these rules be desirable if they were to apply to everyone?

We can probably agree that competence is an important and expected paradigm for care in the health and social services, but we can also acknowledge that it is not standard procedure, or a universal rule. All practitioners in training are practicing outside their competence in order to develop an acceptable level of skills, and the supervision provided in internships and residencies is a necessary but perhaps insufficient effort at ensuring competent care. The second rule (allowing exceptions for competence) may be more realistic and universalizable, but it also opens the door for greater misuse, in that there will always be a rationale for not meeting the competence standard.

When we look at Violet's choices though a deontological perspective, the rule that states people should not practice beyond their competence is likely the one we would prefer to have as a universal law. Each of Violet's choices could be in keeping with this rule.

The utilitarian perspective requires us to consider the consequences of Violet's choices. Choosing to get proper training and accommodate the director's demands would help Violet keep her job, and it would ensure that the new program goes forward and that services are provided to clients in need. The quality of those services, at least at first, is questionable, so we must consider the potential for harm from Violet and other ill-equipped clinicians. On the other hand, perhaps substandard but attentive and caring services are the only alternative to an absence of such services. For those clients who are in need of these services, Violet's decision to stay and work on her skills would be a positive consequence.

What are the consequences of resisting the director's appointment of Violet to the new role? Someone else may take the position, with no guarantee of better preparedness than Violet or a comparable dedication to quality. If no one is able to take the job and the agency loses its contract, clients may lose needed services, and the agency may be put at risk in both the short and long term. If she is branded uncooperative as a result of her resistance, Violet may lose her job, to both her personal detriment and that of her clients. If she decides to resign rather than take on a role she is ill prepared for, she and her clients will be damaged as well, and her prospects for getting a new position may be damaged by the circumstances under which she left this one. On the other hand, a consequence of resigning may be freedom from a problematic practice environment where staff members are forced to take on tasks they are unprepared to do, putting the agency and the clientele at risk.

Social work values appear to support Violet's choices, in that each of her options is a different route in an attempt to ensure quality practice. Competence is one of the six core values of the profession, and the principle related to it states, "Social workers practice within their areas of competence and develop and enhance their professional expertise. Social workers continually strive to increase their professional knowledge and skills and to apply them in practice. Social workers should aspire to contribute to the knowledge base of the profession" (NASW, 1999, p. 2). It appears that her personal values are in harmony with the profession's values, though they are in conflict with those of the director, who apparently values cooperation and organizational growth over worker proficiency. If Violet is mindful of the director's values, however, she may attempt to craft a response that is congruent with his beliefs and imperatives.

The tenets of the NASW *Code of Ethics* cited at the beginning of this chapter support Violet's concerns and her intention not to take the position without proper preparation. Other ethical standards may relate to how she carries out her decision. For example, NASW standards caution clinicians not to abandon clients, and to withdraw "services precipitously only under unusual circumstances, giving careful consideration to all factors in the situation and taking care to minimize possible adverse effects. Social workers should assist in making appropriate arrangements for continuation of services when necessary" (NASW, 1999, 1.16b). Should Violet decide that a resignation is in order, she should be mindful of her clients in the way that she times and carries out her departure.

Standards in the code's section on commitment to employers would also apply to the options she is weighing.

- "Social workers generally should adhere to commitments made to employers and employing organizations" (NASW, 1999, 3.09a).
- "Social workers should work to improve employing agencies' policies and procedures and the efficiency and effectiveness of their services" (NASW, 1999, 3.09b).
- "Social workers should take reasonable steps to ensure that employers are aware of social workers' ethical obligations as set forth in the NASW Code of Ethics and of the implications of those obligations for social work practice" (NASW, 1999, 3.09c).
- "Social workers should not allow an employing organization's policies, procedures, regulations, or administrative orders to interfere with their ethical practice of social work. Social workers should take reasonable steps to ensure that their employing organizations' practices are consistent with the NASW Code of Ethics" (NASW, 1999, 3.09d).

These provisions would support Violet's efforts to educate the director about her concerns and their basis. They would also seem to encourage her to try to make things work at the agency but resist being forced into a role without preparation or support.

Two other standards apply to the director and may be useful to Violet as she makes a case for delaying the program or securing staff development.

- "Social work administrators should take reasonable steps to ensure that the working environment for which they are responsible is consistent with and encourages compliance with the NASW Code of Ethics. Social work administrators should take reasonable steps to eliminate any conditions in their organizations that violate, interfere with, or discourage compliance with the Code" (NASW, 1999, 3.07d).
- "Social work administrators and supervisors should take reasonable steps to provide or arrange for continuing education and staff development for all staff for whom they are responsible. Continuing education and staff development should address current knowledge and emerging developments related to social work practice and ethics" (NASW, 1999, 3.08).

The ethical principles of fidelity and beneficence are also useful in considering Violet's dilemma. Violet should behave in a trustworthy manner toward her director, being forthright about her concerns and constructive in her pursuit of a mutually satisfactory solution. Her choice of whether she can ethically deliver the new service, and her honesty regarding her preparedness to work in the new program, are a hallmark of fidelity. Violet's ultimate decision should uphold the principle of beneficence in promoting the well-being of others and avoiding harm. As such, her efforts to develop skills for effective services or avoid the provision of poor services are preferable to simply leaving in order to remove herself from an untenable situation while allowing poor practices to take place.

As Violet considers her choices, it would be helpful to know what commitments were made in the proposal funding the new program and what stipulations were in place when the contract was granted. Did the director accurately represent the agency's capacity to serve this new cohort of clients? Was the funding agency aware of the training and infrastructure needs that the service requires? Are there state regulations or other policies that might support her in her quest for developing competence in children's services? Affirmative answers to these questions will help Violet get concessions from the director to ensure quality services are provided. In contrast, negative answers, or indications that the director misled the funder in his portrayal of the agency in order to secure the contract, will not bode as well for Violet's prospects as a change agent.

Beyond ethical standards, practical and clinical standards would also support Violet's contention that mental health practice with children and sexual abuse survivors demands specialized training and experience (Lipovsky, n.d.). For example, the *NASW Standards for Social Work Practice in Child Welfare* (NASW, 2005), the *NASW Standards for the Practice of Social Work with Adolescents* (NASW, 2003), and the *Child Welfare League of America's Standards of Excellence for Services for Abused or Neglected Children and their Families* (CWLA, 1999) describe specific areas of knowledge and practice competence that should be held by an individual working with this population. Beyond providing the service, it appears that the director wants Violet to lead the team, which means that others would be looking to her for advice in developing their skills and knowledge. Even if she developed comfort with her own skills, would she feel adequately prepared to provide clinical expertise to others?

Why Is She Selecting a Particular Course of Action?

As Violet narrows her choices, she will need to examine her motivations in selecting one over the others. For example, would her decision to leave the agency be principled in light of her inability to ensure competent services, or is it a self-serving choice to avoid conflict or the effort change requires? If she decides to stay without taking on the new role, is she comfortable with the quality of services others will provide, is she deferring inappropriately to the director's position, or is she reasoning that as long as she's not involved, no ethical dilemma exists?

171

If she decides to take the job and develop the proper credentials for serving children, is she confident that colleagues and mentors will see the wisdom in her decision? Can she deliver the services in such a way that she would be comfortable if she were in the clients' shoes?

How Should Violet Carry Out Her Decision?

In the absence of others who can competently assume the role the director is envisioning for Violet, the most ethically and clinically sound option is for her to get the training needed to develop competence in practice with abused children. To effectively carry out this decision, she must consider her director's needs and those of her clients.

Through consultation, self-examination, and research, Violet should determine precisely what resources are necessary for her and other staff members to develop competence. She should be prepared with the costs associated with developing competence and the time it will require. Also, if there are accommodations that will be needed (reduced caseloads, triaging of cases so that more difficult cases are referred out early on), she should incorporate those elements into her plan. Concurrent with this research, Violet should converse with her colleagues to determine what their needs are and where they stand in relation to her concerns about the new program. In essence, she wants to conduct a force field analysis (Brager & Holloway, 1992) to specify the factors and personnel who will support her position and those who will resist it.

Whatever the analysis reveals, it is likely that the director will be a key in successfully securing the time and resources for the staff to develop necessary skills. If another staff member has a positive history with the director and is able and willing to present the plan to him, that individual may be a more appropriate choice than Violet, a new employee who has already revealed her reservations about the new services. Whoever presents the proposal to the director should employ communication skills, listening, and empathy to try to understand the director's position and the nature of his resistance, if any, to the plan. He or she should present the concerns in a straightforward manner, supporting the request with data on the risks for individuals and the organization if the children's services contract is not carried out with competence. Having anticipated the nature of the director's resistance, the envoy should structure the proposal to mitigate the director's concerns and make it congruent with his values and responsibilities. Uniting his substantive interests and the staff's will increase the likelihood that they can come to a mutually satisfactory agreement (Fisher, Ury, & Patton, 1991). While Violet and the staff may have grave concerns about the consequences if the staff development proposal is not accepted, resorting to dire predictions and threats at this point will not improve their prospects for successful negotiation. This does not mean that they should avoid mentioning their concerns, only that they should be mindful of the timing and manner in which they present them.

If the director agrees to the proposal, the plan should be specified in writing and circulated to those who will be responsible for carrying it out, including the business office or financial manger and supervisors. The implementation phase is sometimes an unexpectedly difficult period for change proposals in that the gains of the change have not been felt, but the costs have, and after the initial enthusiasm for change wears off, staff and administrators may renege on their agreements (Brager & Holloway, 2002). Therefore Violet and her colleagues should be vigilant in pursuing and evaluating the elements of the staff development plan.

In regard to implementing her decision with her clients, Violet should consider what her clients should know about her clinical competence with children and the degree to which that should be part of her informed consent processes. On one hand, clients have a right to know that she is in the process of developing skills in that area so that they can elect not to see her under those circumstances if they wish. On the other hand, too much information may divert the attention inappropriately from the clients' conditions and needs and may unnecessarily undermine their confidence in her. Striking the right balance in the way that conversation is phrased will respect their autonomy and demonstrate trustworthiness while creating a solid foundation for services.

CONCLUSION

Professional competence is a journey, not a destination. While social workers must have an acceptable level of skill and knowledge to address the needs of their clients and service settings, they must also constantly strive to improve those skills to keep pace with workplace demands and the changing knowledge base of the profession. Competent workers are self-aware, they know where their strengths and limits lie, and they ensure that clients and services are not compromised by substandard care. Professionals must also be alert to their own physical and mental health, ensuring that personal difficulties are addressed so their clients are not harmed by worker impairment. And social workers take responsibility for encouraging others to practice with competence. This may mean intervening when colleagues are impaired or unethical or creating professional development opportunities so that areas of incompetence are addressed.

Chapter 9

PROFESSIONALISM

The principles of professionalism and integrity refer to the responsibilities that professionals have to be truthful, to keep their promises, to treat each other fairly, and to behave in a trustworthy manner. In practice this means that practitioners will avoid dishonesty, including lying, presenting information in vague or misleading ways (as in distorting research findings), engaging in false advertising, or misrepresenting competence. Lapses in integrity also include telling half-truths by selectively presenting the relevant facts; leaving false impressions by failing to correct someone's misunderstanding; stealing time, supplies, or money; engaging in fraud; and being "disingenuous, inauthentic or insincere" (Cohen & Cohen, 1999, p. 75).

In this context, integrity also refers to how professionals are expected to treat each other. It means demonstrating respect, using proper channels and processes to resolve disputes, sharing credit and taking responsibility as appropriate, being fair in appraisals of others, and using discretion in the ways that one characterizes one's colleagues. Think of a situation when you considered a colleague's actions and thought, "That's so unprofessional!" and you're on the right track in understanding the elements of this principle. Standards for this principle include:

- "Social workers should not use derogatory language in their written or verbal communications to or about clients. Social workers should use accurate and respectful language in all communications to and about clients" (NASW, 1999, 1.12).
- "Social workers should not exploit clients in disputes with colleagues or engage clients in any inappropriate discussion of conflicts between social workers and their colleagues" (NASW, 1999, 2.04b).

- "Social workers should ensure that their representations to clients, agencies, and the public of professional qualifications, credentials, education, competence, affiliations, services provided, or results to be achieved are accurate. Social workers should claim only those relevant professional credentials they actually possess and take steps to correct any inaccuracies or misrepresentations of their credentials by others" (NASW, 1999, 4.06c).
- "Social workers should uphold and advance the values, ethics, knowledge, and mission of the profession. Social workers should protect, enhance, and improve the integrity of the profession through appropriate study and research, active discussion, and responsible criticism of the profession" (NASW, 1999, 5.01b).
- "Social workers should not engage in solicitation of testimonial endorsements (including solicitation of consent to use a client's prior statement as a testimonial endorsement) from current clients or from other people who, because of their particular circumstances, are vulnerable to undue influence" (NASW, 1999, 4.07b).

UPHOLDING THE STANDARD

Elaine's student Ned wrote an excellent analysis of the Medicare prescription drug program for his final paper in her policy class. Elaine suggested that Ned consider submitting it to a social work journal for publication. She met with him to discuss the specifications for journal publication and the changes he might make to meet those criteria. When he had revised the paper, she reviewed it and gave him feedback. When a colleague heard of their collaboration, she asked Elaine if she planned to be first or second author on the article. "Neither," Elaine replied. "The paper is entirely Ned's. My work with him on it was to help him learn about writing for publication. I was his teacher and editor, not his coauthor."

The NASW *Code of Ethics* (1999) states that "Social workers should take responsibility and credit, including authorship credit, only for work they have actually performed and to which they have contributed" (4.08a). Elaine's interpretation of her role and her refusal to be listed as a coauthor were in keeping with this standard. The code also states that "Social workers should honestly acknowledge the work of and the contributions made by others" (NASW, 1999, 4.08b), so Ned should credit Elaine's assistance in his author's notes and in his conversations about the work.

Sometimes the role distinctions are less clear than they are in Ned and Elaine's case. If, for example, a faculty member's grant led to the creation of a large database from which a student created a study, should the faculty member be listed as a coauthor on articles, reports, or presentations that come out of study? Is the original effort in gathering the data the type of contribution the code intends? Faculty members may rationalize that their colleague's inclusion as an author is justified by the time she spent helping the student and the pressure on the faculty member to acquire publication credits. From the student's point of view, coauthorship credit may duly reflect the faculty member's assistance. It may also seem a small price to pay for the professor's continuing support as a mentor and colleague. Even if the student determines that the coauthorship is unwarranted, he may ultimately feel powerless to resist the professor's insistence on inclusion.

Professionals who wish to act with integrity *and* get proper credit for particular activities have several avenues of assistance. Individuals in academia can refer to guidelines on authorship, which specify the nature of the roles that qualify for different levels of credit (APA, 2002; "Instruction for Authors," 2006; NIH, 1997). Similar resources surely exist for other settings and scenarios. Those with the greatest power in the transaction must be mindful of the fair use of that power and the potential for conflicts of interest. For all social workers striving to uphold the standards of integrity and professionalism, consultation with colleagues will help discern how the field's norms would apply to a particular case. And the tests of right and wrong (smell, mentor, publicity, and reversibility) can also be employed to encourage ethical decision making.

VIOLATING THE STANDARD

Alden worked for a community mental health center for ten years. While he ostensibly resigned in order to start his own private practice, the timing of his departure was influenced by his increasing dissatisfaction with the agency's philosophy. Alden was interested in alternative approaches to physical and mental well-being such as energy-field work, acupuncture, and herbal treatments. He had taken extensive coursework on these topics, and the more he studied, the more concerned he became with the mental health agency's primary emphasis on psychotropic medication. His efforts to get his colleagues and the administration to consider other methodologies that they might suggest to their clients were met with derision. Finally, he decided that it was best to start his own practice as part of a comprehensive wellness collaborative.

Last week, one of his former clients asked her new case manager about Alden's whereabouts and wondered about getting a referral to see him. Cheri, the case manager, replied, "I don't think that's wise. From what I hear, he was let go. That whole witch doctor thing isn't real treatment. He's just asking for a malpractice suit."

Cheri's conversation with the client was both inaccurate and inappropriate. She misconstrues the nature of Alden's departure from the agency, condemns his practice interests, and fails to address the client's request for a referral. The NASW code (1999) states that "Social workers should treat colleagues with respect and should represent accurately and fairly the qualifications, views, and obligations of colleagues" (2.01a). Furthermore, "Social workers should avoid unwarranted negative criticism of colleagues in communications with clients or with other professionals. Unwarranted negative criticism may include demeaning comments that refer to colleagues' level of competence or to individuals' attributes such as race, ethnicity, national origin, color, sex, sexual orientation, age, marital status, political belief, religion, and mental or physical disability" (NASW, 1999, 2.01b).

If Cheri has concerns about the appropriateness of a referral for that particular client or the suitability of Alden's approaches, there are other methods she can use to convey her opinions in a more professional manner. For example, she might forthrightly describe Alden's new workplace and ask the client what interests her about that service. Based on the client's reasons for wanting the referral, she should provide the contact information, as well as that of other resources that might address the interests the client expressed. Cheri might also talk with the client about the outcomes she is seeking in treatment and help her identify some of the signs she can look for in effective serv-ices, with Alden or anyone else. If Cheri has serious reservations about the efficacy of Alden's approach or the appropriateness of that approach for this particular client, she should have a sound basis for those opinions and present them with the client's interests in mind. And she should take care to construe her opinions as opinions, in recognition of the client's right to select services anywhere and out of respect for Alden's status as a fellow professional.

RESOLVING DILEMMAS IN PROFESSIONALISM: A ROCK AND A HARD PLACE

Angela has one child and is seven-months pregnant. The father of her children is a laborer from Mexico whose whereabouts are unknown, though he is being sought by child support enforcement authorities. Angela works six days a week as a housekeeper for a hotel chain. Jeff is her case manager in a welfare-to-work program. In implementing federal welfare reform, the program has high expectations for participants, and it has stiff penalties for those who fail to maintain employment. Because Angela was reported last year for child neglect, she also has a worker in Child Protective Services, and a case plan she must follow to maintain custody of her child.

At this week's appointment, Angela reported to Jeff that she had lost her job. When pressed to explain, she said that she had been late for work on several occasions due to appointments and parenting classes related to her child protection case plan. The final straw for her boss was when she objected to lifting heavy objects and moving furniture because of her pregnancy. Jeff knows it will be difficult for her to find employment so close to her delivery date, yet he also knows that she will be ineligible for benefits. Meanwhile the clock on her lifetime cap for receiving welfare will continue to tick.

When welfare reform was enacted in 1996, the changes were intended to reduce the number of people in the United States on wel-fare by employing a combination of penalties and incentives to encourage recipients to move into the workforce. Each state created different mechanisms and definitions to meet the federal mandate. For example, some states defined education broadly and included those activities in work definitions. Conditions such as pregnancy were treated differently by each state. For example, some states made it an exclusionary criterion for work requirements, while most did not. Proponents of welfare reform note the program's success in reducing welfare rolls by 57 percent (Jansen, 2006). Critics note that many of the recipients have moved into low-wage or part-time jobs that leave former welfare recipients without health care or a living wage.

Angela's difficulties stem from a variety of causes, the most recent of which involves the welfare-to-work provisions. She is a single parent who is unlikely to receive sufficient and consistent child support from the father of her children. Adequate child care is scarce and expensive, particularly for people with multiple children who make a minimum wage, work odd service-sector schedules, and lack reliable transportation. Angela's involvement with Child Protective Services means that she has additional obligations to fulfill in meeting the expectations of the service plan for neglect. While CPS can help Angela access needed resources, it may also put an undue burden on her if a "kitchen sink" approach is taken to developing case objectives (Hepworth et al., 2006). For example, if the charge of neglect stemmed from her need to work irregular hours, resulting in substandard child care arrangements, are parenting classes and regular caseworker meetings an appropriate way to address the problem? The neglect charge may simply be a symptom of the irreconcilable demands placed on Angela and other people with few social supports and financial resources. Sometimes the demands of work and family collide, and low-wage workers rarely have the capacity to meet those demands when, for example, a child is sick, a babysitter quits, bus schedules are suspended for a holiday, or overtime work is required. As a welfare-to-work participant, Angela's success on the job takes on greater importance. As a parent under CPS supervision, she must also place a priority on the care of her child. As a pregnant woman, she is dedicated to her own health and that of her baby. But pregnant women, on welfare or not, are often the subject of workplace discrimination. While it is illegal, it is also difficult to fight and to prove.

Often, these competing and seemingly irreconcilable obligations are invisible to all but the client, who must try to conform to them.

Angela is fortunate to have Jeff's interest and attention in the matter. Jeff's dilemma arises from his role in her double bind. He must hold her accountable for her failure to work even if he suspects that she was wrongfully terminated because of her pregnancy or unfairly terminated because she couldn't reconcile CPS's demands with her job.

Jeff's interpretation of the events also figures into his dilemma. First, he understands the systemic factors at play in her case and looks at the role they play, not simply at her individual responsibility. He also believes in the legitimacy of her actions. That is, he believes that Angela made a concerted effort to comply with the demands placed on her, and that she was right to avoid tasks at work that would jeopardize her pregnancy. Had he taken a derogatory view of her or her decisions on the job, he might be less sympathetic to her predicament, but also less conflicted. What can he do now to treat his client with integrity and carry out his professional obligations? If he can't help Angela, will he act to address the systemic factors that created this cruel double bind?

Who Can Serve as a Resource to Jeff?

In all likelihood, the dilemma Angela's case presents is not unique. The fortunate result is that it opens up multiple avenues for conversation and action. Jeff's supervisor and colleagues at the agency will be first lines of assistance, as they are most familiar with the interpretation of welfare-to-work policies in their state. They will be able to share information on precedents from other cases and the options available to Jeff and Angela. The agency attorney may help Jeff understand the legal limits of his choices. Furthermore, the attorney could address the implications of Angela's termination from the hotel job and any recourse she may have in filing for pregnancy discrimination. Angela's CPS caseworker will be an important contact and a potential ally in ensuring that the units work cooperatively for the best interests of the family.

Jeff might also research welfare rights groups, legal aid, and other organizations to which he could refer Angela for assistance. A consequence, however, might be that some of the resulting advocacy would be directed at him or his employer. Fear of activism should not deter Jeff from letting Angela know about helpful resources—in fact, it may be just the leverage needed to bring attention to problematic agency practices. Jeff should just be mindful of this and prepared for any backlash.

If Jeff takes on the laws and policies that gave rise to this dilemma, he has multiple resources. These include national organizations that are concerned with welfare policies, including NASW (www.naswdc.org); the National Organization for Women (http://now.org); the National Women's Law Center (www.nwlc.org/index.cfm); and local or regional affiliates of these organizations. Jeff may also find that local antipoverty, welfare rights, or women's rights groups in his region offer perspectives and advocacy on the issues Angela is facing.

Jeff might ask key decision makers, such as legislators and the officials in his state who are responsible for welfare policies, to respond to a composite case like Angela's in order to educate them about the effects of particular policies and seek their assistance in making constructive changes (Mizrahi, 2002; Reisch, 2002). Front-line workers in all settings have an important role in putting a personal face on often impersonal policy decisions. However, all workers must be mindful of their role in speaking out about such matters. While all are entitled to engage in public discourse as private citizens, professionalism requires social workers to respect their employers' resources and positions when pursuing social change efforts. It also requires them to ensure the client is protected as the worker moves from case advocacy to cause advocacy. This means being alert to the risks of privacy intrusions, retaliation, or other complications of becoming an exemplar or test case in policy change.

Several provisions in the NASW code apply to Jeff's activism.

- "Social workers should make clear distinctions between statements made and actions engaged in as a private individual and as a representative of the social work profession, a professional social work organization, or the social worker's employing agency" (NASW, 1999, 4.06a).
- "Social workers who speak on behalf of professional social work organizations should accurately represent the official and authorized positions of the organizations" (NASW, 1999, 4.06b).
- "Social workers should facilitate informed participation by the public in shaping social policies and institutions" (NASW, 1999, 6.02).

Organizations and individuals who share Jeff's concerns can inform him of existing efforts to help clients like Angela and of initiatives to improve policies and practices. Jeff can use this information to assist his client and to determine the ways that he can contribute to change efforts.

What Are Jeff's Options?

Jeff has several alternatives that can be exercised individually or in combination in regard to Angela's immediate bind. He can adhere to the policy and count her months of unemployment against her, despite his sensitivity to her plight; seek and pursue options to stop the clock while she maintains unemployment for the duration of her pregnancy; appeal her termination from the hotel or encourage her to seek other work immediately; or subvert the policy and indicate that she is working, although she is not. Whichever action Jeff chooses for Angela's case, he can also pursue systemic changes to address the conditions that created the dilemma, though that alternative won't be weighed as part of the decision-making process.

When Has Jeff Faced Similar Dilemmas?

At the heart of this dilemma are two themes: reconciling the needs of clients with bureaucratic limitations and reconciling the worker's personal beliefs with the standards of the system within which he or she works. The dilemma is characterized by competing interests: the client's, the system's, and the worker's. Jeff's understanding of the essence of the dilemma will help him identify the precedents he can draw on in deciding how to act in this case. Have there been situations in which he took a stand for a client against his employer or another institution? Was that effective? Was it a stance he's proud of? Have there been situations in which he went the extra mile for clients, helping them to access information or resources when his role required much less? Were these efforts fruitful? Did he feel he had done the right thing, professionally and personally? Or, conversely, has it been his habit to draw clear boundaries around his responsibilities, even when individual scenarios required more? Has that stance worked for him, perhaps by helping him maintain balance in his professional roles and avoiding burnout?

Is Jeff inclined to side with the underdog, looking for opportunities to give voice to their needs, even at the risk of his job or well-being? Or does Jeff see every adverse organizational decision as an offense against his clients? Does he have a grudge against his organization, such that he's looking for an opportunity to use clients to advance his cause? Have there been instances in Jeff's personal or professional past where he has been willing to lie for what he perceived to be a greater good?

The self-reflection these questions require will help Jeff identify instances in the past that can guide him today. They also encourage him to examine his motivations in selecting a particular course of action and ensure he is doing the right thing in the right way and for the right reason. Maybe the evaluation will help reveal other needed changes beyond those in Angela's case or the policies that affect her. That is, if Jeff is perennially disenchanted with his agency and eager to take on its policies in the name of client empowerment, an additional ethical question will involve his decision to remain employed by an agency he abhors. Or if he simply finds himself distressed at the decisions he is required to make on a daily basis, perhaps another social work role is more suitable for him. Understanding the dilemmas that Angela's particular case symbolizes will help strengthen Jeff's decision making.

Where Will Ethical and Clinical Guidelines Lead Him?

Let's collapse Jeff's choices into two: he can follow the policy (thereby reducing Angela's benefits and running down her clock while encouraging her to find work or while seeking a formal exception in light of her pregnancy), or he can keep her listed as working, while also encouraging her to regain employment or seeking an exception. The core difference between the two approaches is whether or not Jeff follows the rule about work requirements. Deontology, with its emphasis on universal laws, would endorse rule following over rule breaking. Imagine it as a choice between requiring people to comply with laws, even unfair or illegitimate ones, versus allowing people to comply only with those they support, and you see where the deontological stance comes down.

Utilitarianism, with its emphasis on effects, might support another choice, depending on which consequences are emphasized. Among the outcomes of enforcing the policy are short-term and long-term financial hardships for Angela. Unless she can find a cooperative employer at this late stage in her pregnancy, or an exception to the stated policy, she will face a reduction in benefits, diminished time on her welfare clock, and significant pressure to return to the workforce immediately following the birth of her baby. Each of these is a troubling consequence in and of itself, and a trigger for other potential problems. For example, under pressure to return to work, might Angela take a job that puts her health and ability to care for her children at risk? Might her reduced income or haphazard child care arrangements also jeopardize her children?

Against these scenarios, following the policy also has positive consequences. Complying with the established rules means that Jeff is fulfilling the expectations and trust placed in him by his employer and, in extension, by society, for the measured use of public resources. Compliance means that Angela is being held to the same standard as other welfare recipients in her jurisdiction. Following the rules means that the system is not undermined by individual whims, favoritism, or subversion.

What are the consequences of lying about Angela's work status? It may save her and her children from perilous financial consequences and may keep her from putting herself at risk by taking undesirable jobs late in her pregnancy or soon after delivering. Marking Angela as working when she is not may send the message that she will not be punished for doing the right thing in standing up for her health at the hotel or trying to comply with the CPS mandates. On the other hand, it may also send a message that it is acceptable to defraud the welfare system. Jeff's collusion with it makes that message more destructive, as it puts his reputation (and that of his profession) in question. It may undermine Jeff's authority with Angela and put him at risk of blackmail should she threaten to reveal their secret. Lying at this point may remove Angela's motivation and Jeff's leverage to have her return to work when she is capable of doing so.

If it is revealed, the act of fraud may also result in severe legal penalties for Jeff and his client. Jeff may consider his choice an act of civil disobedience, a necessary evil in calling attention to a flawed system. However, there is no guarantee that his actions will engender the sympathy he hopes for—many Americans scoff at the struggles of those on welfare in light of their own onerous work responsibilities and precarious financial state. And, while Jeff may be willing to endure the consequences of his actions for a greater good, the same may not be true of his client. What voice will/should Angela have in the decision not to hold her accountable to the welfare guidelines?

Even if the plan works and Angela is spared deleterious consequences, Jeff's actions have done nothing to remedy the larger problem. Choosing a more forthright method of addressing the policy would benefit not just one client, but all who share her circumstances now and in the future.

The personal values that might drive Jeff's feelings in the case can be revealed through the process of self-reflection described earlier. Concerns for fairness, loyalty, trustworthiness, empowerment, and righteousness may all come into play as he considers his alternatives. Social work values present a mixed picture. The value of social justice encourages social workers to strive for social change, specifically in areas of poverty and unemployment. However, the value placed on dignity and worth suggests that while social workers must enhance clients' capacities and opportunities, they must be "cognizant of their dual responsibility to clients and to the broader society. They seek to resolve conflicts between clients' interests and the broader society's interests in a socially responsible manner consistent with the values, ethical principles, and ethical standards of the profession" (NASW, 1999, pp. 5–6). This value suggests that the method Jeff is considering for reconciling his client's situation with agency policies is unacceptable. The value of integrity affirms this conclusion. "Social workers act honestly and responsibly and promote ethical practices on the part of the organizations with which they are affiliated" (NASW, 1999, p. 6).

The NASW *Code of Ethics* acknowledges the tension between client interests and societal responsibilities in its first standard. "Social workers' primary responsibility is to promote the well-being of clients. In general, clients' interests are primary. However, social workers' responsibility to the larger society or specific legal obligations may on limited occasions supersede the loyalty owed clients, and clients should be so advised" (NASW, 1999, 1.01).

In reconciling those tensions, the ethical standards, like social work values, endorse truthfulness and trustworthiness.

- "Social workers should not participate in, condone, or be associated with dishonesty, fraud, or deception" (NASW, 1999, 4.04).
- "Social workers generally should adhere to commitments made to employers and employing organizations" (NASW, 1999, 3.09a).
- "Social workers should work toward the maintenance and promotion of high standards of practice" (NASW, 1999, 5.01a).
- "Social workers should uphold and advance the values, ethics, knowledge, and mission of the profession. Social workers should protect, enhance, and improve the integrity of the profession through appropriate study and research, active discussion, and responsible criticism of the profession" (NASW, 1999, 5.01b).

Several standards also offer guidance on addressing troubling organizational practices.

- "Social workers should work to improve employing agencies' policies and procedures and the efficiency and effectiveness of their services" (NASW, 1999, 3.09b).
- "Social workers should take reasonable steps to ensure that employers are aware of social workers' ethical obligations as set forth in the NASW Code of Ethics and of the implications of those obligations for social work practice" (NASW, 1999, 3.09c).
- "Social workers should not allow an employing organization's policies, procedures, regulations, or administrative orders to interfere with their ethical practice of social work. Social workers should take reasonable steps to ensure that their employing organizations' practices are consistent with the NASW Code of Ethics" (NASW, 1999, 3.09d).

While the NASW code could be interpreted as supporting Jeff's concerns, it clearly does not endorse any method of rectifying them that involves dishonesty. The code would support Jeff in raising his concerns and working through available appeals mechanisms on Angela's behalf and through established channels for longer-term policy change.

An examination of ethical principles lends further support to Jeff in upholding the agency's policy. Fraudulent practices, even with good intentions, violate the position of trust that Jeff has been given, misuse scarce resources, and run the risk of doing serious harm to the worker and his client. Putting Angela at risk through fraud, even if it is for her short-term benefit, diminishes her autonomy and long-term opportunities.

Falsely reporting Angela's work status is probably illegal and certainly a violation of agency regulations. Beyond the right-wrong aspect of his choices, are there laws or policies that might allow Jeff to ethically excuse Angela from the work requirements? For example, if Angela's termination from the hotel was, in fact, a violation of the Pregnancy Discrimination Act, does that protect her from penalties under the welfare-to-work program? Women who are pregnant must be treated like any other employee with a temporary medical condition (National Partnership for Women and Families, n.d.). Therefore, if the hotel manager allowed a worker with a broken ankle to reduce his or her activity, then Angela is entitled to the same benefit. If it is determined that Angela was discriminated against, this may indeed constitute good cause for not meeting the work requirements of the welfare program, and she would be allowed to retain her benefits

Might her pregnancy alone constitute a good cause for her to be exempt from penalties for not working until after she delivers the baby? While different locales have different expectations for pregnant women, some states excuse those in the final trimester from the work requirement. No doubt Jeff is conversant with the policy in his area, and it will be pursued. He might also explore whether there are policies in force in Child Protective Services that might be brought to bear on Angela's welfare status at this stage of the pregnancy. Perhaps there are alternate definitions of work (educational programs, for example) for which Angela might qualify, rather than being removed from the rolls for not having a job at this time.

Why Has Jeff Selected a Particular Option?

As noted throughout this section, it is important for Jeff to consider the motives behind his choices for resolving the dilemma. While it is clearly wrong to commit welfare fraud, he might justify his actions through a variety of flawed principles. For example, he might use all-or-nothing reasoning, focusing on the financial losses that Angela will endure in not working, while losing sight of the other risks that will accrue for her if he subverts the policy. He may contend that he is simply acting in his client's best interests, misapplying that concept by focusing only on an individual client, versus the universe of clients in need of welfare funds, and focusing only on her financial interest instead of her need to act lawfully, be treated in a trustworthy manner, and so forth. Jeff may rationalize that his actions follow the spirit, if not the letter, of the law since Angela *wants* to work and *would be* working if she hadn't been mistreated by the hotel manager or the CPS bureaucracy. Such justifications are an invitation to use the smell, publicity, and mom tests, since it is unlikely that the public, his colleagues, or even a loving parent would accept that rationale for deceptive actions. Using the test of reversibility and putting himself in Angela's shoes, Jeff might be grateful for the break from rigid welfare rules, but not likely at the risk that fraud would create.

How Should Jeff Carry Out His Decision?

While it may be tempting to "overlook" Angela's change in work status and fail to document it, such actions are clearly not an ethical avenue for addressing what Jeff perceives to be unfair policies. Jeff must uphold the policy while pursuing options to mitigate the damage. A first step will be informing Angela of the implications of not working and determining her plans and preferences for responding to the change in status. Jeff may offer to intervene on Angela's behalf with her former employer and/or assist her in securing legal assistance for an Equal Employment Opportunity Commission claim for pregnancy discrimination.

Jeff should secure Angela's permission, if he hasn't done so already, to speak with her CPS worker so that their interventions can be coordinated, and incompatible expectations reconciled. The CPS worker may be an ally in any appeals concerning Angela's work status with the welfare program. He or she may also be able to provide funds or resources to supplement the benefits and wages lost while she is unemployed.

Jeff should seek the support of his supervisor in temporarily exempting Angela from the penalties of job loss, using whatever appeal or exclusionary criteria exist within their system. Jeff's careful documentation and clear articulation of Angela's history and circumstances may help to make the case for a good cause exception if any such opportunities exist. He will need to think strategically about his actions so that the exemption is pursued in a timely manner and is not negatively affected by any discrimination claims.

If his efforts are not successful, Jeff can be confident that he did everything in his power to advocate ethically for his client within the system they have. This may be of little comfort if Jeff feels he and the agency are failing clients like Angela through policies that couple unreasonable demands with little opportunity for success. Jeff may find some solace in targeting his interventions at the system rather than the individual client. There may be positions or roles within his agency where he can formally intervene, for example as a legislative liaison or as a representative to coalitions seeking the reform of welfare reform. Alternatively, he may undertake these efforts in his role as a citizen. In either case, he will find helpful guidelines for establishing relationships with decision makers and other change agents, building coalitions, providing constructive resources for policy discussions, communicating effectively, and targeting promising opportunities for change (Mizrahi, 2002; Reisch, 2002).

Even if he becomes an active advocate in efforts to change welfare laws and policies, Jeff may find it difficult to correct flaws in the system or to continue to work in that system. Against such odds, some social workers opt for other careers, and some for other positions or fields of practice where they feel they can best exercise their abilities. The key in such decisions is to have sufficient self-awareness and social support to know when it is no longer possible to be an effective agent of change, and to consider and pursue other opportunities before hopelessness, pessimism, and burnout reveal themselves in practice and erode professionalism. Maslach's findings (2003) on the six domains of work life that may contribute to burnout (workload, control, reward, community, fairness, and values) raise red flags for Jeff's situation. His inability to properly assist deserving clients like Angela may have a detrimental effect on his suitability for practice in that setting.

CONCLUSION

Social workers often find themselves applying or enforcing policies they know are flawed. At times, they struggle for the flexibility to consider individual circumstances in a one-size-fits-all world. The cumulative result of such no-win situations is often cynicism, burnout, and erosion of the reformist spirit that brought many to the field of social work in the first place. While it is difficult to face pain and suffering and live out one's ideals in a world that may not embrace those ideals, the hallmark of professionalism is the ability to face those challenges with integrity. A wide-ranging concept, integrity embodies the qualities of trustworthiness, fairness, and honesty. Social workers are expected to exercise these qualities in their dealings with clients, colleagues, and the general public. Professionalism doesn't require social workers to maintain a happy facade in the face of troubled individuals or troubling policies. Rather, it sets norms for resolving those disputes in a transparent and above-board manner.

Lapses in professionalism have repercussions beyond the individuals involved. Unhealthy organizational norms can develop where problems are not handled in a forthright fashion. The erosion of the public trust can damage an agency's reputation and take decades to repair (Shepard, 1992). Unprofessional conduct reflects negatively on all members of the profession, as all members pay the price for the actions of a few. Clients who are treated unprofessionally develop a disdain for professional interventions that may carry over into subsequent helping relationships.

Despite its long history and noble aims, social work is an often misunderstood and poorly regarded profession. All members of the profession must be mindful that their actions speak for their employers and their field, not only for themselves as individuals. Acting with integrity ensures that social workers are endeavoring to do the right things the right way for the right reasons.

Chapter 10

NONDISCRIMINATION AND
CULTURAL COMPETENCE

Social work requirements regarding nondiscrimination and cultural competence are related to principles enforcing the dignity and worth of all persons and the responsibilities to treat clients fairly and support the equitable distribution of resources (justice). This means that helping professionals "ensure that their work does not reflect personal or organizational biases or prejudices" (Fisher, 2003. p. 60). This "work" refers not just to that done on behalf of clients but also to the roles of supervisors, educators, administrators, and researchers. Social workers must be alert to biases and act to prevent discrimination in all aspects of professional practice.

Related to this is the area of cultural competence, which is defined as "a set of congruent behaviors, attitudes, and policies that come together in a system, or agency, or among professionals and enable the system, agency or professionals to work effectively in cross-cultural situations" (NASW, 2000b, p. 61). It "refers to the process by which individuals and systems respond respectfully and effectively to people of all cultures, languages, classes, ethnic backgrounds, religions and other diversity factors" (NASW, National Committee on Racial and Ethnic Diversity, 2001, p. 11). One could argue that this should be considered a subset of the other areas of professional competence addressed earlier. However, cultural competence is inextricably linked to principles of fairness and nondiscrimination. The failure to comprehend and respond to the features associated with diverse populations may lead to inaccurate and unfair conclusions in clinical assessments, to the use of inappropriate or biased tests or procedures, or to policies that disadvantage whole classes of clients or potential clients. Beyond the helping relationship, cultural competence is required in professional transactions such as those among colleagues, and between supervisors and staff. The NASW *Code of Ethics* (1999) addresses cultural competence through the following standards:

- "Social workers should understand culture and its function in human behavior and society, recognizing the strengths that exist in all cultures" (1.05a).
- "Social workers should have a knowledge base of their clients' cultures and be able to demonstrate competence in the provision of services that are sensitive to clients' cultures and to differences among people and cultural groups" (1.05b).
- "Social workers should obtain education about and seek to understand the nature of social diversity and oppression with respect to race, ethnicity, national origin, color, sex, sexual orientation, age, marital status, political belief, religion, and mental or physical disability" (1.05c)
- "Social workers should act to prevent and eliminate discrimination in the employing organization's work assignments and in its employment policies and practices" (3.09e).
- "Social workers should not practice, condone, facilitate, or collaborate with any form of discrimination on the basis of race, ethnicity, national origin, color, sex, sexual orientation, age, marital status, political belief, religion, or mental or physical disability" (4.02).
- "Social workers should promote conditions that encourage respect for cultural and social diversity within the United States and globally. Social workers should promote policies and practices that demonstrate respect for difference, support the expansion of cultural knowledge and resources, advocate for programs and institutions that demonstrate cultural competence, and promote policies that safeguard the rights of and confirm equity and social justice for all people" (6.04c).

As the standards indicate, cultural competence results from the interaction of knowledge, attitudes, and actions. Social workers cannot be expected to possess knowledge about every aspect of every culture represented by their clients and colleagues. They are, however, expected to value diversity, understand their own culture and the hazards of ethnocentrism, actively seek to enhance their familiarity with different cultures and customs, and recognize the heterogeneity that exists in all groups (Community Toolbox, 2003; Mason, Benjamin, & Lewis, 1996; NASW, National Committee on Racial and Ethnic Diversity, 2001). Beyond having an attitude of acceptance and curiosity and a dedication to knowledge acquisition, social workers are expected to put those tools into action. Nondiscrimination means eliminating policies and practices that expressly disadvantage particular classes of people and those that appear neutral but have a disparate impact on members of a particular race, gender, faith, sexual orientation, or any other background (Noe et al., 2002). It also means accepting an active role in support of social justice.

UPHOLDING THE STANDARD

Nelson is an MSW student doing his field placement at a Native American men's center. He is a member of the Mille Lacs Band of Ojibwe and is dedicated to helping to ameliorate the social conditions that have damaged the well-being of so many members of his community. Nelson has applied for entry into a doctoral program in public policy where Sarah, his research professor, is a member of the admissions committee. The application is a multifaceted process requiring the applicant to submit GRE scores, letters of recommendation, undergraduate and graduate GPAs, personal statements, and writing samples. The committee strives to select candidates who hold promise for successful graduate study and the capacity to effectively evaluate and influence public policy.

Nelson's portfolio presents a mixed picture. His writing, personal statements, recommendations, and graduate-level grades are superb. His GRE score and undergraduate GPA are significantly below those of other applicants. Several members of the admissions committee, in an effort to streamline and quantify the selection process, have suggested that GRE scores be used as the sole criteria for differentiating candidates. Sarah objected vigorously. "There are many ways in which applicants show promise for our program. If the only thing that counts is the GRE, why do we ask for everything else?"

The chair replied, "You are just trying to advocate for Nelson because of your soft spot for him. Should we loosen the criteria for everyone?"

"I don't see it as weakening the standards. I see it as appropriately using the criteria we have. Nelson, and perhaps some other candidates, overcame significant odds, including a poor preparation for college, to get where he is today. His experience in social services, his grades from graduate school, and his legislative advocacy on policy change all are indicators of his promise. I'm saying we shouldn't discount those for any of the candidates."

Other committee members nodded their assent and began to develop a schema to evaluate all the candidates using all the sources of data in their applications.

The consideration of race in college and graduate school admissions is a highly charged social issue (Boddie, 2005). The arguments in support of racial considerations or quotas cite the historical disadvantages some groups have faced and the importance of advanced degrees for individual and community development. These advocates contend that certain indicators of merit such as SAT or GRE scores reflect institutional biases that will always yield classes that are not racially or socioeconomically diverse (Young, 2003). In 2003 the United States Supreme Court "reaffirmed that the educational benefits of diversity were a compelling interest under federal law" (Bell, Coleman, & Palmer, 2005, p. B9). In fields such as social work, the argument for racial considerations in admissions may be linked to the profession's values for human diversity, and the desirability of matching the racial characteristics of social work clientele. Those who oppose race-conscious admissions argue that race is a socially constructed schema that becomes even less meaningful as the proportion of multiracial citizens increases (Connerly, 2000). Some also suggest that racial preferences are prejudicial, since they imply that some classes of applicants cannot successfully compete for admission without additional assistance (Schmidt, 2006). And such systems may work against the goal of broadening access to education in that the presumption of historical disadvantage based on race may benefit well-to-do applicants of color at the expense of poor whites whose schools and family backgrounds provided a shaky platform for higher education. An additional argument against taking race into account for admissions is simply that it is fundamentally unfair. Those who are given extra points for certain characteristics may be favored

195

over others who scored better on measures of merit or achievement (Connerly, 2000).

Between these two "for" and "against" positions is a third that asks what other measures could be substituted for race to achieve the ends of a diverse student body and improved access to higher education for all citizens. Rather than asking about race, are there proxies for disadvantage that can be identified and credited in an applicant? For example, is he or she the first generation in the family to attend college? What is the quality rating of his or her high school? Has the applicant overcome personal adversity, such as prejudice, socioeconomic disadvantage, family tragedy, or violent surroundings, in striving for a college or graduate education?

Another tactic is to structure a system where race is identified but is credited in a specific proportion with other admissions criteria. The arrangement making race one factor among many was supported in the recent Supreme Court ruling in *Grutter v. Bollinger* and appears to be reflected in the admissions criteria described in this vignette. Sarah and the other members of the admissions committee have created a system where multiple achievements and experiences are weighed in the application process. Their system intends to create a class that blends academic achievement and life experiences so that both "head" and heart" are present in the classroom by valuing a variety of "ways of knowing." Other schools may certainly select and weigh criteria differently, depending on what they value and what kinds of applicants are expected to succeed in their particular program.

Sarah's argument that the committee should utilize all the sources of data it seeks from candidates demonstrates several ethical principles, including integrity, nondiscrimination, and cultural competence. Depending on the qualifications of the other applicants, the schema that the committee develops may not necessarily lead to Nelson's admission, but it will ensure that his abilities and experiences are accounted for as the committee determines his promise for doctoral education.

VIOLATING THE STANDARD

Jane is a twenty-three-year-old social work student in the first week of her internship at a veterans' hospital. Her clientele is predominantly men over the age of forty who are suffering acute bouts of posttraumatic stress disorder. Mr. Carter, her first client, has just undergone an amputation of his arm following repeated failed surgeries to treat a wound he received in the first Gulf War. He has a history of homelessness but no predominant psychiatric problems. Jane's responsibility is to arrange the rehabilitation services and adaptive devices he will need upon discharge.

At their first meeting, Mr. Carter is sullen and resistant to Jane's suggestions. When asked about his arm, he reports that he can still see it there and feels as if it is still attached. He is discouraged that after all the hospitalizations, he still lost the arm. Jane replies matter-of-factly, "But the reality of the situation is that you have lost it, so what can we do to get you functioning again?"

Mr. Carter explodes. "Listen, sister, I am functioning! You have no clue what I've seen, what I've been through. You and your privileged little cocoon can't do nothin' for me!"

Jane replies, "Well, that's certainly your choice," and ends the interview. In her treatment notes for the case record, Jane writes, "Mr. Carter appears to suffer from an explosive disorder. His hallucinations should be explored further as evidence of possible psychosis. His lack of motivation and resistance to service indicate a poor prognosis for success post-discharge." Her supervisor, who was not part of the interview, takes Jane's analysis at face value and fails to explore other factors at play in the interview.

The vignette doesn't reveal all the sources of difference between Jane and Mr. Carter, but it does indicate that they differ in age, ability, and gender, and presumably in military experience. Bridging such differences to build a trusting helping relationship takes effort, time, and compassion. Successful cross-cultural practice requires a high degree of self-awareness on the part of the worker, a commitment to learn more about others and their cultural experiences, and a willingness to acknowledge mistakes and misunderstandings and work to overcome them. Nondiscrimination means that clients aren't penalized by the worker's lack of sensitivity, lack of knowledge, or abuse of power (Lieberman & Lester, 2004; NASW National Committee on Racial and Ethnic Diversity, 2001).

In the interaction with Mr. Carter, Jane appears insensitive to his experience and more focused on her agenda than the needs of her client. Perhaps their differences exacerbated Mr. Carter's reaction. His presumptions about Jane and the intensity of his response indicate outrage at not being heard or respected, and perhaps disbelief in her capacity to help him, given their differences. Rather than ending the session, Jane could have defused the situation by acknowledging her error. "You are right, Mr. Carter. I apologize for focusing on the future instead of what you'd just told me. Can we start over?" In addition to providing assistance with his immediate needs, she could also use their sessions to learn more about him and his background, establishing the trust necessary for a helping relationship, especially one where the participants come from very different worlds (NASW National Committee on Racial and Ethnic Diversity, 2001). Beyond helping Mr. Carter, such conversations would help broaden and deepen Jane's cultural awareness.

Instead, Jane cuts off further communication, and her treatment notes reflect a lack of empathy toward Mr. Carter's position, and poor awareness of her own role in the transaction. Her ignorance of the physical phenomena that accompany amputations results in an inappropriate diagnosis. Her supervisor's superficial review means that there is no opportunity for Jane to learn from the incident and devise strategies to salvage her work with Mr. Carter. It also means that her flawed treatment notes stand as written and risk taking on a life of their own, as the workers on other shifts and those who read them in subsequent admissions or referrals may come to believe her account and respond to Mr. Carter accordingly.

RESOLVING DILEMMAS IN DISCRIMINATION AND CULTURAL COMPETENCE: THE TELLTALE OFFICE

Mary is a social work supervisor at a multiservice mental health center. Susan is a student intern who began placement at the agency three weeks ago. Yesterday Susan asked to meet with Mary and upon doing so expressed her distress and disgust at the office decor of her supervisor, George. The agency is located in a large metropolitan area where one of the professional sports teams has a Native American nickname and mascot. Like many employees, George is an avid fan of the team. His office reflects his interests and is full of memorabilia supporting the team. Susan voiced her objections to the display to George, and now to his supervisor, on the grounds that it is derogatory to indigenous people, perpetuates damaging stereotypes, and violates social work values about human dignity and respect. She finds it offensive and distracting and wonders if clients might not feel the same, though none have voiced such concerns.

Mary thanks Susan for taking the initiative to share her concerns and promises to take it up with George. When she does, he is decidedly less open to Susan's request that he remove the sports memorabilia. George maintains that the team is a source of civic pride, and that the decorations help clients relax in his office and create a bond with him. Furthermore, he notes that the logo and mascot are fixtures throughout the city on buses, billboards, sportswear, and bumper stickers. Removing them from the office, he says, would be "political correctness run amok. And, Mary," he adds, "if you are going to tell me how to decorate my workspace, will you do the same with Alice's religious paraphernalia and slogans, or Joan's incense and New Age posters? Or is it only Susan's sensitivities that matter here?"

Susan's questions about the appropriateness of George's office decorations raise several issues that Mary must address. She must contend with the relationship between the supervisor and supervisee, which is at risk of rupture given Susan's interpretation of George's decorations, his refusal to change them, and his reactions to her complaint. Regardless of what she decides to do about George's office, Mary must determine if and how the supervisory relationship can be saved. She must also address the issue sparked by Susan's complaint: who decides when office decor is offensive or inappropriate? Moreover, what norms or policies should be in place at the agency in order to foster a welcoming and inclusive environment? This section focuses primarily on resolving the ethical dilemma embedded in the issue of office decor, though the strategy for assisting Susan and George will be considered as well.

Who Can Assist Mary in Determining the Ethics of Office Decor?

In deciding how to respond to Susan's original complaint and George's rejoinder about others' offices, Mary should consult her own supervisor about agency policies and about the process for addressing the issue. If the agency has a policy, does it clearly resolve the question regarding decorations such as George's? Or is it worded in such a general way (requiring "modest and tasteful decorations," for example) that its interpretation is open to dispute?

Whether or not the policy is clear, if it exists and has not been enforced, perhaps Mary's supervisor can explain why and advise her on bringing attention to it. Key questions include who else will be affected if the policy is imposed and what will result if the policy is enforced after it has been dormant for some time. The agency's human resources department may also be helpful in interpreting the policy or crafting a new one. HR staff can also describe other agency policies that may relate to Mary's dilemma, such as those on the use of agency property or criteria for what constitutes a hostile work environment under sexual harassment or discrimination provisions.

Mary may want to consult with other supervisors at her agency. Have they experienced similar dilemmas? How do they perceive George's office environment? If her colleagues represent diverse backgrounds, it may be useful to hear their perspectives on office environments in general, and the intentional and unintentional messages that are sent. Perhaps there is also merit in surveying current and former clients about the agency environment and their perceptions of the cultural competence reflected there.

Colleagues in other settings may be an additional resource. Given the visibility of the team logo in the city, it is likely many other organizations—corporate, nonprofit, and otherwise—have struggled with similar questions, and it will help to benefit from their wisdom.

Have leaders in the Native American community spoken out about the logo and mascot? Have they said that they feel it is insensitive or off-putting? If official pronouncements have been made, to what extent do they help with Mary's decision? Tribal leaders in some regions of the country have approved the use of their names by local teams (for example, the Seminoles at Florida State University). If that is the case with the team in Mary's area, does that mean such decor is acceptable there but not in other regions where tribes have come out against the practice? Do those official sanctions mean the decorations George and others use are automatically rendered inoffensive?

Beyond the message sent by the logo, how much latitude do other employers offer staff in decorating their workspace? How would they handle a dispute when one worker is upset with another's decor? The HR staff at Mary's agency may be able to take the lead in conducting research on the standards in other organizations.

Mary should also talk further with her own staff about the issue of office decor, moving it away from Susan's complaint about George. What norms would the group wish to develop to create a welcoming workplace? Where would they draw limits in individual choice? What are the clinical implications of certain signs and symbols? If clients are in distress and disempowered when they appear for service, might they feel inhibited about voicing concerns about decorations they find unsettling? How can the staff be sensitive to those perceptions?

Other policies and consultations may serve as resources to Mary as she tries to resolve her dilemma concerning Susan and George's supervisory relationship. Since Susan is a student, the social work program that placed her at the agency likely has a contract that specifies how disputes are supposed to be addressed. Has George or Susan spoken to the school's field liaison about the friction between them? Should Mary meet with George and Susan to determine if the issue of office decor is inhibiting a constructive supervisory relationship and help to create a remediation plan if it is? Should she be in contact with Susan's social work program about the problem?

Beyond the student placement contract, Mary should determine what policies the agency has for addressing supervisory disputes. There may be a grievance process or mediation assistance that either party can access. Or there may be a process for reassigning supervisees. Whether or not any of these are called for at this time, Mary should be aware of her options.

What Are Mary's Choices?

Mary must decide whether George's office decorations are inappropriate because they are racially insensitive, upsetting to clients or coworkers, or just plain excessive. If she decides that they are, she will have to consider whether his is the only office that raises such concerns or whether other offices reflect similar problems. If she decides it is just George, she should deal with him individually and discuss with him both the office itself and any related concerns about cultural competence.

However, if George's office is only one example of insensitive or potentially offensive office décor, Mary must create or enforce a policy that would address his decorations and those of other workers. Finally if Mary decides George's office decor is not inappropriate, she must deal with Susan's feelings and with the effects on her relationship with the agency.

When Has Mary Faced a Similar Dilemma?

In past evaluations of the agency as a sensitive environment for a multicultural clientele, the leadership team has audited the surroundings and made adjustments to convey a message of inclusion. Recently the waiting area was redecorated with signs in three languages and prints by African American, Asian, and Native American artists to send a welcoming message to the agency's diverse clientele. As part of that team, Mary clearly believes that decor sends a message to clients and that everything from the selection of reading material in the waiting area to the languages spoken on the voice mail service should encourage clients of all backgrounds to feel at home there. If the discussions in the environmental audit addressed individual offices, that information would impinge on her current thinking about George's office. Certainly, the agency's attention to the importance of artwork, signage, and the like, would indicate that it views decoration as a significant matter.

Mary's experiences as a supervisor, and specifically as George's supervisor, will aid her in this situation. How has she handled supervisory disputes in the past? What interventions have proved successful? At what point does Mary think she must become involved because the two parties can no longer effectively address the issue? And how does Mary experience George? To what degree does she believe his office reflects a larger cultural insensitivity? Do service statistics and client feedback indicate that he has difficulty connecting with clients of different backgrounds? Is he typically resistant or defensive when presented with feedback from Mary or his colleagues? Is he respectful of agency policies and willing to follow them even if he doesn't wholeheartedly agree?

This particular ethical decision also requires Mary to reflect on her own experiences with oppression or discrimination. How do her history and worldview shape her appraisal of the degree to which George's office (and others) is offensive? Can she put herself in a client's shoes and examine the messages that are conveyed by the surroundings? Has she experienced the type of outrage or marginalization Susan felt when her concerns with George's sports memorabilia were rebuffed? How did Mary handle those experiences? Can she draw on them in this situation?

Perhaps Mary has had experiences with students whose zeal and moral clarity conflict with the realities of contemporary service delivery. Has Mary's response been to demean or temper the students' good intentions or explain why things are, immutably, the way they are? Or has she helped students both to understand the workplace and to be constructive agents of change? In these ways, too, Mary's past experience provides a basis for her current decisions.

Where Will Ethical and Clinical Guidelines Lead Her?

Three rules are clearly embedded in Mary's choices: "Office decorations should not be offensive to clients or staff," "Office decor should not demean others on the basis of race, gender, or religion," and "Employees have a right to decorate their offices any way they want to." Of these, the last is the most troubling when taken to an extreme. If we chose it to be a universal law, we'd be supporting the office occupant's individual rights over those of everyone else, and permitting any decor that suits that individual's taste. On what basis would we want to support such a rule? Is an individual's control over his or her workspace compelling enough for the agency to give up its voice in the matter? Is the risk of abuse so slight that the right to free reign is warranted?

The first two rules are probably already reflected in the organization's norms: staff members are expected to treat others with respect and avoid offensive characterizations of others' backgrounds. If George's decorations were not affiliated with a famous sports team, he would probably view them as inappropriate and demeaning. The fact that they are tied to the sports team may explain why he and others are attracted to the logos and mascots, and inured to their offensive symbolism. This suggests an additional option: can George's office decor reflect his loyalty to the team without using the logos and mascots, that Susan (and others) finds distasteful? Whether or not this compromise works, the deontological perspective would encourage Mary to take action concerning provocative office decor to encourage a nondiscriminatory and respectful work environment.

Taking a utilitarian perspective, what are the possible consequences of Mary's choices? If the agency develops or enforces a policy about office decor, the result could be more uniformity in the offices and an environment in which the risk of offending or alienating any client is reduced. An unintended result may be sterile environment where workers and clients feel ill at ease because of the lack of personality and individualism in the clinicians' workspaces. Whether George alone is targeted or the policy is directed at all staff, Mary can expect backlash from those who are strongly attached to the work environments they have created. Perhaps there will also be retribution toward Susan as the perceived instigator of the change.

A failure to address concerns about the decor may mean that individual workers' offices are so highly personalized that they prove distracting or upsetting to clients. The offices may be the province of the workers, but they are the property of the agency: the organization has a stake in the decor, particularly given its efforts at inclusive messages in the common agency space. Doing nothing may send the wrong message to the staff about their individual workspaces. It will also prove a grave disappointment to Susan, who could continue to fight the battle over decor with her social work program and with human rights agencies outside the placement setting.

Of these consequences, the most grave for the agency's mission is the potential for clients to be disaffected. As such, it seems Mary should at least initiate conversations in the agency about decor and its effect on clinical services. Hopefully the resulting discussion will lead to norms or policies that balance the employees' interests with those of the people they serve.

A number of values warrant consideration in this case. Clearly George and the other workers value the autonomy to create environments in which they are comfortable. Susan, too, wants to be comfortable in the offices she visits at the placement. We might assume too that the agency's administration and staff value respect for clients and for culturally sensitive approaches to service.

The ethical principle of justice states, "Social workers pursue social change, particularly with and on behalf of vulnerable and oppressed individuals and groups of people. Social workers' social change efforts are focused primarily on issues of poverty, unemployment, discrimination, and other forms of social injustice. These activities seek to promote sensitivity to and knowledge about oppression and cultural and ethnic diversity. Social workers strive to ensure access to needed information, services, and resources; equality of opportunity; and meaningful participation in decision making for all people" (NASW, 1999, p. 5). The value upholding individuals' dignity and worth would also apply to this case, in that the principle behind it states, "Social workers treat each person in a caring and respectful fashion, mindful of individual differences and cultural and ethnic diversity" (NASW, 1999, p. 5).

Sports memorabilia at one nonprofit agency may seem a minor concern in light of the vast historical and contemporary mechanisms of oppression and discrimination. However, if office decorations make clients and coworkers ill at ease about biases or stereotypes concerning race, religion, gender, sexual orientation, or other characteristics, overlooking them on any scale would seem inconsistent with social work values. Social work values suggest that Mary should take action.

Ethical standards also support action. In addition to those on nondiscrimination and cultural competence stated at the outset of the chapter, the following tenets may be applicable to this case:

- "Social work administrators should take reasonable steps to ensure that the working environment for which they are responsible is consistent with and encourages compliance with the NASW Code of Ethics. Social work administrators should take reasonable steps to eliminate any conditions in their organizations that violate, interfere with, or discourage compliance with the Code" (NASW, 1999, 3.07d).
- "Social workers should not permit their private conduct to interfere with their ability to fulfill their professional responsibilities" (NASW, 1999, 4.03).

The first standard encourages Mary and her superiors to take seriously the code's provisions on respect and nondiscrimination. Several options might constitute "reasonable steps" to address conflicts with the code, for example, holding meetings to craft a policy about office space, discussing strategies to best serve a diverse clientele, offering staff development around cultural competence, and encouraging open communication among paid and nonpaid staff about ways to enhance the organizational environment.

The second standard might be relevant to George or other workers who consider their offices an extension of themselves and an expression of who they are. "Private conduct" may go beyond activities on the employee's personal time to include individual expression through one's appearance or surroundings. At its essence the standard asks social workers to give priority to their professional responsibilities when private interests might infringe on those duties. This is in keeping with the value of "service to others above self interest" (NASW, 1999, p. 5). A worker whose office is laden with family photos, or another who routinely wears jewelry with religious symbols, may be sending a message of "This is who I am." But as professional social workers, they must also be mindful of the message received by the clients they encounter: "I don't belong here," "Can this person understand me?" or "Will this person be able to help me?" Even if only a fraction of the clientele is put off or put down by those messages, is that a worthwhile trade-off for the freedom of expression at work?

Embedded in this tension is the principle of autonomy and the balance between policies that support the workers' rights with those of the clients. In this case, the clients are in a less powerful position, in that they likely have little choice in which workers they see at which agencies, and limited ability to take issue with aspects of service they find disconcerting. Mary's choice should help to maximize the autonomy of all involved, but particularly that of the least powerful members of the transaction, the clients.

Which option represents fidelity and justice? Mary must consider promises made to employees, to Susan and other students, and directly or indirectly to clients. She must act in a manner that is congruent with stated policies and encourage others to do the same. The process she uses for making and implementing her decision should be transparent and reinforce her trustworthiness. And her decision must meet the standards of fairness. In this she should be particularly careful in singling out George and his office for scrutiny. If her rationale for acting to limit the personalization of offices has to do with exclusive messages for clients and colleagues, she should be certain that all offices meeting that criterion are addressed as well. If Mary determines that George's office is not out of line, fairness demands that she be certain that no precedents exist where workers in the organization were disciplined for similar issues.

The principles of beneficence and nonmaleficence would look to enhance the goods in the case and minimize the negative effects. While it is good for workers to be happy in and comfortable with their office environments, the greater good is for clients to be comfortable there, and the greater damage occurs when they are not.

While the laws about discrimination don't encompass office decorations, numerous statutes and regulations address discrimination in the workplace. Title VII of the Civil Rights Act of 1964 prohibits employers from discriminating against or harassing people on the basis of sex, race, color, religion, or national origin (Milkovich & Boudreau, 1997). Subsequent interpretations of the statute and rulings of the Equal Employment Opportunity Commission have shaped the application of this law in areas such as dress codes, holiday decorations, work schedules, and proselytizing (Atkinson, 2004). An understanding of the characteristics of unequal treatment of employees and the unequal impact of ostensibly neutral policies will be essential as Mary and her colleagues respond to this case and craft new organizational guidelines.

Beyond information on nondiscrimination, Mary may also review policy and position statements on Native American mascots. For example, a position statement by the United States Commission on Civil Rights (2001) states that

> The Commission assumes that when Indian imagery was first adopted for sports mascots it was not to offend Native Americans. However, the use of the imagery and traditions, no matter how popular, should end when they are offensive. We applaud those who have been leading the fight to educate the public and the institutions that have voluntarily

discontinued the use of insulting mascots. Dialogue and education are the roads to understanding. The use of American Indian mascots is not a trivial matter. The Commission has a firm understanding of the problems of poverty, education, housing, and health care that face many Native Americans. The fight to eliminate Indian nicknames and images in sports is only one front of the larger battle to eliminate obstacles that confront American Indians. The elimination of Native American nicknames and images as sports mascots will benefit not only Native Americans, but all Americans. The elimination of stereotypes will make room for education about real Indian people, current Native American issues, and the rich variety of American Indians in our country.

Similarly, the president of the National Congress of American Indians states, "The National Congress of American Indians strongly condemns the use of sports team mascots that claim to portray Native Americans and Native cultures in a positive light. . . . It is only with Native Americans that this practice continues. It is a national insult and does nothing to honor the Native peoples of this country" (National Congress of Indians, n.d.). Statements such as these provide support for Susan's complaint and for Mary's efforts to take action on George's office. However, they don't remedy other forms of offensive decor, nor do they address any underlying concerns about cultural competence.

Might office decorations be considered a form of free speech and thus be protected from intrusions by the employer? While the First Amendment of the Bill of Rights prohibits the government of the United States from abridging free speech, the expressions of that right are continually defined and redefined by laws, court decisions, and social policies (American Civil Liberties Union, n.d.). If the agency is not a governmental entity and the actual office space is the private property of the organization, it seems unlikely that the First Amendment applies in this case. However, if Mary expanded her efforts to address personal appearance (such as religious insignias or jewelry), the workers' First Amendment protections might apply.

How do practice norms apply to this case? Some clinicians' decisions about their office decorations are dictated by their theoretical orientations, in that some perspectives would encourage more worker self-revelation, and others less. Some workers are guided by pragmatic considerations—they choose not to reveal very much about themselves in order to reinforce attention to the client, or they share office space and have determined that neutral furnishings are in order. Other workers create a culturally welcoming space by purposefully selecting furnishings to convey a particular message or worldview (Mason et al., 1996). Beyond the norms about decoration, there appears to be scant published information about what decor should *not* be encouraged or the strategies supervisors and administrators can use to ensure compliance with agency standards.

Why Is Mary Selecting a Particular Course of Action?

The information we have about the case and the ethical analysis support Mary in taking action about George's office and other offices as needed, not only on the basis of Susan's discomfort but because such decor contradicts agency values and may be troubling or distracting to those the agency serves. Her decision is reinforced by a consideration of the various errors in judgment had she made a different decision. For example, choosing to do nothing would certainly be easier for her and would preserve her relationship with her staff, even at the expense of her relationship with the student intern. But it places those relationships above her responsibility to clients and to culturally sensitive practice. It allows her to avoid the search for acceptable compromises and privileges some workers' rights over those of their colleagues and clients.

How will her decision fit with the principle of publicity? Maybe George is right that it smacks of political correctness and a tendency to allow the sensitivities of a few to dictate the actions of the majority. If this perception is shared by others, Mary's efforts could be met with derision inside the agency and in the professional community. Nevertheless, there is also power in the messages sent by her attempt to enhance cultural competence: we care about what people think, we care about the comfort of others, and when in doubt, why not err on the side of sensitivity?

If George and the other staff could imagine themselves in their clients' shoes, complete with apprehensions about treatment, histories of powerlessness and marginalization, and limited authority at the agency, what option would they choose? Can the principle of reversibility help them appreciate the need to make accommodations for others? Does it reinforce Mary's conviction that she should act for change? As she considers what feels appropriate, and what her mentors might do, is she confident in her decision?

How Should Mary Carry Out Her Decision?

Mary will need to engage the agency's leadership in this situation. If she finds that the problem only involves George's office, she will want to be sure that she has the administration's support and guidance for the actions she takes. If this is a systemic problem, then the administration and other supervisors must be involved to craft an agency-wide strategy.

The change effort itself is likely to be most successful is if it inclusive of all personnel and if the rationale for change and the implementation process are fair and transparent. Mary and others must be careful not to make Susan the scapegoat for the change but rather acknowledge that she brought to attention an issue that is of concern to the organization. Those promoting the change should emphasize that the policy is in the interests of the agency and its workers, in that it makes it a more welcoming and effective workplace. Their change strategy should consider various options that reconcile the interests of the workers and their desire for personalized and unique office space with the need for a culturally sensitive workplace. That may mean limiting the proportion of personal furnishings in an office or requiring workers to convey their interests in an inoffensive way (for example, team memorabilia without the troubling mascot or logo). Whatever strategy they employ, Mary and the leadership should also strive to evaluate the change and document that it had the desired effects. If it does not, they should refine it accordingly.

CONCLUSION

Ethical standards on nondiscrimination require social workers to treat their clients, employees, students, and colleagues in a fair and unbiased fashion. The commitment to social justice obliges social workers to advocate for improved social conditions and policies to eradicate inequality. Cultural competence goes beyond nondiscrimination to encourage an array of activities to help workers understand and respond sensitively to various forms of diversity. Effective social work requires an ongoing commitment to learning more about others and incorporating that knowledge into practice.

Professionals should be mindful of the messages sent by their dress, surroundings, and behavior. Do those messages foster trust and convey a sense of helpfulness and acceptance of difference? Are they congruent with the agency's mission and the intentions of the professionals involved? While culturally sensitive surroundings are important, office furnishings and decor should be an authentic expression of interests, not window dressing advertising a competence that does not exist.

A healthy organizational environment invites open discussion of differences and concerns and adopts practices benefiting the organization's clientele and workforce. Even in effective agencies, conversations about racism and discrimination can be difficult. So too is reconciling the rights and interests of various parties. However, those efforts can help to strengthen the workplace, improve morale, and develop a culture where diverse perspectives are honored and valued.

Chapter 11

Sustaining Ethical Habits

Hopefully this book has given you greater familiarity with ethical decision making and enhanced your confidence in your own decisions. Still, you may be weary of all the considerations, equivocations, and ambiguities involved in determining ethical actions. I trust that this fatigue is a sign of your strengthened understanding and abilities in this area, not a feeling of futility. Given the complexities of social work practice, the settings in which the field is represented, and the roles social workers play, it's easy to understand why some may feel the thoughtful examination of dilemmas is aggravating or, worse, pointless. While there are endless permutations of the cases you have encountered in this book, the effort you make in carefully and critically resolving dilemmas can be viewed as an investment in the resolution of future dilemmas. As indicated in the decision-making model, past judgments provide precedents for solving subsequent problems. In short, good decisions should beget better and easier decisions. They help us to make a habit of ethical decision making.

IMPEDIMENTS AND AVENUES TO ETHICAL HABITS

The will and capacity for ethical excellence are often imperiled by a variety of circumstances and considerations, including preoccupation with risk, intrapersonal characteristics, environmental characteristics, and the disuse and misuse of decision-making skills. Let's close by examining each of these threats and some ways to avoid or diminish their destructive effects.

Risk Aversion

I've tried to make the case in this text that thoughtful, well-supported decisions can mitigate risk. However, they will never eliminate it.

In truth, anyone can take issue at any time with the way professionals conduct their practice. Clients may be dissatisfied with the outcomes of their care, the type of services they received, or the way they were treated. Supervisees may take offense at direction, performance appraisals, or assigned tasks. Payers may question the rationale for services or their cost. The possibilities are endless. They can also be paralyzing.

Clinicians who practice from a risk-averse stance may limit their clientele to avoid complex cases or particular pathologies. Overly cautious practice may be fear driven, leading workers to avoid necessary confrontations with clients or overreact to troubling information. They may set policies that are conservative but unresponsive to client needs, for example, refusing all gifts, thus missing opportunities to acknowledge the client's kindness or explore the intent behind the gift. In their concern for self-protection, risk-driven decision makers may emphasize their security over client needs, in effect, increasing some risks by trying to eliminate others. The worker who feels compelled to notify a client's spouse about his infidelities so that she can protect herself from sexually transmitted infections is incurring other harms in exchange for his or her own peace of mind.

The question, I think, is not how to *avoid* risk, but rather how to put it in the proper place in our decision making. Here are some suggestions. Invite it in, give it a seat at the table, acknowledge it, articulate the fear, and use it as a method to anticipate the specific harms you fear. A former colleague of mine used to say, "That which cannot be put into words cannot be put to rest." Ignoring or denying fear, or internalizing it as the basis for one's decision making, limits our capacity for creative, responsible decisions.

Another way to cope with fear is to appreciate the ways that our humanity and our dedication to the profession are diminished in a risk-avoidance paradigm. Consider the price we pay for defensive, "risk-proof" practice. What client groups are avoided, what services are withheld, what conversations are not pursued in the interest of a largely false sense of safety? This is not an invitation to be dense or rash. To the contrary, it is an invitation to engage in mindful (versus self-conscious) practice, where carelessness is shunned and prudence is encouraged. It is an appeal to look at our work with a wider lens, appreciating the implications when we choose a defensive posture over an affirming and inclusive one.

Wrestling with risk also requires us to confront our willingness to act on principle, to *do the right thing* rather than simply *know the right thing to do*. This is not a simple task. By definition it entails hazards and demands courage. Whether we are putting our physical well-being at risk by confronting an abusive parent, or our personal comfort at risk by confronting a disrespectful colleague, we are committing an act of courage. And physical and moral courage do not mean that the person has no fear but rather that he or she acts in spite of those fears (McCain & Salter, 2004). When we uphold ethical principles, even at the risk of condemnation, litigation, or alienation, we are acting with moral courage.

When we avoid upholding principles in the name of risk avoidance, we must always contend with the possibility that our rationale is moral cowardice in disguise. I recognize that "cowardice" is a strong word. My intent in using it is not to shame or bully people into action, but rather to recognize it as a phenomenon with which we all must contend. I suspect we all can recall times when we have not acted as our best selves, or when we have failed to speak up and regretted the failure later. Sometimes we don't calculate the risk to our conscience in making a risk-avoiding decision. As John McCain puts it, "I can recall all too well those times I've avoided the risk of injury or disappointment by overruling the demands of conscience. . . . Remorse is an awful companion. And whatever the unwelcome consequences of courage, they are unlikely to be worse than the discovery that you are less a man than you pretend to be" (McCain & Salter, 2004, pp. 70–71).

Risk is real, and good decision making takes all forms of risk into account. Sometimes ethical action requires that we act in spite of risk, and sometimes ethical action is really *in*action—demonstrating restraint, keeping confidences, allowing due process. Upholding moral and ethical principles despite risks and fears demands courage, but even lapses in courage can serve as a basis for learning and an impetus to do better the next time around.

Intrapersonal Characteristics

Risk may lie not in those things external to us (the client's pathology, the nature of our services, the community in which we practice), but within us. Like risk aversion, personal traits can also undermine ethical habits. Workers may have power issues, hubris, and compelling needs (the need to be liked, to be right, to be in control, or be successful, for example) that override those of the client or the role. While each of these characteristics can be used in social work to constructive ends, they can also lead to dangerous deviations from accepted practice. For example, insecurity or an aversion to conflict can keep the worker from setting appropriate boundaries. Shame or pride can keep the worker from seeking case assistance. The needs for control and achievement can result in the practitioner overriding the client's wishes or rejecting clients whose success is not guaranteed.

Another assault on ethical habits comes from poor self-awareness on the part of the professional. Practitioners who do not have a good understanding of their own zeal, habits, and personal histories are ill equipped to use them purposefully when they are called for or rein them in when they have the potential to be destructive. For example, perhaps a worker has been drawn to the field due to personal experience with child abuse or volunteer or work experiences in that area. As a result, the worker's passion is in righting wrongs and standing up for this vulnerable population.

These experiences may prove beneficial in a variety of ways. They may create a vocal and impassioned advocate in child protective services, someone who is willing to work in a difficult field and who will stay in that field even when the going gets tough. The result may be extraordinary empathy for the victims of child maltreatment and uncommon dedication to social change. However, this profile of experiences also has a down side. It may blind the individual to other perspectives in the case and inhibit his or her ability to work effectively with other personnel in cases of abuse. The worker's zeal may lead to an ends-justify-the-means outlook and a whatever-it-takes determination, in which rights and processes are sacrificed in service of the worker's perceptions of justice.

The acquisition of self-knowledge and the management of personal characteristics and inclinations are a prerequisite for effective practice in the helping professions, including the practice of ethical decision making. It is a lifelong quest. The attention to self that is so much a part of professional development can become obscured over the course of a career. Our workplaces, personal responsibilities, and achievements can divert attention from ourselves, as we lack the time, impetus, inclination, and opportunities required for self-examination. Our personal characteristics themselves can undermine our examination of them. Take a trait such as insecurity. Workers who are insecure in their knowledge or abilities may live in fear that those vulnerabilities will be discovered. As a result, they may fail to seek the very advice or input that could help bolster their capacities and increase their confidence. The trait of confidence, too, can lead to the same problematic spiral. The excessively confident worker may not see any need for consultation or may ignore the suggestions of others and refuse to second-guess his or her own decisions. Driven not by fear but by ego, the person with all the answers forecloses opportunities for growth and change.

How do we overcome our internal barriers to developing ethical habits? Sometimes events will demand reexamination in spite of our inertia or resistance. These events can come in the form of personal crises that call for self-reflection, or organizational or community catastrophes that result in wholesale reviews of personnel and processes. Regardless of the catalyst for self-examination, the process of honest self-appraisal should not be derailed by quests to assign or avoid blame or to put the crisis quickly to rest and move on. On the contrary, a climate of intentionality, trust, and affirmation creates the safe space in which people can examine their actions, take responsibility, and make plans for change.

It is not necessary to wait for a divorce, demotion, client death, or public scandal to engage in critical self-reflection. An honest and involved network of colleagues, friends, and family can make us aware of who we are, who we want to be, and how well our choices are aligning with those aspirations. Our civic involvements and faith communities can perform the same function.

216

Environmental Factors

Beyond attending to their personal characteristics, those who aspire to ethical action must contend with their environments as well. Social service, health-care, and other settings must address organizational needs and strategic imperatives in order to survive and thrive. Some of these imperatives are evident in cases throughout the book: policies that restrict access to care, funding and programming changes that fail to account for staff capabilities, and pressures to meet outcome standards, regardless of the means needed to do so. It is easy to understand how workers might find themselves torn between the organization's expectations and the needs of those they serve.

In the absence of a clear moral compass and the capacity for independent decision making, workers may capitulate to the organization's expectations without critically examining the ethical risks involved. Ethical action requires professionals to be assertive in examining organizational directives, taking steps to address those that are ethically or legally compromised. As indicated in the cases in this book, as agents of change, workers in these positions must strategically utilize their skills and resources. They must be able to articulate the principles on which their concerns rest and manage the tensions inherent in the internal advocate role. They must also be mindful of the short-term and long-term consequences of their activism. The successful agent of change will help to make the organization a stronger and more effective service entity. Even those who are unsuccessful in pressing their case on a particular issue may ultimately be able to effect other positive long-term changes in an organization. But those individuals who find that their ethical concerns are consistently rebuffed may ultimately need to move on to a healthier setting. While all organizations must balance their needs with those of their clientele, not all manage those tensions in a way that jeopardizes ethical, legal, and personal standards.

Misuse

Just as our ethical habits can be enhanced by those around us, so too can they be diminished. Individuals with a firm moral compass and a sound history of decision making may drift from those moorings in a sea of corruption. It's not always easy, though, to perceive this turbulence. The principle of just noticeable difference, also known as the boiled frog phenomenon, suggests that when the changes around us are subtle and gradual, we adjust to those conditions without appreciating the distance we have come or the peril in our current surroundings. Most individual and corporate scandals are years in the making and follow a rather predictable trajectory from minor, well-rationalized transgressions to increasingly more serious, harmful, and indefensible errors. Individuals who are able to avoid being swept up in the tide of wrongdoing typically have mechanisms (friends, interests, creeds) that call their attention to an ethical dilemma and reinforce their commitment to do something about it. That something may involve speaking up or in some other way endeavoring to be an agent of change. It may also involve "voting with one's feet" and leaving the untenable situation or calling a halt to dishonest personal behavior.

The phenomenon of groupthink poses another threat to ethical habits. An artifact of extreme cohesion, groupthink results when individual members are inhibited from introducing contrary opinions. In essence, members are reluctant to rock the boat because of the influence of powerful members or the approbation of their fellow group members. Decisions tainted by groupthink can be recognized by characteristics such as insufficient attention to alternatives, a lack of attention to the risks of the preferred choice, failure to reevaluate initially rejected alternatives, a poorly conducted search for information, and biases in weighing and processing that information (Tropman, 1997).

Catastrophes such as the NASA space shuttle crashes and the Enron collapse have been attributed to groupthink. Other troubling actions result when the phenomenon plays out on a smaller scale. Groupthink can lead to poorly considered decisions, such as the failure of a treatment team to weigh an array of service options or a board's acceptance of a policy that disenfranchises specific racial or ethnic groups. It can also lead to the compounding of errors when attempts to cover up mistakes lead to greater errors, ruined reputations, and violations of trust.

The same intra- and interpersonal resources that help individuals avoid the boiled frog phenomenon can provide support in avoiding groupthink. Changes in organizational and team culture can help too. For example, groups can develop norms that tolerate dissent or create procedures where minority positions are solicited and considered. Individuals can weigh in and support those who, in acting with moral courage, speak up to say, "Perhaps we haven't considered all the downsides of this plan" or "Let's think this through more carefully." Boards or committees can make a commitment to address divergent opinions within the group, rather than following a path of silent acquiescence when troubling actions are taking place. Group members can be alert to messages and behaviors that shut down debate or that discourage careful examination of issues and options.

This is probably daunting advice for anyone who spends much time in group or committee meetings. It is easy to dismiss it as unrealistic, inefficient, and problematic. But, in keeping with our discussion of risk, let's be mindful of the costs in time, energy, and reputations of decisions that are superficially supported, poorly considered, and potentially hazardous.

Disuse

Ethical decision making, like any skill, becomes strengthened through practice and weakened by disuse. The lack of opportunities to practice ethical decision making may be an artifact of our success at it; that is, we are so adept that it no longer requires much effort at all. Think of it as hefting a two-pound barbell when you are ready for a ten-pound weight. Our opportunities for ethical decision making may also be limited because we fail to see novel opportunities for applying our skills. How do we apply understood concepts to new settings, populations, issues, or technologies? Think of this challenge as using the weights on only one area of the body rather than exercising different muscle groups.

Keeping our ethical habits from getting rusty does not mean going out in search of dilemmas to solve, at least not literally. However, we can seek opportunities to apply and refine our skills by using them imaginatively in the situations we confront in our daily lives. We can help others with their ethical dilemmas. We can test our judgments against those of the ethics and advice columnists in our daily newspapers. We can envision our responses to dilemmas portrayed in novels, films, television, and other media. In doing so, we ask: "What would I do in a given circumstance? On what basis did I decide that was a good thing? Where would I turn for assistance? Is this particular decision consistent with others I have made and with my overall framework for ethical action?"

I know, I know—you've worked all day, and now I'm ruining your free time by making it into an intellectual exercise. It's not my intent to turn recreation into work, or every TV plot into a Socratic debate. All I'm asking is that you carry an ethical lens that you can train on dilemmas as they arise (even those of which you are not a part), using those observations to build on the ethical habits you've already established. In truth, most of us do it anyway. When a therapist on *Law and Order* surrenders client information to detectives or Jack Bauer is torturing a suspect on *24*, I think our instinct is to declare those actions right or wrong. Exercising ethical habits just gets us to examine why we think that way and generalize the situation to the times we may be called on to make similar judgments.

Of course, ethical habits can be enhanced by more direct means, including reading texts on topics such as philosophy, courage, cheating, morality, and decision making. I encourage people to participate in ethics Listservs or discussion groups, subscribe to free electronic digests such as the *Ethics Newsline* from the Institute on Global Ethics (www.globalethics.org), or participate in "moral communities" with other therapists (Doherty, 1995). Each is an opportunity to further our knowledge, examine our thinking, articulate our positions, and apply our beliefs to real-life quandaries, including those in other fields. While the specifics of dilemmas in corporate America, international diplomacy, sports, or politics may differ from those encountered in the helping professions, the essential tensions are often the same: due process versus expedience, honesty versus strategic advantage, the well-being of an individual or group versus that of another, and so on.

THE INTEGRATED SELF

Our decisions shape others, and we are shaped by our decisions. As we make decisions and grapple with ethical dilemmas, they become part of who we are. This book has argued for self-evaluation and decision evaluation in service of the development of ethical habits. It has also argued for moral citizenship and courage, based on the notion that our decisions are not ours alone. They have reverberating effects on the organizations in which we serve, and the colleagues, citizens, and clients with whom we interact. Healthy, helpful, and affirming decisions contribute to a better culture, and our resulting actions fulfill the promise and privilege that our professional status provides. Inaction, bad decisions, and unethical conclusions can also have reverberating, and detrimental, effects.

As we engage in the journey of integrating the decisions we must make daily with our individual moral framework, let's be mindful not only of the challenges but of the possibilities. Some dilemmas and choices will fit seamlessly with our existing value framework, and others will challenge our beliefs, at times changing our belief system and at other times capitulating to it. The tensions in reconciling the two, the effort required to develop ethical habits and arrive at good decisions, and the pressures of the practice environment can all conspire to portray ethics as idealistic, naïve, or irrelevant. But I think in our hearts, even the most cynical among us knows better. Our humanity is enhanced or diminished by the decisions we make. Let's take advantage of the tools at our disposal to make the best decisions we can and strive for improvement when we fall short.

REFERENCES

American Academy of Pediatrics. (1995). Informed consent, parental permission, and assent in pediatric practice. *Pediatrics, 95*(2), 314-317.

American Civil Liberties Union. (n.d.). *Free speech.* Retrieved May 23, 2006, from http://www.aclu.org/freespeech/index.html

American Counseling Association. (2005). *ACA code of ethics.* Alexandria, VA: American Counseling Association.

American Psychological Association. (2002). *The ethical principles of psychologists and code of conduct.* Washington, DC: American Psychological Association.

Appelbaum, P. S., Lidz, C. W., & Meisel, A. (1987). *Informed consent: Legal theory and clinical practice.* New York: Oxford University Press.

Atkinson, W. (2004, December). Religion in the workplace: Faith vs. liability. *Risk Management Magazine*, 18-23.

Barna Update. (2002). Retrieved September 16, 2006, from http://www .barna.org/FlexPage.aspx?Page=BarnaUpdate&BarnaUpdateID=120

Bell, A., Coleman, A. L., & Palmer, S. R. (2005, May 27). Race and diversity practices for the post-"Grutter" era. *The Chronicle of Higher Education, 51*(38), B9.

Berman-Rossi, T., & Rossi, P. (1990). Confidentiality and informed consent in school social work. *Social Work in Education, 12*(3), 195-207.

Boddie, E. (2005, July 1). An insidious attack on affirmative action. *The Chronicle of Higher Education, 51*(43), B16.

Boisen, L. S., & Bosch, L. A. (2005). Dual relationships and rural social work: Is there a rural code? In L. H. Ginsberg (Ed.), *Social work in rural communities* (4th ed., pp. 189-203). Alexandria, VA: Council on Social Work Education.

Brager, G., & Holloway, S. (1983). A process model for changing organizations from within. In R. M. Kramer & H. Specht (Eds.), *Readings in community organization practice* (pp. 198-208). Englewood Cliffs, NJ: Prentice-Hall.

Brager, G., & Holloway, S. (1992). Assessing prospects for organizational change: The uses of force field analysis. *Administration in Social Work, 16*(3/4), 15-28.

Brager, G., & Holloway, S. (2002). *Changing human service organizations: Politics and practice.* New York: Free Press.

Buchanan, A., Brock, D.W., Daniels, N., & Wikler, D. (2000). Eugenics and its shadow. In *From chance to choice: Genetics and justice* (pp. 27-60). New York: Cambridge University Press.

Bullis, R. K. (1996). *Spirituality in social work practice*. Washington, DC: Taylor & Francis.

Burkemper, E. M. (2005). Ethical mental health social work practice in the small community. In L. H. Ginsberg (Ed.), *Social work in rural communities* (4th ed., pp. 175-188). Alexandria, VA: Council on Social Work Education.

Burton, R. V., & Kunce, L. (1995). Behavioral models of moral development: A brief history and integration. In W. M. Kurtines & J. L. Gewirtz (Eds.), *Moral development: An introduction*. Boston: Allyn & Bacon.

Canda, E. R., & Furman, L. D. (1999). *Spiritual diversity in social work practice: The heart of helping*. New York: Free Press.

Caplan, A. (2000). What's morally wrong with eugenics? In P. Sloan (Ed.), *Controlling our destinies* (pp. 209-228). Notre Dame, IN: University of Notre Dame Press.

Carson, V. B., & Arnold, E. N. (1996). *Mental health nursing: The nurse-patient journey*. Philadelphia: W. B. Saunders.

Center for Reproductive Rights. (2002). *Briefing paper: Reproductive rights and women with disabilities*. Retrieved May 26, 2006, from http://www.crlp.org/pdf/pub_bp_disabilities.pdf

Chemtob, C. M., Hamada, R. S., Bauer, G., Kinney, B., & Torigoe, R. Y. (1988). Patients' suicides: Frequency and impact on psychiatrists. *American Journal of Psychiatry, 145*(2), 224-228.

Child Welfare League of America. (1999). *CWLA standards of excellence for services for abused and neglected children and their families*. Washington, DC: CWLA.

Cohen, E. D., & Cohen, G. S. (1999). *The virtuous therapist: Ethical practice of counseling and psychotherapy*. Scarborough, Ontario: Wadsworth.

Cohen, R. (2002). *The good, the bad and the difference: How to tell right from wrong in everyday situations*. New York: Doubleday.

Community Toolbox. (2003). *Cultural competence, spirituality, and the arts and community building: Cultural competence in a multicultural world*. Retrieved July 16, 2006, from http://ctb.ku.edu/tools/en/tools_toc.htm

Confidentiality of Alcohol and Drug Abuse Patient Records, 42 C.F.R. § 2.1 (2002).

Congress, E. P. (1996). *Social work values and ethics*. Chicago: Nelson-Hall.

Connerly, W. (2000). *Creating equal: My fight against race preferences*. San Francisco: Encounter Books.

Cooper, C. (1995). Patient suicide and assault: Their impact on psychiatric hospital staff. *Journal of Psychosocial Nursing, 33*(6), 26-29.

Corey, G., Corey, M. S., & Callanan, P. (2003). *Issues and ethics in the helping professions* (6th ed.). Pacific Grove, CA: Brooks/Cole.

D'Aprix, A. S. (2005). Ethical decision-making models: A two phase study. *Dissertation Abstracts International, 66* (05), 1957A. (UMI No. AAT 3177652).

Devettere, R. J. (2000). *Practical decision making in health care ethics: Cases and concepts* (2nd ed.). Washington, DC: Georgetown University Press.

Dickson, D. T. (1998). *Confidentiality and privacy in social work: A guide to the law for practitioners and students.* New York: Free Press.

Dobrin, A. (2002). *Ethics for everyone: How to raise your moral intelligence.* New York: John Wiley and Sons.

Doherty, W. J. (1995). *Soul-searching: When psychotherapy must promote moral responsibility.* New York: Basic Books.

Dudley, J. R., Smith, C., & Millison, M. B. (1995). Unfinished business: Assessing the spiritual needs of hospice clients. *American Journal of Hospice and Palliative Care, 12*(2), 30-37.

Ebert, B. W. (1997). Dual-relationship prohibitions: A concept whose time never should have come. *Applied and Preventative Psychology, 6,* 137-156.

Epstein, R. S., & Simon, R. I. (1990). The exploitation index: An early warning indicator of boundary violations in psychotherapy. *Bulletin of the Menninger Clinic, 54*(4), 450-465.

Erickson, S. H. (2001). Multiple relationships in rural counseling. *The Family Journal: Counseling and Therapy for Couples and Families, 9*(3), 302-304.

Fisher, C. B. (2003). *Decoding the ethics code: A practical guide for psychologists.* Thousand Oaks, CA: Sage.

Fisher, C. D. (2004). Ethical issues in therapy: Therapist self-disclosure of sexual feelings. *Ethics and Behavior, 14*(2), 105-121.

Fisher, R., Ury, W., & Patton, B. (1991). *Getting to yes: Negotiating agreement without giving in.* New York: Penguin Books.

Franklin, C., & Jordan, C. (2002). Effective family therapy: Guidelines for practice. In A. R. Roberts & G. J. Greene (Eds.), *Social worker's desk reference* (pp. 256-263). New York: Oxford University Press.

Freeny, M. (1998). *Terminal consent.* Orlando: William Austin Press.

Freundlich, M., & Gerstenzang, S. (2004). Ethics and adoptive family recruitment. *Adoptalk.* Retrieved May 21, 2006, from http://www.nacac.org/newsletters/ethics.html

Freundlich, M., Gerstenzang, S., & Blair, E. (n.d.). *Lasting impressions: A guide for photolisting children.* Retrieved May 26, 2006, from www.adoptuskids.org/images/resourceCenter/**photolisting**.pdf

Frey, G. (1990). Framework for promoting organizational change. *Families in Society, 7*(3), 142-147.

Gabbard, G. O. (1996). Lessons to be learned from the study of sexual boundary violations. *American Journal of Psychotherapy, 50*(3), 311-322.

Gartrell, N. K., & Sanderson, B. E. (1994). Sexual abuse of women by women in psychotherapy: Counseling and advocacy. *Women & Therapy, 15*(1), 39-54.

Gilligan, C. (1982). *In a different voice: Psychological theory and women's development.* Cambridge, MA: Harvard University Press.

Gottlieb, M. C. (1994). Ethical decision making, boundaries, and treatment effectiveness: A reprise. *Ethics and Behavior, 4*(3), 287-293.

Gottlieb, M. C. (1996). Some ethical implications of relational diagnoses. In F. W. Kaslow (Ed.), *Handbook of relational diagnosis and dysfunctional family patterns* (pp. 19-34). New York: Wiley.

Graham, G. (2004). *Eight theories of ethics.* New York: Routledge.

Gumpert, J., & Black, P. N. (2005). Walking the tightrope between cultural competence and ethical practice: The dilemma of the rural practitioner. In L. H. Ginsberg (Ed.), *Social work in rural communities* (4th ed., pp. 157-174). Alexandria, VA: Council on Social Work Education.

Gustafson, K. E., & McNamara, R. (1987). Confidentiality with minor clients: Issues and guidelines for therapists. *Professional Psychology Research and Practice, 18*(5), 503-508.

Haas, L. J., & Malouf, J. L. (1995). *Keeping up the good work: A practitioner's guide to mental health ethics* (2nd ed.). Sarasota, FL: Professional Resource Exchange.

Halligan, P., & Corcoran, P. (2001). The impact of patient suicide on rural general practitioners. *British Journal of General Practice, 51*, 295-296.

Halverson, R. (1992, July 6). Sears nixes commission pay in light of fraud charges—Sears Roebuck and Co., auto services. *Discount Store News.*

Hepworth, D. H., Rooney, R. H., Rooney, G. D., Gottfried, K., & Larsen, J. (2006). *Direct social work practice: Theory and skills* (7th ed.). Belmont, CA: Thomson Brooks/Cole.

Health Insurance Portability and Accountability Act. 45 C.F.R. § 164 (1996).

HIPAA Medical Privacy Rule. (2003). Retrieved May 1, 2004, from http://www.socialworkers.Org/hipaa/medical.asp#

Hogan, R., & Emler, N. (1995). Personality and moral development. In W. M. Kurtines & J. L. Gewirtz (Eds.), *Moral development: An introduction* (pp. 209-228). Boston: Allyn & Bacon.

Houston-Vega, M. K., Nuehring, E. M., & Daguio, E. R. (1997). *Prudent practice: A guide for managing malpractice risk.* Washington, DC: NASW Press.

Hutchison, E. D. (1999). *Dimensions of human behavior: The changing life course.* Thousand Oaks, CA: Pine Forge Press.

Institute for Global Ethics. (2001). *Leading with values: Ethics training for nonprofits.* Camden, ME: Institute for Global Ethics.

Instructions for authors. (2006, January 4). *Journal of the American Medical Association, 295*(1), 103-111. Retrieved May 23, 2006, from http://jama.ama-assn.org/ifora_current.dtl

Jansen, B. (2006, July 10). Welfare changes threaten funding. *Portland Press Herald/Maine Sunday Telegram.* Retrieved July 11, 2006, from http://pressherald.mainetoday.com/news/state/060710welfare.shtml

Josephson, M. (1991). *Ethical values and decision making in business.* Marina del Rey, CA: Josephson Institute of Ethics.

Kaczynski, D. (2005). My brother; the Unabomber: An interview with David Kaczynski. *Free Inquiry, 25*(5), 12.

Kelly, J. (2002, December 30–January 6). The year of the whistleblowers. *Time, 160,* 8.

Kenyon, P. (1999). *What would you do? An ethical case workbook for human service professionals.* Pacific Grove, CA: Brooks/Cole.

Kidder, R. M. (1995). *How good people make tough choices: Resolving the dilemmas of ethical living.* New York: Simon and Schuster.

Kidder, R. M. (2005). *Moral courage: Taking action when your values are put to the test.* New York: William Morrow.

Kidder, R. M., & Bracy, M. (2001). *Moral courage.* Camden, ME: Institute for Global Ethics.

Kitchener, K. S. (1988). Dual relationships: What makes them so problematic? *Journal of Counseling and Development, 67*, 217–221.

Kleespies, P. M., Penk, W. E., & Forsyth, J. P. (1993). The stress of patient suicidal behavior during clinical training: Incidence, impact, and recovery. *Professional Psychology: Research and Practice, 24*(3), 293–303.

Koenig, T. L., & Spano, R. N. (2003). Sex, supervision, and boundary violations: Pressing challenges and possible solutions. *The Clinical Supervisor, 22*(1), 3–19.

Kohlberg, L. (1984). *The psychology of moral development: The nature and validity of moral stages.* San Francisco: Harper & Row.

Koocher, G. P., & Keith-Spiegel, P. (1990). *Children, ethics, and the law: Professional issues and cases.* Lincoln: University of Nebraska Press.

Koocher, G. P., & Keith-Spiegel, P. (1995). *Ethics in psychology: Professional standards and cases.* New Jersey: L. Erlbaum.

Koocher, G. P., & Keith-Spiegel, P. (1998). *Ethics in psychology: Professional standards and cases* (2nd ed.). New York: Oxford University Press.

Kurtines, W. M., & Gewirtz, J. L. (1995). *Moral development: An introduction.* Boston: Allyn & Bacon.

Kutchins, H. (1991). The fiduciary relationship: The legal basis for social work responsibilities to clients. *Social Work, 36*(2), 106–113.

Kuther, T. L. (2003). Medical decision-making and minors: Issues of consent and assent. *Adolescence, 38*(150), 343–358.

Lacayo, R., & Ripley, A. (2002, December 30–January 6). Persons of the year: The whistleblowers. *Time, 160,* 30–33.

Ladany, N., O'Brien, K. M., Hill, C. E., Melincoff, D. S., Knox, S., & Petersen, D. A. (1997). Sexual attraction toward clients, use of supervision, and prior training: A qualitative study of predoctoral psychology interns. *Journal of Counseling Psychology, 44*(4), 413–424.

Lazarus, A. (1994). The illusion of the therapist's power and the patient's fragility: My rejoinder. *Ethics and Behavior, 4*(3), 299–306.

Legal issues: Child custody and sex claims trigger more malpractice suits. (2003, September). *Psychotherapy Finances, 29*(9), 1-3.

Lieberman, A. A., & Lester, C. B. (2004). *Social work practice with a difference: Stories, essays, cases, and commentaries.* Boston: McGraw-Hill.

Lipovsky, J. A. (n.d.). *Treatment of child victims of child abuse and neglect.* Retrieved July 16, 2006, from http://childlaw.sc.edu/frmPublications/treatment_114200441012.pdf

Locke, B., Garrison, R., & Winship, J. (1998). *Generalist social work practice: Context, story, and partnerships.* Pacific Grove, CA: Brooks/Cole.

Loewenberg, F. M., Dolgoff, R., & Harrington, D. (2000). *Ethical decisions for social work practice* (7th ed.). Itasca, IL: F. E. Peacock.

Madden, R. G. (1998). *Legal issues in social work, counseling, and mental health: Guidelines for clinical practice in psychotherapy.* Thousand Oaks, CA: Sage.

Maltsberger, J. T. (1992). The implications of patient suicide for the surviving psychotherapist. In D. Jacobs (Ed.), *Suicide and clinical practice* (pp. 169-182). Washington, DC: American Psychiatric Press.

Manning, S. S., & Gaul, C. E. (1997). The ethics of informed consent: A critical variable in the self-determination of health and mental health clients. *Social Work in Health Care, 25*(3), 103-117.

Manning, S. S., & Van Pelt, M. E. (2005). The challenges of dual relationships and the continuum of care in rural mental health. In L. H. Ginsberg (Ed.), *Social work in rural communities* (4th ed., pp. 259-282). Alexandria, VA: Council on Social Work Education.

Mason, J. L., Benjamin, M. P., & Lewis, S. A. (1996). The cultural competence model: Implications for child and family mental health services. In C. A. Heflinger & C. T. Nixion (Eds.), *Families and the mental health system for children and adolescents: Policy, services, and research* (pp. 165-190). Thousand Oaks, CA: Sage.

McCain, J., & Salter, M. (2004) *Why courage matters: The way to a braver life.* New York: Random House.

McKinney-Vento Homeless Assistance Act, Pub. L. No. 100-77. 42 U.S.C. (1987).

Menninger, W. W. (1991). Patient suicide and its impact on the psychotherapist. *Bulletin of the Menninger Clinic, 55*(2), 216-227.

Milkovich, G. T., & Boudreau, J. W. (1997). *Human resource management* (8th ed.). Homewood, IL: Richard Irwin.

Mill, J. S. (1967). *Utilitarianism.* Indianapolis, IN: Bobbs-Merrill. (Original work published in 1861)

Miller, W. I. (2000). *The mystery of courage.* Cambridge, MA: Harvard University Press.

Mizrahi, T. (2002). Community organizing principles and practice guidelines. In A. Roberts & G. Greene (Eds.), *Social worker's desk reference* (pp. 517-524). New York: Oxford University Press.

Morreim, E. H. (1988). Cost containment: Challenging fidelity and justice. *Hastings Center Report, 18*(6), 20-25.

Moulton, J. F. (1924). Law and manners. *Atlantic Monthly, 134,* 1-5.

National Adoption Information Clearinghouse. (2004). *Use of advertising and facilitators in adoptive placements: Summary of state laws.* Retrieved May 25, 2006, from http://naic.acf.hhs.gov

National Association of Social Workers. (1999). *Code of ethics.* Washington, DC: NASW.

National Association of Social Workers. (2000). Cultural competence in the social work profession. In *Social work speaks: NASW policy statements* (pp. 59-62). Washington, DC: NASW Press.

National Association of Social Workers. (2003). *NASW standards for the practice of social work with adolescents.* Washington, DC: NASW.

National Association of Social Workers. (2004). *NASW standards for social work practice in palliative and end of life care.* Washington, DC: NASW.

National Association of Social Workers. (2005). *NASW standards for social work practice in child welfare.* Washington, DC: NASW.

National Association of Social Workers National Committee on Racial and Ethnic Diversity. (2001). Specialty practice sections: Credentials. *NASW standards for cultural competence in social work practice.* Retrieved July 15, 2006, from http://www.socialworkers.org/sections/credentials/cultural_comp.asp

National Association of Social Workers National Council on the Practice of Clinical Social Work. (1994). *Guidelines for clinical social work supervision.* Washington, DC: NASW.

National Center for HIV, STD, and TB Prevention. (2005). *The Tuskegee timeline.* Retrieved June 1, 2006, from http://www.cdc.gov/nchstp/od/tuskegee/time.htm

National Congress of American Indians. (n.d.). *Position statement: Antidefamation and mascots.* Retrieved May 28, 2006, from http://www.ncai.org/ncai/resource/documents/governance/NCAIposis.htm

National Institutes of Health. (1997). *Guidelines for the conduct of research in the intramural research programs at NIH.* Retrieved May 28, 2006, from http://www.nih.gov/news/Irnews/guidelines.htm

National Partnership for Women and Families. (n.d.). Know your rights: On the road from welfare to work: Pregnancy discrimination. Retrieved July 27, 2006, from http://www.nationalpartnership.org/portals/p3/library/WorkplaceDiscrimination/PregnancyDiscriminationGuideOct03.pdf

National Public Radio. (2002). *Remembering Tuskegee: Syphilis study still provokes disbelief, sadness.* Retrieved May 26, 2006, from http://www.npr.org/programs/morning/features/2002/jul/tuskegee

National Resource Center for Foster Care and Permanency Planning. (n.d.). Retrieved June 28, 2006, from http://hunter.cuny.edu/socwork/nrcfcpp.html

Nickell, N. J., Hecker, L., Ray, R., & Bercik, J. (1995). Marriage and family therapists' sexual attraction to clients: An exploratory study. *American Journal of Family Therapy, 23*(4), 315-327.

Noe, R. A., Hollenbeck, J. R., Gerhart, B., & Wright, P. M. (2004). *Human resource management: Gaining a competitive advantage* (4th ed.). Boston: McGraw-Hill.

Patterson, K., Grenny, J., McMillan, R., & Switzler, A. (2002). *Crucial conversations: Tools for talking when stakes are high.* New York: McGraw-Hill.

Pearlman, T. (1992). Response to: When a patient commits suicide. *American Journal of Psychiatry, 149*(2), 282-283.

Piaget, J. (1932). *The moral judgement of the child.* New York: Harcourt, Brace Jovanovich.

Practice basics: Avoid legal trouble with custody evals and boundary issues. (2005, March). *Psychotherapy Finances, 31*(3), 4-5.

Protecting the privacy of patients' health information. (2003). Retrieved May 1, 2004, from http://www.hhs.gov/news/facts/privacy.html

Quinlan, K. (1997). Director of Isaiah House, Rochester, NY. Personal Communication.

Rachels, J. (1980, June). Can ethics provide the answers? *Hastings Center Report, 32-41.*

Rachels, J. (2003). *The elements of moral philosophy* (4th ed.). Boston: McGraw-Hill.

Reamer, F. G. (1998). *Ethical standards in social work: A critical review of the NASW code of ethics.* Washington, DC: NASW Press.

Reamer, F. G. (1999). *Social work values and ethics* (2nd ed.). New York: Columbia University Press.

Reamer, F. G. (2001). *Tangled relationships: Managing boundary issues in the human services.* New York: Columbia University Press.

Reamer, F. G. (2006). *Social work values and ethics* (3rd ed.). New York: Columbia University Press.

Reisch, M. (2002). Legislative advocacy to empower oppressed and vulnerable groups. In A. Roberts & G. Greene (Eds.), *Social worker's desk reference* (pp. 534-539). New York: Oxford University Press.

Richards, D. F. (2003). The central role of informed consent in ethical treatment and research with children. In W. O'Donohue & K. Ferguson (Eds.), *Handbook of professional ethics for psychologists* (pp. 377-390). Thousand Oaks, CA: Sage.

Rowling, J. K. (1997). *Harry Potter and the sorcerer's stone.* New York: Scholastic.

Saltzman, A., & Furman, D. (1999). *Law in social work practice.* Chicago: Nelson-Hall.

Scarth, S. (2004). Straight talk about photolisting. *Adoption Council of Canada.* Retrieved May 25, 2006, from http://www.adoption.ca/news/050101edphoto0403.htm

Schacht, T. E. (1992). Response to: When a patient commits suicide. *American Journal of Psychiatry, 149*(2), 282.

Schank, J. A., & Skovholt, T. M. (1997). Dual relationship dilemmas of rural and small-community psychologists. *Professional Psychology: Research and Practice, 28*(1), 44–49.

Schmidt, P. (2006). Civil-rights group challenges CUNY's efforts to help black men. *The Chronicle of Higher Education, 52*(34), A32.

School Social Work Association of America. (2001, March 15). *School social workers and confidentiality.* Retrieved July 13, 2006, from http://www.sswaa.org/about/confidentiality.html

Schuerger, K. (2002). Information packet: Child-specific recruitment. *National Resource Center for Foster Care and Permanency Planning at the Hunter College School of Social Work.* Retrieved on June 28, 2006, from http://www.hunter.cuny.edu/socwork/nrcfcpp

Sendor, V. F., & O'Connor, P. M. (1997). *Hospice and palliative care: Questions and answers.* Lanham, MD: Scarecrow Press.

Shepard, C. E. (1992, February 28). United Way head resigns over spending habits. *Washington Post,* p. 3.

Sinclair, C., Simon, N. P., & Pettifor, J. L. (1996). The history of ethical codes and licensure. In L. J. Bass, S. T. DeMers, J. R. P. Ogloff, C. Peterson, J. L. Pettifor, R. P. Reaves, et al. (Eds.), *Professional conduct and discipline in psychology* (pp. 1–15). Washington, DC: American Psychological Association, & Montgomery, AL: Association of State and Provincial Psychology Boards.

Smith, D. (2003). Ten ways practitioners can avoid frequent ethical pitfalls. *APA Monitor, 34*(1), 50.

Social workers and psychotherapist-patient privilege: *Jaffee v. Redmond* revisited. (n.d.). Retrieved March 2, 2005, from http://www.socialworkers.org/ldf/legal_issue/200503

Spandler, H., Burman, E., Goldberg, B., Margison, F., & Amos, T. (2000). A double edged sword: Understanding gifts in psychotherapy. *European Journal of Psychotherapy, Counseling and Health, 3*(1), 77–101.

Spohn, W. C. (2000). Conscience and moral development. *Theological Studies, 61*(1), 122–138.

Staller, K. M., & Kirk, S. A. (1997). Unjust freedom: The ethics of client self-determination in runaway youth shelters. *Child & Adolescent Social Work Journal, 14*(3), 223–242.

Stefan, S. (n.d.). *HIPAA facts: Parent and minor rights.* Retrieved June 24, 2006, from http://www.ftnys.org/HIPAA%20rights.pdf#search=%22Stefan%20and%20Hipaa%20facts%22

Steinman, S. O., Richardson, N. F., & McEnroe, T. (1998). *The ethical decision-making manual for helping professionals.* Pacific Grove, CA: Brooks/Cole.

Strom-Gottfried, K. J. (1999). Professional boundaries: An analysis of violations by social workers. *Families in Society: The Journal of Contemporary Human Services, 80*(5), 439–449.

Strom-Gottfried, K. J. (2005). Ethical practice in rural environments. In L. H. Ginsberg (Ed.), *Social work in rural communities* (4th ed., pp. 141-155). Alexandria, VA.: Council on Social Work Education.

Strom-Gottfried, K., & Mowbray, N. D. (2006). Who heals the helper? Facilitating the social worker's grief. *Families in Society: The Journal of Contemporary Social Services, 87*(1), 9-15.

Swanson, J. W., Swartz, M. S., Ferron, J., Elbogen, E. B., & Van Dorn, R. A. (2006). Psychiatric advance directives among public mental health consumers in five U.S. cities: Prevalence, demand, and correlates. *Journal of the American Academy of Psychiatry & Law, 34*(1), 43-57.

Tropman, J. (1997). Obstacles to and guidelines for working together in community development. In *Successful community leadership: A skills guide for volunteers and professionals* (pp. 3-13). Washington, DC: NASW Press.

United States Commission on Civil Rights. (2001, April 13). *Commission statement on the use of Native American images and nicknames as sports symbols.* Retrieved May 22, 2006, from http://www.aics.org/mascot/civilrights.html

United States Department of Education. (2002). *Education for homeless children and youth: Grants for state and local activities.* Retrieved May 8, 2006, from http://www.ed.gov/programs/homeless/legislation.html

United States Department of Health and Human Services. (2003a). *Office for civil rights: HIPAA.* Retrieved August 4, 2003, from http://www.hhs.gov/ocr/hipaa

United States Department of Health and Human Services. (2003b, April 14). *Protecting the privacy of patients' health information.* Retrieved May 1, 2004, from http://www.hhs.gov/news/facts/privacy.html

Van Hoose, W. H., & Paradise, L. V. (1979). *Ethics in counseling and psychotherapy: Perspectives in issues and decision-making.* Cranston, RI: Carroll Press.

Young, J. R. (2003). Researchers charge racial bias on the SAT. *The Chronicle of Higher Education, 50*(7), A34.

Zsonai, L. (1998). Rational choice and the diversity of choices. *Journal of Socio-economics, 27*(5), 613-622.

INDEX